Praise for *Creativity for Life*

"Eric Maisel has taught me more about the creative life and how to live it successfully than any other author. *Creativity for Life* is for anyone who has ever dared to live an extraordinary and fully exposed life."

— Sharon Lebell, author of
The Art of Living: The Classic Manual on Virtue, Happiness, and Effectiveness

"Using simple and straightforward principles, Eric Maisel offers an inspiring guide to living an artful, art-filled, and art-committed life."

— Kari L. Pope, coordinator, Arts and Disability Network for California

"*Creativity for Life* offers an insider's journey into the marvels of creative expression. Read it, and personal clarity and commitment will be your gifts!"

— Gail McMeekin, LICSW, author of
The Twelve Secrets of Highly Creative Women

"*Creativity for Life* helps readers who are regularly in contact with artists and creative persons develop a deeper understanding of them. And for those who are already art-committed, this book is recommended for the nightstand."

— Martine Vanremoortele, president,
Centre for the Development of Creative Thinking (COCD), Belgium

"*Creativity for Life* goes far beyond typical surface discussions on the act of creativity. It is a serious investigation into all aspects of being and functioning as a working artist."

— Nancy Fletcher Cassell, visual artist and writer

"Maisel's work has changed the way I work. His methods and strategies are sensible, crystal clear, and completely un-goofy. No other writer-psychologist practicing today 'gets' artists as purely and wholly as Eric Maisel does."

— Heather Sellers, PhD, author of *Georgia Under Water* and *Page After Page*

"*Creativity for Life* offers wise and life-changing advice for anyone who wants to be more creative. Maisel's innovative approach illuminates the way toward finding the courage and resilience to make magic with your art."

— [illegible], author of *Return of the Condor*

"Both creative and practical, *Creativity for Life* is an exciting, engagingly written book. I immediately appreciated its value and utility for my clients, my colleagues, and myself."

— Kate F. Hays, PhD, author of *You're On!: Consulting for Peak Performance*

"If you are an artist who wants to get a project finished, read this book. It gave me new understanding of my artist personality and why I put things off. Most important, it gave me new courage to forge the path I know I have to take."

— Coleen Rajotte, documentary filmmaker

"This is the most comprehensive book on creativity that I have encountered. I will make this book required reading for the students in my creativity coaching training as well as for clients embarking upon a creative path."

— Jill Badonsky, MEd, creativity coaching trainer and author of *The Nine Modern Day Muses (and a Bodyguard)*

"Eric Maisel warrants special praise. He demonstrates unique sensitivity to the issues artists face and provides practical guidelines for artists whose mental health and creative outputs must be protected and promoted."

— Richard Lippin, founding president, International Arts-Medicine Association

"This is an ideal guide and companion for all artists. It describes the artist's struggle for expression, recognition, and survival with singular tenderness and depth."

— Peggy Salkind, pianist and piano department chair, San Francisco Conservatory of Music

"At last, a book that does justice to the ambitions, conflicts, struggles, frustrations, and achievements of creative and performing artists."

— Peter Ostwald, former director, UCSF Medical Center Health Program for Performing Artists

"Eric Maisel speaks as the artist's friend and ally. His book will serve as a powerful encouragement for people who undertake the courageous and often lonely adventure of finding, protecting, and nourishing their creative voice."

— Stephen Nachmanovitch, author of *Free Play: The Power of Improvisation in Life and the Arts*

Creativity
for Life

ALSO BY ERIC MAISEL

Creativity for Life

Practical Advice on the Artist's Personality and Career
from America's Foremost Creativity Coach

Eric Maisel, PhD

New World Library
Novato, California

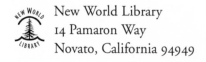
New World Library
14 Pamaron Way
Novato, California 94949

Parts of this work were originally published as *A Life in the Arts* (Jeremy P. Tarcher/Putnam, 1994).

Author photograph on page 347 by Tim Porter
Text design and typography by Tona Pearce Myers

Library of Congress Cataloging-in-Publication Data
Maisel, Eric.
    Creativity for life : practical advice on the artist's personality and career from America's foremost creativity coach / Eric Maisel, PhD.
        p.   cm.
Includes index.
ISBN 978-1-57731-558-2 (pbk. : alk. paper)
    1. Creative ability.   2. Creation (Literary, artistic, etc.)   I. Title.
BF408.M2324 2007
153.3'5—dc22   2006101775

First printing, April 2007
ISBN-13: 978-1-57731-558-2
Printed in Canada on acid-free, partially recycled paper

g New World Library is a proud member of the Green Press Initiative.

10 9 8 7 6 5 4

For Ann

Contents

PART THREE:
THE CHALLENGES OF RELATIONSHIPS

PART FOUR:
STRATEGIES AND TACTICS

INTRODUCTION *Lifelong Creativity*

The phrase "creativity for life" means three quite different things. First, it means that creativity can permeate one's life, that a person can be creative in the way she handles her job, solves problems around the house, plans menus for dinner parties, or takes in a sunset. She manifests the qualities of a creative person, like imagination, resourcefulness, self-direction, and so on, and shines them like a beacon on whatever she thinks about or tackles. Our shorthand, in this book, will be that she is "everyday creative" or engaged in "artful living."

Second, it means that people who love things like art, music, literature, science, and, more broadly, gorgeous, thought-provoking, evocative things, want them in their lives. They want a life full of foreign movies, intellectual puzzles, and natural beauty. They love it that bookstores, museums, and concert halls exist, and they love it that they can fill their living space and their spare time with art. Our shorthand for this is an "art-filled life" or "art-filled living." In this sense, having "creativity for life" means filling all your days with art and the joy that art brings.

Third, it means that a person can spend a lifetime creating in a particular domain, a domain to which she decides to devote herself. She can be creative as a violinist and devote herself to music. She can be creative as a writer and devote herself to writing novels. She can be creative as a research biologist and devote herself to scientific inquiry. Our shorthand for this is an "art-committed life" or "identifying as an artist." This third avenue is the main focus of this book.

When you use a phrase like "creativity for life," you likely mean all three things: that you want to be generally creative, because that is the way you manifest your potential, make meaning, and feel alive; that you want art in your life, you want to experience the joy of reading a novel or listening to music; and that you want to be creative in a particular area, because you feel love there, because you want to express yourself there, and perhaps because you consider it your most important meaning-making avenue. You want to be everyday creative and surrounded by art, but you also want to be an actor, say, or a screenwriter, and a successful one, at that.

An artful life, an art-filled life, and an art-committed life are not mutually exclusive ideas or ways of being. But they do present different challenges. This book focuses on the challenges that arise for the person who decides to identify as an artist (in the broad sense) and commit to a life in the arts. A different version of this book first appeared in 1992 as *Staying Sane in the Arts*, and a few years later it was updated in paperback as *A Life in the Arts*. Those titles describe my focus in this new expanded and updated edition. I also want to present core ideas about how you can manifest your creative potential in everything you do: that is, how to live an artful, as well as an art-committed, life.

As soon as you decide to be creative in a particular domain and that you mean to live as a novelist, biochemist, actor, or sculptor, you introduce a set of profound challenges that you would not have confronted if you had "settled" for artful living and an art-filled life. It is one thing to make an interesting pumpkin soup; it quite another to dream about becoming a chef and to live out that dream in the trenches. It is one thing to decorate your apartment with found objects that tickle your fancy; it is quite another to set your mind on becoming a "found object" artist. When you decide to devote yourself to creativity in a specific area, you raise the stakes tremendously, you organize your life around that dream, and you find that your emotions rise and fall with your successes and failures.

If, for example, you decide to be creative in a scientific specialty and you want to advance that specialty through your creative efforts, then suddenly it vitally matters that you get to study with the preeminent practitioners in your field, get funding for your lab, keep abreast of breakthroughs, avoid dead-end alleys (and theories) that waste years of your time, and so on. Because you want to be creative *here*, suddenly all *that* appears. If you don't really care and decide not even to try, then the challenges evaporate. But if you do care, then each challenge is magnified in direct proportion to your hopes for yourself in that domain.

That is the subject of this book. When you commit to a life in the arts or to any field that demands your full creative involvement and your largest meaning investment — whether as a research physicist, inventor, poet, activist, investigative reporter, or country-western singer — then you have made a deal with yourself that you will spend years, decades, even a whole lifetime in the pursuit of real results, excellence, and success, however you might define or measure these. You have said to yourself, "I am authentically involved in this. This matters to me." You have made a move at the level of meaning and identity; next come the repercussions.

AN ART-COMMITTED LIFE

Let's ground these ideas by looking at the challenges that arise as soon as you identify yourself as, say, a classical musician. Perhaps you have trained on the oboe and would love to play the oboe as your life's work. In our culture, this means that you will need to make money from playing the oboe, marry someone who will support you as you play the oboe, have the good sense to be born into wealth, or somehow cobble a life of settling customer complaints at your day job and keeping your quartet afloat in the evenings. That is, you will have to deal with the real, pressing, and persistent challenges that arise as a consequence of wanting to play the oboe as your life's work.

As someone in this position, you will find yourself confronted by the following challenges:

- *Getting it right.* You will want and need to hit the right notes as you play. This alone is difficult. You will need to produce a pleasant sound. Anyone who has ever tried playing the oboe knows that this too can be difficult. You will need to come in on time when the music calls for your entry — every single time. If you are setting your sights high and want to make music, rather than "just" play the notes right, then you will need to rise to a level of practice, expertise, care, imagination, and personality management that taxes your resources and will sometimes seem quite beyond you.

- *Getting it right in public.* Because of your choice, you have made a pact with yourself to put yourself on the line in front of audiences, where everything about you and your playing can and will be scrutinized. You may find yourself a victim of performance anxiety, which may accompany you as an unwanted lifelong companion. You will certainly fall victim to subtle criticism (like a lukewarm round of applause at the end of a concert) and overt and sometimes hostile criticism (at the hands of reviewers, a caustic parent, an envious peer, a former teacher), and so your choice has made you a public figure, with all that entails.

- *Having sufficient talent.* You will need to deal with aspects of your being that amount to the thing we call "talent," factors as diverse as the distance your fingers can reach, your lung capacity, your passion, your intuitive musical understanding, your healthy narcissism, and so on. Whatever the word *talent* means for you, it is a concept that will never be far from your mind and that will likely plague you. You may feel that you have an insufficient amount of it ("I'm just not that talented"), or maybe that you possess it but are failing to manifest it ("I have all this raw talent but I just can't seem to harness it").

- *Accessing your internal resources.* To play your instrument with feeling, you will need to feel, which is a stretch for many people. For reasons having to do with familial injunctions and cultural imperatives, as well as with individual personality differences, many people remain walled off from their feelings and operate in a superficial, matter-of-fact, literal way that, as it pertains to their music-making, causes them to play mechanically, without richness or depth. As our oboist, a challenge that you may never recognize, and so may never adequately address, is the fact that the quality of your music-making is related as much to your beating heart (and your internal psychological landscape) as it is to your moving fingers.

- *Having some successes and feeling successful.* For you to feel good about your journey, you will need opportunities to play — and you will need the right opportunities. Playing in a quartet that performs during Sunday brunch in the lounge of a fancy restaurant may feel fine when you are twenty, but it is unlikely to feel fine when you are forty. You are apt to consider yourself a success if: you are part of a symphony orchestra; it is a good orchestra; you are the principal oboist; you also get to play personally resonant music with a chamber group or as a soloist; you are recorded; you are considered a "top oboist"; and so on. Conversely, it will not feel good to play "second fiddle" to other oboists, to languish in long-term obscurity, or to remain on the far fringes of the oboe world.

- *Dealing with the repertoire.* Because you have decided to play the oboe as your life's work, you must learn the pieces that you will be playing, even if you don't love some of them, even if you find some of them devilishly hard, and even if it bores you to repeatedly play the same passages thousands of time in practice and in performance. Wittingly or not, you have tied your life, your days, and your future to particular pieces of music, and if you have fallen in love with the sound of the oboe but not with the oboe literature, then you may find yourself in lifelong conflict as you play music that taxes you and that you do not love.

- *Competing.* To get what you want, you will need to compete. You may not want to compete, you may not feel that you are actively competing, and you may shy away from competing, but you are nevertheless embedded in a world that is simple in its Darwinian survival-of-the-fittest logic. There are only so many openings for symphony oboists; there are only so many slots for principal oboists; there are only so many classical recordings that sell; there are only so many venues for your quartet; there is only so big a pie. If you were playing mountain music with your neighbors in the backwoods of rural America, this issue would not exist. You would just pull up a chair and play. But because of your choice, which inevitably involves you in auditions, comparisons, interpersonal dynamics, and every aspect of competition, you must either successfully compete or fall by the wayside.

- *Relinquishing control.* If you were sitting at home writing oboe music, you would be in complete control of your creative life, in a manner of speaking. To be sure, real limitations and challenges will arise as you try to compose; and the second you want your oboe piece publicly performed, you will lose all illusion of control and find yourself at the mercy of the marketplace. But there is still a real difference between the freedom and control a composer experiences and the lack of freedom and control felt by a performer. As a performer you must take direction; you must follow the music; you must play at a pace consistent with that of your fellow musicians; you must accept that you have tied your rope to this orchestra and now must travel with it to Berlin, or to Boise. You never really meant to relinquish control in this way, but your love of the oboe has led exactly to this dependency and to all these restrictions.

- *Dealing with people like yourself.* By virtue of your decision, you have also set yourself up to deal with people exactly like you, people who are ambitious, driven, competitive, sensitive, complex, eccentric, moody, self-absorbed, histrionic, and grandiose. Without intending it, you have landed yourself in a dramatic world of diva conductors, fanatic soloists, arch patrons, and other colorful — and difficult — characters. Will you land in bed, literally or figuratively, with a temperamental flautist or an anxious violinist? Quite likely — and with all the repercussions one would naturally expect.

As our oboist, what other challenges must you face? You must contend with the dead time between performances, the feelings that arise when you hear an oboist whom you consider better, the orchestra's indifference as it plays a chestnut it has played too many times already, the fact that your salary does not quite make ends meet and your realization that you must somehow make more money, the criticism the woodwinds receive from the high-handed visiting conductor (criticism that, unfortunately, is justified), your lack of motivation to practice, and the nagging depression whose source you can't quite identify though you know it has something to do with your choice to make a career in music. It isn't that you can't contend with these challenges and all the others that inevitably arise, but meeting them is anything but easy.

We will devote a lot of attention to the challenges of living an art-committed life and to the strategies you can employ to deal with those challenges. However, let's spend at least a minute on the rewards! It doesn't cheapen words like *sacred* or *miraculous* to say that creating a great symphony is miraculous and something like a sacred act, that penning a life-changing book is glorious for the writer and a boon to its readers, that curing a horrible disease is as good as good deeds get, that exposing high-level fraud by muckraking is as serious, worthy, and courageous an act as human beings are capable of performing. Because we have genuine meaning-making needs that can't be minimized and because enterprises like medical research, novel writing, and documentary filmmaking, to name just three of many artistic pursuits, are substantial places to make meaning, we naturally gravitate toward these enterprises as lifelong loves. And it is a good thing that someone does!

ATTENTION AND PRACTICE

Having outlined the challenges that are the subject of this book, I would like to make an important point at this early juncture: whether your goal is artful living, an art-filled life, or an art-committed life, the two keys to success are attention and practice. We tend to do an amazingly poor job of paying attention to our realities; we seem genetically programmed to repeat our days without improving our circumstances or deepening our awareness. Nor do we tend to commit to the lifelong, patient apprenticeship required of anyone who wants to translate her love of an art form into mastery and a body of work. In other words, we pay too little attention, and we don't practice enough.

A novelist works too little on her novel, leaving the writing after a few minutes because she isn't sure what comes next. The next day the same thing happens. Every day for a year she writes too little, until the time comes when, depressed and defeated, she throws in the towel and abandons the novel. Why didn't a loud alarm go off that first day? Why didn't she say, "Writing for two minutes, bad-mouthing myself, and then running off can't be the way"? Why did the scales tip in favor of defensiveness and avoidance rather than self-encouragement, self-awareness, and the courage to continue?

I think that the image of a tipping scale provides us with an important clue. We live in a precarious balance between truly caring about our art-making and not caring about anything, between feeling real desire and feeling empty and dull, between trusting our abilities and not trusting them at all. We live in a precarious balance between acknowledging that we must make mistakes and messes if we are to venture into the unknown and refusing to acknowledge that mistakes and messes come with the territory. We stand poised between paying attention and not paying attention, and between committing to lifelong practice and refusing to make that commitment. Every day the scales tip one way or the other, but usually in the direction of avoidance.

It is an act of courage to maintain awareness. If you are feeling courageous, I invite you to engage in the guided writing program presented in part 4. More simply, I invite you to tell yourself the truth. If your truth is that writing a novel feels scary, admit that, rather than telling yourself things like "I have no imagination" or "It's too late to start." If your truth is that your life is out of control and creativity is just one of the many things that you aren't attending to, stand up and admit that to yourself, even if it means that you must change everything. Nor can you do this truth telling just once or twice: you need to do it today, tomorrow, and forever.

Pay attention. And practice. You will feel more positive, motivated, and on track if you commit to a daily practice that connects to your creative discipline. This means, if you are a writer, writing every day, turning to your work even when you don't feel equal to it, refusing to get up from your writing even when you feel anxious or uncertain, eliminating the dodges that you customarily employ to avoid writing, accepting the trials that come with attempting to write well, attempting to write often, attempting to get published, and so on. In part 4 I describe the elements of a creativity practice. The challenges that we face as art-committed human beings are so great that unless we commit to lifelong practice, we have little chance of handling them. I hope that you will start your creativity practice very, very soon.

My goal with this book is to help the working artist in the real world (and the would-be artist who hasn't yet taken the plunge). That artist is often uncertain about his talent, wants to do art his own way but must also do business and factor in the demands of the marketplace, is hard-pressed to make a living from his art, possesses a personality that sometimes does not serve him well, frequently suffers from bouts of depression, and in general faces as tough an uphill battle as one can imagine.

In this context, I define as successful the self-aware, resourceful artist who understands her personality, her chosen life, and the world so well that she can maintain her spirits, her relationships, and her creativity even as she wrestles with the day-to-day challenges confronting her. While she is not without anxieties and eccentricities, black spells, periods of inactivity, and crises of faith, she weathers these and returns to champion her art.

There's no such thing beneath the heavens as conditions favorable to art. Art must crash through or perish.

— SYLVIA ASHTON-WARNER

I did not write this book as a dirge to accompany the artist's life. Rather, it is a celebration of the artist's heroism. A participant in one of my workshops, a poet and small-press editor, felt reminded by day's end of the importance of honoring the hard and courageous work she did as an artist. She said, "I leave here feeling stronger and more joyous about the choices I've made, the work I've done, and more confident about the work I'll continue to do." I hope that you will feel that way, too, as you meet the material in this book head-on.

As society's visionaries and rebels, artists often remain unthanked and unheard. I hope that as you read this book you will feel recognized and, in some small measure, rewarded for committing to the artist's life. I also firmly believe that you will have greater success as an artist and will simply feel better if you take the time to carefully process the material presented here. There are many ways to do this — by discussing the issues with your peers, by bringing them up in therapy, by using your medium as a tool of exploration, and especially by committing to the self-awareness and creativity practices outlined in part 4.

I am guessing that you want to manifest your creative nature in the three ways mentioned above: that you are interested in artful living, in an art-filled life, and in an art-committed life. You want to use your brain every day for real stretches of time and not just on the occasional Thursday for twenty minutes. You want to go deep into yourself and into the nature of reality. You want to feel proud of your meaning-making efforts. If we understand the word to include everything that we've been discussing, you want to be an *artist*. Anything less feels like a waste of your potential and a violation of your understanding of what life's about. Good, then! Let's plot your course in the direction of lifelong creativity.

PART 1

The Challenges of the Artistic Personality

1 *Creativity* and *Talent*

Songs are all written as part of a symphony.

— BOB DYLAN

You are a creative or performing artist. You love to sing, dance, make images. You cherish the written word. Acting thrills you. Your pulse races when you drum. Your darkroom is a magical laboratory. But will you be able to spend the rest of your life pursuing your passion in the face of the many significant challenges that confront you? Can you carve out a career in art, achieve the level of success you dream of, secure some measure of comfort, and find time both for art-making and for living? Can you survive the artist's life?

We are talking about nothing less than survival here, for few creative and performing artists in contemporary Western society can even earn a living from their art. Disturbing figures about visual artists, poets, short story writers, playwrights, novelists, independent filmmakers, pop singers, potters, jazz musicians, rock musicians, classical composers, art photographers — for all groups of creative and performing artists — could be quoted. According to a Rockefeller Panel report commissioned to take an in-depth look at the financial realities of the performer's life,

> the miserable income of the majority of performing artists reflects both a shortage of jobs and the brief duration of employment that is available. In all except the small handful of our major and metropolitan orchestras, musicians earn an average of only a few hundred dollars a year from their professional labors. During an average week in the winter season, only about one-fifth of the active members of Actors' Equity Association, the theatrical performers union, are employed in the profession. Of the actors who do find jobs, well over half are employed for only ten weeks — less than one-fifth of the year. For most opera companies the season lasts only a few weeks. The livelihood of the dancer is perhaps the most meager of all.

This is not a pretty picture. Why would a smart, ambitious, talented person choose such a life? Why have you chosen to struggle with cattle-call auditions, rejected fiction, indifferent gallery owners, a lack of recognition, and the other challenges that artists face?

The answers are severalfold. First, your need to express yourself and to manifest your creativity springs from very deep sources. Like a devout believer, you are profoundly moved by art. Your connection to art is reverent, intellectually alive, viscerally deep. You experience *rasa*, the Sanskrit word for the mood or sentiment evoked by a work of art. In you, what Alfred North Whitehead called the "impulse to originate" is stirred. You want to present to the world what the Navajo call *hozh'g*: the beauty of life, as seen and created by a person.

You value art and are hopeful about the contributions you can make in art. These needs and values translate into a sense of mission, even something like a religious fervor. You consider the task sacred and the calling noble, and you are willing to make sacrifices and even martyr yourself for art. Emily Carr, the Canadian painter, explained: "Once I heard it stated and now I believe it to be true that there is no true art without religion. The artist himself may not think he is religious but if he is sincere his sincerity in itself is religion."

British poet Stephen Spender wrote: "It is evident that a faith in their vocation, mystical in intensity, sustains poets. From my experience I can clarify the nature of this faith. When I was nine we went to the Lake District, and there my parents read me some of the poems of Wordsworth. My sense of the sacredness of the task of poetry began then, and I have always felt that the poet's was a sacred vocation, like a saint's."

You feel that you have a special, vital role to play in society. From a considered vantage point outside society, you observe, witness, and judge. As the German Expressionist painter Georg Baselitz put it, "The artist is not responsible to anyone. His social role is asocial."

You also feel the simple joy of applying paint to canvas, of making music, of playing a part with other actors. You discover that you are good at it — good with words, good on your feet, good with your voice or your fingers, good at images. Art makes you feel alive. You find that the process of art-making — be it the quietly absorbed practicing, the rollicking rehearsing, the intense poetry writing, or the tempestuous encounter with a blank canvas — buffers you against the ordinariness of the world. "Painting is a way of forgetting oneself," said visual artist Joan Mitchell. Sculptor Louise Nevelson confided, "In my studio I'm as happy as a cow in her stall."

You may also choose the artist's life because you are using art as a tool to help heal childhood wounds or as a means of expressing the pain in your life. Painter Barbara Smith said, "The intent of my work is to break out of a dark place." Nancy Spero, also a painter, offered the following self-description: "I am the angry person sticking out her tongue." The painter Harmony Hammond explained, "I want my work to demand your attention because I can get it no other way."

You may also perceive a career in art as a way to gain recognition, to stand out, to become known as a special and talented person. No doubt you feel you have valuable, innovative, beautiful work to do. Quite possibly you're hoping for fame and fortune. You may harbor the hope that people will one day applaud your achievements and call you great.

Last, you pursue the artist's life because you believe you could be the exception who proves the rule when it comes to money and success. Perhaps like the French painter Chaim Soutine, you'll be discovered by a passing dentist, or like Jean Harlow you'll be discovered sipping soda in a drugstore. You see your novel making a mark and being hailed as a work of genius. You imagine yourself becoming a star and going from rags to riches overnight. The possibility that success may strike quickly and out of the blue sustains you.

You begin your journey as an artist out of sacred motives, with dreams and high hopes, and also, perhaps, you embark from a place of painful turmoil or other inner necessity. From these powerful drives comes your conscious decision to pursue a life in art, your resolve to call yourself an artist, whatever the consequences. You nod in agreement with painter John Baldessari, who said, "Art is about bloody-mindedness. It's not about living the good life. In the end, it's just you and the art."

You identify yourself as an artist. But just how good an artist are you? How good can you become? Are you confident that you have the necessary skills and abilities to master your medium? Do your paintings capture your passion and your ideas? Are you a virtuoso actor or pianist? Can you create characters and handle plot to your liking? Are you creative and talented enough to accomplish the artistic tasks you've set yourself?

Indeed, creativity and talent are the first challenges we need to examine. To feel good about yourself as an artist, you need to manifest your creativity and make appropriate use of your talents. These are hard tasks to accomplish in their own right, made even harder by the fact that *creativity* and *talent* are both such puzzling terms. Let's examine them in some detail.

CREATIVITY AND THE ARTIST

It would be vain to try to put into words that immeasurable sense of bliss which comes over me directly [when] a new idea awakens in me and begins to assume a definite form. I forget everything and behave like a madman.

— PYOTR ILICH TCHAIKOVSKY

Over the centuries, artistic creativity has been related to divine inspiration, madness, sheer genius, unnameable life forces, and cosmic powers. In modern times it has been linked to unconscious processes, the working out and sublimating of sexual instincts, attempts at wish fulfillment, and incipient neurosis. It has also been linked to the natural associational tendencies of a special mind, to the self-realizing and self-actualizing efforts of some individuals, and to the accidental presence of a certain collection of personality traits.

The psychiatrist Lawrence Hatterer described the Freudian view in *The Artist and Society*: "The dominant theory of the creative person and act stems from Freud's concept of sublimation. Freud hypothesized that the creative act is rooted in transformed sexual energy, in the diversion of these energies to higher, more socially acceptable aims. Creativity, he felt, arose out of the artist's unconscious need to rid himself of mental tension."

The Freudian view is provocative, and so are the humanistic positions regarding self-realization and self-actualization championed by psychologists Carl Rogers and Abraham Maslow. Trait theory also has something important to tell us about creativity, as do the existential theories of Rollo May, Victor Frankl, and others.

In my view, the most useful definition of creativity is the following: people are artistically creative when they love what they are doing, know what they are doing, and actively engage in art-making. The three elements of creativity are thus *loving*, *knowing*, and *doing*; or heart, mind, and hands; or, as Zen Buddhist teaching has it, great faith, great question, and great courage.

Creativity is no more mysterious than that. This hardly means, however, that manifesting one's creativity is easy. Artists, in order to be creative, are challenged to love enough, to know enough, and to do enough, and these tasks are as real and challenging as any human endeavor can be.

Loving

Love is the spirit that motivates the artist's journey. The love may be sublime, raw, obsessive, passionate, awful, or thrilling, but whatever its quality, it's a powerful motive in the artist's life. The actor Derek Jacobi distinguished this special, deeply rooted drive from mere desire: "You have to have an absolute obsession and compulsion to act, not just desire; it's just not enough to have talent and want to express it; it's not enough. It's got to be more deeply rooted, more abrasive. The fire in the belly has got to be there. If there's no fire, you can't do it."

What is it that the artist loves? It is first and foremost the sheer power of whichever medium has attracted her. This is why she is a painter or a novelist or an archaeologist: an art form (in the broad sense) has gotten under her skin. It may be the power of the book that gripped her, the power of dance, the power of music, the power of the image, the power of the play, the mystery of ancient cultures, the very secrets of the universe.

I could list various artists' expressions of this deep love and passion endlessly. Visual artist Diane Burko said, "I love putting paint on canvas, I love pouring it and watching new colors happen in my margarine containers." The painter Hans Hofmann claimed that "as an artist, you love everything of quality that came before you." Pianist Jorge Bolet said, "My gods were [Josef Casimir] Hofmann and [Sergey Vasilyevich] Rachmaninoff. Every time I heard Rachmaninoff play, I said to myself, '*That* is what *I* want to sound like.'" Artist François Gauzi wrote of Vincent van Gogh, "When discussing 'art,' if one disagreed with him and pushed him to the limit, he would flare up in a disturbing way. Color drove him mad. [Eugène] Delacroix was god, and when he spoke of this painter, his lips would quiver with emotion."

Your love is also a love of the great masters, a love of the human being who had it in her to write the novel that transfixed you or who flew across the stage to the strains of music. It is a love of Mozart's music and a love of the man, too — not a love of his personality, necessarily, but of his ability to express human potential.

The artist who does not love ardently may fall far short of his creative potential. He may not have enough "lubricating juice," as Virginia Woolf called it. He may move from piano lessons and small recitals to a good conservatory to a concert tour, mastering his technique and honing his skills along the way, but if he remains out of love with music, his is a career, not a love affair.

We see again and again in the lives of special artists a profound youthful infatuation with their medium, with everything and anything connected with it — the good, the bad, and the indifferent. If books have mesmerized them, they will read everything; if paintings have, they will frequent every gallery, running to every visiting show. They may have no idea that they are about to devote their lives to those media; they simply feel in love. The actor Len Cariou described his relationship to movies: "I didn't have any thoughts about being an actor. I always was an actor. I'd go to films every Saturday. I had an insatiable appetite for films. You could see four films and a serial for half a buck. In 1959 when I read an ad in the local paper, 'Young actors wanted for summer stock,' all of a sudden I knew; there was a crunch in my head."

In the beginning, the artist may love indiscriminately, in a regular wash of infatuation. Many critics observe, for instance, that as a youth Van Gogh consistently admired and respected the work of a host of minor artists; he praised better and worse artists in the same breath. When Van Gogh was twenty, for example, he wrote to his younger brother, Theo, from London: "There are clever painters here, among others Millais, who has painted the 'Huguenot.' His things are beautiful. Then there is Boughton, and among the old painters, Constable, a landscape painter who lived about thirty years ago; he is splendid, his work reminds me of Diaz and Daubigny; and there are Reynolds and Gainsborough, who have especially painted very beautiful ladies' portraits; and Turner. I see you have a great love of art; that is a good thing, lad. Admire as much as you can; most people do not admire enough."

Critics have felt that such passages point to a noncritical streak in Van Gogh's nature. But to call this a lack of critical ability is to misunderstand the early infatuation of the artist. If we recognize that the artist is embarking on a love affair, into which one day he will throw his whole being, then these moments become not only understandable but also absolutely predictable. They have about them the feeling of puppy love, as the young person suspends his discriminating abilities in the pursuit of passion.

The artist therefore inflates the painting, the book, the piece of music in question because it has moved him. He calls it great because it has struck a great chord in him. If we remember the books or paintings or pieces of music that we loved as children and young adults, if we remember how we were moved by them in the moment, we may feel loathe to look back and recognize that a certain book was poorly written, that a particular painting was sentimental. In the moment we experienced that book or that painting, we were surely in love.

Chopin, experiencing Paris for the first time at twenty-one, wrote this to a friend: "I doubt whether anything so magnificent as *Robert le diable*, the new five-act opera by Meyerbeer, has ever before been done in the theater. It is the masterpiece of the modern school. There are devils, immense choruses singing through tubes, and souls rising from the tomb. The most extraordinary thing of all is the organ, the sound of which, coming from the stage, delights and astonishes one and almost drowns the orchestra."

The artist is transported by her medium, delighted and astonished. That her medium is able to speak to her in this way is a special affirmation in the realm of the spirit.

Knowing

The young artist gobbles up everything she can in her medium because she has a need to know. Much of her knowing comes from this early period. The young singer listens to all of Billie Holiday's records and begins to learn the blues. The young writer reads all the works of Shakespeare and learns how language and drama operate. Throughout her life as well, the artist is driven to know enough, to take in everything she needs to take in, even if, in the language of Zen, she must forget much of what she knows in order to work.

Knowing is intuitive and rational, tonal and factual, conscious and unconscious. Actors as well as playwrights and directors, soloists and ensemble players as well as composers and conductors, carry inside them the work they are doing; they operate at multiple levels. They create the version of the piece they will play even as they peel potatoes for dinner. This ongoing inner learning and knowing are no different for the creative artist or for the re-creative artist, such as a musician or actor. Jorge Bolet, for instance, described his process of learning new piano pieces: "I never solved a major mechanical or interpretive problem *at* the keyboard, only *away* from it. Even when I sometimes become so completely baffled that I am utterly struck for a direction in which to go, I return to the *music* and piece it out."

This is a knowing based on immersion. If you're an actor you immerse yourself in a role, living and breathing the character. If you're a dancer you become the deer or the swan. If you're a writer you inhabit the scene of your novel. If you're a pianist you live inside the sonata.

All artists are immersed in different waters, to be sure, and their art reflects these differences. One is immersed in abstraction, another in realism. One is immersed in jazz, another in traditional Andean flute music. But each, insofar as he or she is deeply creative, is deeply immersed. As psychologist E. W. Sinnott put it, "Inspiration, it is well recognized, rarely comes unless an individual has immersed himself in the subject. He must have a rich background of knowledge and experience in it."

Of course, what you know as an artist shifts and changes. You learn more, forget, change your mind. What you do today informs and alters what you knew yesterday; or, as the visual artist Frederick Franck put it, "I have learned that what I have not drawn I have never really seen." These shifts in knowing can produce frustrations. You're happy with a poem you've just written; when you reread it you note its flaws. You're happy with a morning's painting; in the afternoon the work looks dull. As the sculptor Stephen De Staebler recollected of Alberto Giacometti,

> Giacometti once visited a friend and saw one of his plaster heads that he'd given the friend as a gift. He immediately pulled out a pen knife and began carving away at the head. It would never be right.
>
> The quest for the unattainable drives all artists. It has nothing to do with what others say about your work. Sometimes you get a glimmer, you feel you've really touched something. Then the next day you look at it and wonder what it was you saw.

Knowing is not a cold and mechanical holding of a universe of facts, a strictly left-brain enterprise. Rather, it involves intuitions as well as ideas, feelings as well as beliefs. One artist may stress the importance of ideas in his work, and that may be a true self-appraisal. Another may stress intuition. The painter David Ligare, for instance, wrote, "Making paintings is a passion for me, but it is a passion of ideas rather than just pigment." Conversely, painter Jane Freilicher said, "I believe I rely rather heavily on intuition and depend on an intuitive response from my audience."

While you may belong to one camp or the other, asserting that the idea is higher than the intuition or vice versa, on the sidelines we may speculate that there are more than a few ways of knowing.

Doing

Loving is the heart of creativity, knowing is its brain, and doing is its musculature. Doing is effort of the sort described by Tchaikovsky in a letter to a friend:

> We must *always* work, and a self-respecting artist must not fold his hands on the pretext that he is not in the mood. If we wait for the mood, without endeavoring to meet it halfway, we easily become indolent and apathetic. We must be patient, and believe that inspiration will come to those who can master their *disinclination.* A few days ago I told you I was working every day without any real inspiration. Had I given way to my disinclination, undoubtedly I should have drifted into a long period of idleness. But my patience and faith did not fail me, and today I felt the inexplicable glow of inspiration of which I told you; thanks to which I know beforehand that whatever I write today will have power to make an impression, and to touch the hearts of those who hear it.

Doing is also execution, of the sort described by the Spanish painter Francisco Goya: "An artist, seeing a man fall from a third-story window, should be able to complete a drawing of him by the time he hits the ground."

A person is not an artist until he works at his art, no matter how eloquently he speaks during the cocktail hour or how fine the images are that come to his mind. As David Salle, the visual artist, put it, "It's easy to be an artist in your head." We, as artists, know this. We realize that often we are not able to translate our vision into splendid art. Even the finest artists write books that are not great, paint pictures that are not great, compose pieces that are not great, give performances that are not great, involve themselves in projects that are not great. But the artist can only try — and she must.

When you love what you are doing, know what you are doing, and do it, a confidence is bred in you that is the best stretcher of limits. Then you can say, as visual artist June Wayne did, "Now, when I start something, I expect to carry it off." Decades of loving, knowing, and doing are the hallmarks of the person committed to art and devoted to lifelong creativity.

TALENT AND THE ARTIST

Creativity is human potential made manifest. But what is talent? *Webster's New World Dictionary* informs us that *talent* is "any natural ability, power, or endowment, and especially any superior, apparently natural ability in the arts or sciences or in the learning or doing of anything."

This definition is revealing on several counts. First of all, it defines talent in terms of abilities and powers. It suggests that an artist can answer the question, "Am I talented?" in the affirmative if she can point to certain endowments that she possesses.

But which ones should she point to? Which are most important in her discipline? How many of them does she need in order to do good work? Do they all matter equally? Which, if any, are absolutely necessary? How much of a desired ability does she need — how great a vocal range, how long a leap, how fine a hand?

If we look at just a few art disciplines we see how difficult it is for artists to answer these questions. Is it more important, for instance, for a pianist to possess virtuosity and to be able to race her fingers up and down the keyboard or to possess the ability to interpret music and express emotion through her playing? Is the talented actor the one who has the ability to be himself (and who perhaps can't be anyone else) or the one with the widest range? Is it more important for a painter to be able to render a likeness, compose a painting and balance its parts, possess a fine color sense, have a knack for new images or ideas — or to paint something that evokes a powerful response in the observer?

As difficult as these questions are, an artist must nevertheless grapple with them. In making this attempt he will gain a greater awareness of the demands and requirements of his field, of the skills and powers he brings to the task and of those he may still need. Only then will he be able to determine what talent means in the context of his discipline. If he does not possess the requisite talent to achieve his goals, recognizing this will put him in a better position to make a strategic career decision.

For example, after such an assessment an artist may say to himself, "Well, I understand better what's needed in my art and what I have to offer. I think I'm talented — except in one, unfortunately important, area: I can't draw a straight line. Should I lie to myself and ignore the problem? Should I get out of art? If talent is innate, and I haven't a drawing talent, what am I supposed to do?"

Fortunately, the dictionary definition of talent points to a possible way out of this dilemma. That definition begins by asserting that talent is one or another innate ability of the individual but goes on to call talent in the arts only an *apparently* innate ability. This is of crucial significance, because it allows the artist to put the following question on the table: "Is there a chance that I might develop more talent?"

Consider Van Gogh, for example. Van Gogh's drawings show a truly remarkable improvement over the two years he set aside to intensely practice drawing. At the start of that period his sketches look clumsy and amateurish. With great ardor, thoughtfulness, and effort — by manifesting his creativity, in short — at the end of those two years Van Gogh was producing drawings showing not only that he had mastered elements of technique but also that he had educated himself in ways that moved him far ahead of his classically trained peers.

Van Gogh's progress excites the artist. It seems to clearly imply that by acting creatively, an artist may significantly increase his talent or make manifest significant talent he didn't know he possessed. Maybe a brilliant novel *is* within his grasp. Maybe he *can* achieve a breakthrough in the visual arts. Maybe he *can* play his instrument like a god.

The artist is comforted. But his good mood is interrupted by a new thought. He realizes that when he questions whether he is talented, as often as not he is comparing himself to the greatest or most talented artists of all time, or even comparing his talent to a level that no one has yet achieved — to some Platonic ideal of perfection. In doing that, he suddenly wonders, isn't he setting himself up for disappointment and failure? Won't he end up thinking of himself as a marginal talent or a minor artist, even if he realizes a sizable portion of his potential?

He sees the fruits of such unfortunate comparing in the words of the late novelist Jerzy Kosinski: "There's no greater punishment than an insufficient talent. I have always been a very marginal novelist. A lesser talent. Yes, there's nothing wrong with that. Ninety-nine percent of mankind is, even in this I am typical. Would I like more talent? Yes. But you cannot get more talent. But I'm no different than most lesser talents. We're all lesser talents."

Rather than priding himself on his novels, such as *The Painted Bird* and *Being There*, Kosinski put himself down. Perhaps his ironic self-indictment is more a piece of misanthropy than a statement about talent. It may even be a kind of convenient shorthand to describe a bankrupt artistic life. But it's just as likely that Kosinski spent his adult life comparing himself to the giants of literature and feeling like a failure by comparison.

The artist, thinking about this issue, has to mutter to himself, "Wonderful. I want to increase my talent and manifest my creativity — in short, I want to do great work. But I mustn't set up the immortals in my field as a yardstick against which to compare my work, because if I do, I risk growing profoundly dissatisfied with my own accomplishments. I'll end up back at a place of not really feeling talented. And — worse yet! — when I make a mistake or produce a bad book or a bad painting, flub my lines or drop notes, I'll feel really terrible, having fallen so very far short of the ideal!"

Taking some time to consider this issue, the artist realizes how easy it is to disparage his talent and to lower his self-esteem in the process. He realizes also that when he calls another artist a marginal talent, he invariably means it as a criticism. Yet he knows in his heart that art is hard to do and that we should each be forgiven our very human limitations. Miracles of art do occur, but limits can only be stretched, not transcended. Even though he feels extraordinary when he senses brilliant music or a brilliant poem coursing through him, he is nevertheless all too aware of his own great ignorance and insufficiencies.

What should he do? Should he set his sights lower and not judge himself and others against the very highest standards? Should he regularly confess to frailty and ordinariness and act generously when he sees the frail and ordinary works of other artists? Or should he set his sights extremely high and risk almost certain disappointment?

The artist, puzzling over this matter, arrives at an answer. He determines that he means to shoot for the sky and to judge himself and others by the highest standards, come what may. He recommits himself to manifesting his creativity and talent. But just like that, in the next second, he's struck by another troubling question. "What," he wonders, "if being talented doesn't matter after all? What if it isn't the issue? What if it's even a hindrance?"

This question has troubled him before; it regularly plagues most artists. The screenwriter, the pop singer, the painter, the songwriter, and the television writer look around them and everywhere see mediocrity rewarded, even demanded. The artist, already in turmoil as he tries to address the many sides of the talent issue, now thinks, "Here I am, doing everything I can to manifest my creativity and make use of my talents — and the public really only wants comedy that comes with a laugh track, fiction to take to the beach, and music driven by the beat of a drum machine! Why should I challenge myself if the public wants cat art and homilies?"

The artist now feels furious. He wonders if there is any way he can get even with the audience. He is reminded of a certain kind of modern artist, a John Cage or an Andy Warhol, who, perhaps also infuriated by this demand for mediocrity, throws the matter back in the face of his audience and mocks it with visions of ordinariness. Such an artist will try anything, for who's to say what's good and bad, and isn't she likely to garner applause even for her most ridiculous efforts?

Like Warhol, who painted soup cans and pastel-colored prints of Marilyn Monroe, such an artist ironically declares, as Warhol did, "I want everybody to think alike. I think everybody should be a machine." Like Yoko Ono, the artist gives a "silent concert," demanding that the audience supply the music. No matter what he does — whether he plays radio static as his concert piece or crafts clay turds as his museum piece — the artist can't shock or wake up the public or succeed in irony. The audience simply doesn't get it. As the French Dadist artist Marcel Duchamp put it, "I threw the bottle-rack and the urinal in people's faces as a challenge, and now they admire them for their aesthetic beauty."

The artist now finds himself in a fine stew. But suddenly a new question intrudes: "Isn't all this brooding about my talent really pretty disgusting? Am I really so ego driven and narcissistic?" Feeling much too self-involved, he announces to himself, "No, I won't allow talent to be the issue any longer! I'm going to stop massaging my ego and acting prideful. In fact, there's so much important social and political work to be done in the world, I'm going to make use of the talents I possess, just as they are, in the service of a good cause."

He decides that he will no longer hold individual expression in higher esteem than community or global welfare. He nods in vigorous agreement at the writer and painter Suzi Gablik's call for a more socially minded art:

> Today, there is still a pervasive sense that only by divorcing themselves from any social role can artists establish their own individual identity. But it strikes me that, as the dangers to planetary survival escalate, the practical consequences of such an attitude are becoming increasingly apparent. Our modernist notions of freedom and autonomy, of art answering only to its own laws, the pure aesthetic without a function, begin to seem a touch ingenuous. We simply cannot remain committed to our disembodied ideals of individualism, freedom, and self-expression while everything else in the world unravels.

For reasons flowing from the same sort of argument, the artist may decide to use her art to make a political statement. She may decide, for instance, to give up painting and devote herself to what was previously denigrated as "craft" work, as a protest against male privilege and gender-based inequities. As Elaine Reichek, the American visual artist, put it, "It's political to choose a form that is a craft — not painting, not sculpture, not in the tradition of high white art."

The artist may or may not arrive at this or a similar place, and may or may not long remain there. What is certain, however, is that throughout her career she will question herself about the issues of talent, perhaps subconsciously if the issue is too dangerous or painful, but no less closely for that. She will question herself, doubt herself, and brood about the sufficiency of her talent, no matter how talented she happens to be. She may be gifted with a voice like Maria Callas's but still doubt her ability to hit the high notes in a Puccini aria. She may have the command of language of a Virginia Woolf, the drawing skills of a Picasso, or the melodic touch of a Mozart, but, falling short with a given book, painting, or sonata, label herself a failure.

She will question herself throughout her career, but most likely in a haphazard, self-critical, and confused way. Almost certainly she'll avoid interrogating herself systematically about the matter, especially if she's unhappy with the way her art is going or if she fears that she's untalented.

But in fact such a systematic examination is the most profitable way for an artist to deal with the question of talent.

The matter needs to be put squarely on the table and given conscious attention. For you do need to know what abilities are required in your art discipline, in what measure they are required, and in what measure you possess them. You may learn that drawing isn't what matters, but expressive power is. You may learn that your "talent to amuse" is more valuable than you'd imagined. You may finally understand the real nature of your strengths and discover how to make yourself into an even stronger artist.

Once you've accomplished this assessment, and unless it turns out that you're lacking such an important endowment that you really must alter your sights or change your career plans, it becomes far more profitable for you to focus on creativity than on talent. For it is within your power to become more creative, no matter what the upper limits of your talent may be. And by being creative you make the most of your talents.

If you make every effort you can to bring your passion, knowledge, and will to bear on your art-making, you will become more creative and manifest your talent. If you challenge yourself to love enough, to know enough, and to draw on your knowledge, to work at your art and to master your disinclination to work, your questions about your talent are likely to be answered. Continue to dream and continue to believe yourself special, for if you stop dreaming you lose your motivational energy, you love less, and you grow less creative. Continue to learn, practice, and explore. Ultimately the question of the sufficiency of your talent may melt away as you manifest your creative nature.

STRATEGIES

Ask yourself the following questions about the issues raised in this chapter.

ON CREATIVITY:

1. What do I mean by *creativity*? How is it different from talent?

2. Do I believe that I can be more creative? In what ways? What must I do to become more creative?

3. Do I love my art enough? Do I feel passionate about my art?

4. How can I test whether I love art enough? (Might I base one test on the poet Rilke's advice to a young friend: If I can imagine doing something other than write poetry, might I be better off not pursuing the poet's life?)

5. If I feel less ardent than I think I should, how can I increase my love for my art? How can I really and truly fall in love with my medium (or fall in love with it again)? (One approach might be to ascertain whether I ever really chose to be an artist, or if it was something that just happened. Consciously choosing, perhaps even in a ceremony I devise for the occasion, may liberate my passion and start my lubricating juices flowing.)

6. Do I know enough to work creatively? Am I lacking in any knowledge? Am I insufficiently aware of traditions, the technical aspects of my medium, the current trends and fashions? Given that it is impossible to know everything, is there one area of knowledge that would be really beneficial for me to increase?

7. Do I work hard enough at my art? Do I spend enough hours at it? Do I give it enough consideration?

8. Have I developed ways of mastering my disinclination to work? Do I have a repertoire of strategies? If not, will I put such a repertoire together?

ON TALENT:

1. What do I mean by *talent*? How would I define it?

2. What does it mean to be talented in my field? What skills and abilities does someone in my field need? How many of them do I need to do good work? Do they all matter equally? Are any absolutely necessary?

3. How talented am I? What are my strengths and weaknesses? To what extent do I possess the skills and abilities I need?

4. Do I consider the skills or abilities I lack to be the kinds that one

either innately does or does not possess? Or do I believe that they can be acquired or enhanced through practice or learning?

5. Does the matter of talent, in my case, seem to revolve around one or a few certain abilities that I possess in insufficient measure? Will I create a plan to test myself for those abilities? Will I work hard at manifesting them before deciding that I don't possess them?

6. Having assessed my talent as best I can, what do I see as the right fit between my talent and my career aspirations? Am I setting my sights too high or low?

7. Against which great masters do I compare myself? Against what set of ideals do I compare my talent? Will I consider myself insufficiently talented if I fall short of matching the accomplishments of some great master or the requirements of some set of ideals?

8. Because I see that mediocrity sells in the marketplace, do I doubt that talent is really an issue in my field? Do I need to concern myself with matters other than talent in order to have a career?

9. Because of the path I've chosen to take as a community artist (or a collaborative artist, a craftsperson, a pop artist, a postmodernist, and so forth), how much or how little should the matter of talent concern me?

Next, consider the following nine strategies:

Examine creative blockage. Perhaps what you perceive as your insufficient talent may really be a matter of blockage. Does anxiety, guilt, fear, or ignorance prevent you from manifesting your full talent? If so, you can access your native talent by eliminating those blocks.

One creativity coaching client, a singer, added several notes to both ends of her vocal range by learning to quell her performance anxiety. Another client, previously censoring the contradictions in his nature, began to paint more powerfully when he allowed himself to "tell dark stories" as he painted self-portraits. These are but two of the myriad ways blockage and talent can interconnect. You will learn more in chapter 6, which focuses on blockage, and in chapter 7, which focuses on its cousin, resistance.

Work on a mighty theme. What's the biggest subject you'd like to tackle?

The most important book? The most ambitious painting? The most complicated film? What's the most amazing piece of music to add to your repertoire? What existentially resonates for you?

You may doubt that you can realize your grandest ideas. But doubt is only a certain kind of thinking. If you work attentively on a mighty theme for just a short while, honoring the difficulties but courageously returning to the work, you will grow more creative. Attempt your *Crime and Punishment* or your Ninth Symphony.

Affirm that you can create or perform. Affirm that you can pull off what you attempt. Don't give your fears a second thought. One client, a singer who doubted her ability to form her own band, learned to assert herself by affirming that she was competent to do whatever needed to be done. She auditioned musicians, put together a set, searched out gigs, and performed in the band named after her. Your affirmations can be spoken or written, general or specific. "I can do it" and "No problem," said under your breath, are examples of powerful affirmations.

Carry your work differently. Much of the artist's work, including that of the performer, is done out of conscious awareness. Your fictional characters first speak to one another, then they speak to you. The emotional point of the concerto you're learning comes to you in a dream.

But for the work to get done that way, you need to have a spacious place in your unconscious where it can gestate. If you disown the work or treat it with indifference, it will have no life within you. If, however, you're enthusiastic about the work, curious about its outcome, and disturbed or obsessed by it, and if you're committed to birthing it, it will live within you even as you balance your checkbook.

Periodically surprise yourself with the question, "Where is my work?" Sense if it's nearby or far away. How quickly does it come back? In a split second? If you can't bring it back immediately, spring the question on yourself more often. Nag yourself. The nearer the work is, the more attention it is being given just out of conscious awareness.

If you are a performer, also create. If you're tired of auditioning for inferior roles, roles that you don't respect or that bear no resemblance to your inner reality, write your own performance piece. If you're tired of your band playing only cover tunes, compose. If you're an ensemble player, consider writing a quartet. If you act, consider directing. Don't restrict your creativity by labeling yourself a servant and not a master.

Change formats. Paint larger. Paint smaller. Work within the limits of the sonnet or concerto form. Work outside those limits. Write a novel in the first person. Write a short story in the second person. Put down your flute and pick up a piccolo. Each such change affords you a new piece of knowledge and forcibly shifts your perception of the limits of your medium and the limits of your talent.

Turn things on their ears. Do a painting in the Cubist style. Put new colors on your palette. Play one note and draw out its sound; hear it as if for the first time. Play an emotion on your oboe — improvise. Write naked. Take your band to the beach and play by the water. Redesign your flute so that it fits your fingers. Write the shortest story you have ever attempted — one paragraph long.

Take a new look at the world and at the art you make or perform. If you break free of your habitual ways of thinking, seeing, hearing, and doing, you may be led to an artistic and personal revolution. Have you underestimated your talent? Are you disconnected from what you know and love? Turn everything on its head. You may turn over a rock and find your powerful painting style or fresh fictional character underneath.

For example, are you an accomplished musician who still has trouble sight-reading? You may simply have never grasped the logical relationship between written notes and the keys of your instrument.

Discover ways of working more deeply and effectively. Notice attention leaks. What distracts you? How do you handle distractions? How might you handle them more effectively? What thoughts disturb or derail you? Inoculate yourself against them. Fend them off. Dispose of them. Write them down on scraps of paper, then drop them in an elegant little box you keep on the corner of your desk for that purpose.

Recognize how you work best. Are you flooded with images on train trips? Grab a pad and ride the trolley out to the ocean. Is it important for you to remember your past successes? Keep a framed copy of the cover of your last book where you can see it. Is it important to focus on an upcoming deadline or to purposely forget about it? Do you work best with Vivaldi on in the afternoon but in complete silence in the morning? Create the conditions that elicit your best work.

Track your creativity. Even the most persistently creative person can sink or meander into long, unpleasant, and dispiriting uncreative periods. Keep tabs on your creativity. Remember the three components of creativity: loving, knowing, and doing. You can propel yourself into a creative outburst by choosing any of the three as a starting point. Find your creative spark by working, by choosing a project and launching into it. Rekindle your creative spirit by learning something new — an unusual photographic technique or repertoire piece, the ins and outs of a new brand of oil pastels. Or rejuvenate yourself by falling in love with art again, by spending time with a masterwork.

2 | *The Puzzle* of *Personality*

I have inside me an unchanging, undying need to be somebody else.
That, however, is paradoxically coupled with the unchanging desire to
express myself.

— LAWRENCE LUCKINBILL

There is no one right way to look at personality, an artist's or anyone else's. Personality is in a class by itself and is larger than our attempts to describe it. To suppose that any theoretical orientation — psychoanalytic, behavioral, systems, and so on — can more than partly, and poorly at that, capture the essence of human personality is to make the logical mistake known as reductionism.

Therefore the following discussion of the artist's personality should be considered merely as one way to approach the question, How are artists different from nonartists? Here we'll think of the artist's personality as if it were constructed of certain building blocks, using an approach known as personality trait theory.

At one time trait theory was a popular alternative to the type-and-drive personality theories of Sigmund Freud and other psychodynamic thinkers. To this day the majority of personality inventories and intelligence tests used by psychologists are based on the assumption that particular traits can be meaningfully named and reliably assessed. This approach to personality theory especially fascinated many of the researchers interested in understanding creativity and the makeup of the creative individual. A large literature grew up chronicling attempts to determine which traits, taken together, added up to creativity in the individual or distinguished creative people from less creative people.

This is a fruitful approach for several reasons. First, it helps us to understand the powerful dynamism present in the artist's personality. It seems contradictory to call an artist both shy and conceited, introverted and extroverted, empathic and self-centered, highly independent and hungry for community — until we realize that all these qualities can be dynamically present in one person.

Indeed, this dynamism regularly perplexes and buffets the artist. She may begin to consider herself crazy for longing to perform, even though public performance frightens her, or neurotic for feeling competent at the piano but incompetent in the world. She may come to possess the vain hope that she can live quietly, like other people, her personality statically integrated in some fashion, and then feel like a failure when the contradictory forces at play within her prevent her from feeling relaxed even for a minute. Once she realizes, however, that this puzzling contradiction is her personality, she will be better able to accept herself and to understand her motives and actions.

Second, this approach to personality offers us an additional way to understand what it means to call an artist "difficult." By that label we usually mean that an artist is narcissistic, high-strung, flamboyant, arrogant, or self-involved, but we can also rightly mean that the artist is difficult in the same sense that a complex novel or string quartet is difficult. The artist lives in a state of greater dynamic tension than the nonartist and so is likely to demand more, desire more, withdraw further into herself, witness better, laugh harder, and bellyache louder. This may not be easy for anyone to take

— the artist included — but it reflects not just one quality like selfishness or narcissism but a whole array of interactive qualities.

The ten personality traits we will examine below have been culled from the creativity literature, from the biographies and autobiographies of artists, from my conversations with artists, and from my work with artist clients. As you read about them, you might profitably ask yourself the following questions:

- In what sense is it desirable for an artist to possess this trait?
- Does an artist in my discipline particularly need this trait?
- What might be the repercussions of having too much of this trait?
- What might be the repercussions of having too little of this trait?
- Is this trait equally useful in my art life and my everyday life?
- If this trait is valuable to me as an artist but an impediment in my everyday life, how will I manage this contradiction?

The following, then, are the traits we'll consider:

1. Intelligence
2. Introspective stance
3. Discipline
4. Honesty
5. Empathy
6. Self-centeredness
7. Self-direction
8. Assertiveness
9. Resiliency
10. Nonconformity

Let's examine each of these in some detail.

INTELLIGENCE

How mad should Hamlet be?

— SIR JOHN GIELGUD

Though intelligence and creativity are not directly correlated, artists typically possess a keen intelligence. In experimental studies writers have been shown to score higher on a variety of intelligence tests than do lawyers, doctors, or college professors.

Intelligence, of course, is not a single ability but a cluster of abilities. Among them are cognitive flexibility, intellectual playfulness, an analytic capacity, a proficient memory, a rich imagination, and a penchant for originality. Each has its particular value for the artist and each its particular shadow side.

For example, cognitive flexibility, the ability to see two or more sides of an issue and, especially, to tolerate ambiguity, is generally considered one of the hallmarks of the emotionally healthy person. The unpleasant vibration that attends to complexity — to complex international situations, moral situations, or interpersonal situations — causes the average person to seek refuge in slogans and rote positions. Artists, in contrast, are often able to see many sides of an issue and feel duty-bound to acknowledge and affirm ambiguity.

Artists whose nature or upbringing prevents them from maintaining a wide-ranging flexibility are in danger, in life and in their art, of adopting rigid and airless positions. Such artists are less free to experiment, to let go of a genre, to allow ambiguity to enter their work. Yet artists who are more able to tolerate complexity and ambiguity are themselves confronted by a variety of risks, including the possibility that they will become passive as a result of their excellent understanding. The writer who sees into the heart of his villain as clearly as he sees into the heart of his hero may find his plot slipping away from him, his book coming not to a climax but to an ambiguous ending.

Intellectual playfulness is another aspect of intelligence that artists regularly exhibit. It is a quality apparent, for instance, in the paintings of Paul Klee or Joan Miró, the architecture of Antonio Gaudí, the elegant humor of Jane Austen, the ironic stance of Dostoyevsky, and the music of Mozart.

When the painter Chuck Close says, "In my work the blurred areas don't come into focus, but are too large to be ignored," we imagine him spending time focusing and unfocusing images in his mind's eye, just as a child might spend time focusing and unfocusing images in the viewfinder of her first camera.

The less playful artist is in danger of producing art that will be labeled heavy or dull. The more playful artist is in danger of producing art that will be labeled shallow or silly. All artists are destined to veer in one direction or the other and consequently will have to deal with one label or the other throughout their careers.

If playfulness is a right-brain aspect of intelligence, then a capacity to analyze is a left-brain aspect. It's the capacity reflected in the jazz musician Ornette Coleman's observation: "If I play an F in a tune called 'Peace,' I don't think it should sound the same as an F that is supposed to express sadness." The artist with a capacity to analyze is able to use logic, to compare and contrast two styles or two works of art, and to appraise the strengths and weaknesses of her work.

Artists relatively lacking in these analytic qualities are like miners who have trouble distinguishing among ores. They may happen upon gold and not know it, or they may be seduced by anything that glitters. Artists who are most able to analyze, however, may be challenged by their own high standards. They may be all too aware of the shallowness of the words their character is forced to speak in the play they are performing in, too aware of their instrument's imperfections, too aware of their failure to handle green shades subtly. Their hyperawareness may turn into hypercriticality, so that their output dwindles badly. As Dorothy Parker put it, "I can't write five words but that I change seven."

Artists also possess a special sort of memory. For instance, they can hold in their memory the essence of all the books they've ever written, without remembering the name of a single character in them. Writer Molly Keane said, "If you were to give me some old book of mine, I'd read it with great surprise as though I had no connection with it at all." Your memory is specialized and miraculous. Part of the miracle lies in your ability to let go of what you no longer need to remember, and part of it lies in your refusal to take in what has no value for your art.

Your memory is more selective than the nonartist's. While the nonartist collects facts, you collect glances, glimpses, nuances, images, and tonalities. You remember the essences of performances that stirred you. You have snapshot memories of Gothic churches seen from the train and of schoolgirls huddling in the rain and laughing in the piazza. These are not memories you can draw on to make conversation during the cocktail hour, but they have extraordinary value in your creative life, and this is why you retain them.

That your memory works this way can disable you, however, when it comes to doing business. The splendid image of that Gothic church, which you can bring up at will, is not the image to conjure with as you try to interest an editor in a new idea. For such tasks you must access other parts of your memory banks — parts in which you may have stored precious little information.

Imagination, like memory, is one of the miracles of human consciousness. Its essence is captured in the joyous words of the young Russian writer Natalya Baranskaya: "My imagination takes me so many places — it flies and I fly with it!" But the imaginative life is not available in equal measure to every human being, not even to otherwise intelligent people; nor is the possession of an intense and fiery imagination without its dangers.

If you are an artist with too little imagination, you may produce work that you realize is hackneyed and trite. Or you may pride yourself on your dexterity, fluency, and competency, playing music or writing with commendable technical skill, but you may balk at engaging your own imaginative faculty. The more your personal and cultural traditions demand that you act by the letter of the law, in constrained and safe ways, the more afraid you are to rebel, the more your imaginative faculties may wither away, and the more passive and conforming an artist you may become.

If, however, you have too vivid and untrammeled an imagination, you're in danger of being led about by your imaginings. Withdrawing into a world of fantasy, you may wall yourself off from the world. The artist who lives too deeply in her imagination is less able to find peace than the artist whose imagination is united with real-world purposes. Painter Francisco Goya's dictum applies here: "Fantasy abandoned by reason produces impossible monsters; united with her, she is the mother of the arts and the origin of their marvels."

Artists, bringing their imagination, analytic ability, memory, and the rest of their intelligence to bear on an artistic question, arrive at original ideas and strive for originality in their work. As the painter Georges Braque put it, "The poet can say: the swallow knifes the sky. Thereby he makes a knife out of a swallow."

Performing artists, too, are eager to put their stamp on a role or a piece, no matter how much they admire some past performer's interpretation. Whereas surgeons want to replicate their past operations and lawyers want to make use of their boilerplate documents and their previously successful arguments, artists typically prefer not to repeat themselves.

The artist in whom this impulse is weak may be satisfied with a formulaic way of working, which limits her creativity but may cement her success. The artist in whom this impulse is great will be troubled by his doubts about whether his reckless and exhilarating voyage into the unknown will lead him to success or to disaster.

While intelligence is generally valuable to artists and necessary for their success, it is also a risky possession. Artists who can look deeply into the mysteries of the universe may feel out of step with their culture and may recognize that their culture fails to prize intelligence. They may also experience their artworks as imperfect vehicles for communicating their thoughts.

This latter problem may be particularly vexing. The artist must do more than think: he must successfully manipulate his medium in order to convey in concrete fashion all that his intelligence has to offer. He must not only fathom the universe but also find the means of expressing that knowledge. This is a problem akin to the one Sir Isaac Newton confronted when, on arriving at an intuitive understanding of the motion of the planets, he then had to invent calculus in order to prove the correctness of his vision.

The less intelligent artist will perhaps be less bothered by the need to invent calculus but will also have a less profound understanding of the universe. The highly intelligent artist, however, may be quite bothered and may brood about whether her art has successfully made manifest her ideas. Does her monochromatic painting, her epic poem, her meditative sonata, or her eccentric performance really capture what she had in mind? These are questions that, if long brooded on, inevitably lead to depression.

INTROSPECTIVE STANCE

*What I am seeking, in fact, is a motionless movement, something
equivalent to what is called the eloquence of silence, or what St. John
of the Cross meant, I believe, by dumb music.*

— JOAN MIRÓ

It's one thing to be intelligent and quite another to enjoy thinking, to relish the time spent alone with one's thoughts, to happily muse, imagine, and analyze. Artists, who are introspective by nature, typically enjoy spending time in this fashion and may even prefer solitude to the company of others. Able to work by themselves, artists are often lost in a state of dreamy thoughtfulness of the sort described by painter Hans Hofmann when he wrote, "The first red spot on a white canvas may at once suggest to me the meaning of 'Morning redness,' and from there I dream further with my color."

Artists are not introspective — meditative, thoughtful, lost in time and space — because they wish to ignore the world. They're introspective because out of that attitude artistic answers flow. The artist who is made uncomfortable by this special silence will produce much that is superficial and unrealized. The challenge for the artist who loves this silence with all his heart, however, is that he must sometimes rejoin the world; the world, after all, has much to offer.

Artists bring this state of dreamy thoughtfulness with them wherever they go. As the Russian composer Modest Mussorgsky put it, "Whatever speech I hear, no matter who is speaking nor what he says, my mind is already working to find the musical equivalent for such speech." When we liken the artist to a dreamer, we are referring to this aspect of personality.

The artist who has least permission from herself to dream in this fashion may find herself growing tired of art-making, for by not dreaming she is growing old. The thoughtful dreaming of the artist serves as a fountain of youth. The artist who most evidences this thoughtfulness may, however, be relatively lost to the world. Especially if his reveries have an obsessional edge to them, so that he can't escape them — so that he is *always* dreaming of the musical equivalent of speech or *always* calculating how to capture the image before him — then he is bound to find himself intensely distanced from other human beings.

The editor Burton Rascoe wrote, "What no wife of a writer can understand is that a writer is working when he is staring out the window." In fact, a writer's wife or husband understands this perfectly well. What he or she finds hard to countenance is the artist's bold delinquency in staring out the window so long and so often, while the needs of those around the artist go unmet.

DISCIPLINE

When you're in the theater, you must work incredibly hard. Your life is regimented and you must store up your energy for that one burst of light.

— VERA ZORINA

Artists have available to them two working states, absorption and concentration, and each feels qualitatively different from the other. When artists are absorbed they are lost in time and space and oblivious to their surroundings. As the dancer Kay Mazzo described it, "You prepare and prepare for a role, but the minute you're onstage, you are lost, lost in what you are doing." This is a trance state in which the artist finds the hours slipping silently past as she writes, paints, practices, or performs.

That this state of absorption is valuable goes without saying. Inspiration flows from it. Choreographer Maurice Béjart wrote, "When I start work, I have a total vision of the final work — this vision lasting but one second." The absorbed mind sees whole books, whole ballets, whole movies in a flash.

Concentration, in contrast, is much more of an effortful state. Artists force themselves to concentrate when they feel no particular inspiration and have no real desire to work but nevertheless want to work in a disciplined fashion. If the artist in a trance works with an unfurrowed brow, the concentrating artist's brow is furrowed and her jaw set. While absorption is the ideal creative state, an artist must also be able to concentrate, to work in the face of distractions, for often absorption will elude her.

The Puzzle of *Personality*   33

Some artists never realize that they must sometimes demand this discipline of themselves. They may simply leave their work too quickly. The concentrating artist, who is too aware of her surroundings, of time passing, of the hardness of the work, and of the silence around her, may announce to herself that she is wasting her time and may leave her work, not realizing that the trance state she desires is only minutes or seconds away.

Every so often I lead all-day workshops for writers who consider themselves blocked. Most have struggled for months — sometimes years — producing little or no writing. In the workshop I present didactic material about creating an environment conducive to writing and committing to a particular piece of writing, the day's "mission piece." Then, for the rest of the day, participants write. Invariably, they lose themselves in their writing. When the time for a promised break arrives, I call for another half hour of writing, and then another — and everyone continues writing, stopping only to shake out a tired arm.

Why is this? How is it that they can easily, fully, and dramatically lose themselves in a workshop setting but not in their own environments?

Part of the answer is perhaps obvious. These writers are ready to work; by committing to the workshop, by publicly acknowledging their blockage, by setting aside a Sunday, they've readied themselves to write. Perhaps the supportive group feeling also encourages them (although I do the same work in individual sessions, with similar results). It may be that by sitting with them for those hours, not writing and not daydreaming and doing *nothing* except holding the idea that the group will write, I make it possible for them to remain undistracted and absorbed.

But something of a mystery remains. If blocked artists are so close to working in an absorbed fashion, so close that after an introductory hour they can work steadily all day long in a workshop, what prevents them from making that same leap into absorption in their own homes? It is a mystery that a long discussion of blocks would still not answer. It appears as if the gulf between the productive artist and the blocked or frustrated artist may in reality be tiny — while, at the same time, remaining enormously difficult to cross.

HONESTY

I still put romance in films when I can, but the realities of materialism, corruption, and injustice interfere. I try to reflect how I see things, not create a fantasy world.

— RAINER WERNER FASSBINDER

You have the desire to honestly communicate the truth as you understand it. Frequently you're the only one in your neighborhood making such an effort. You're the one who must tell your grandmother's story, your father's story, or your own story as best you can. And since the truth is frequently painful and rarely profitable, few except you are interested in championing it.

In this regard you are society's primary holder of positive human values. You agree with visual artist Ben Shahn, who said, "I hate injustice, and I hope to go on hating it all my life." Standing apart, holding your own counsel, attuned to both the beautiful and the moral, you are the one able and willing to point out the naked emperor, the stench coming from the closet, the starvation right around the corner, the colors of the far mountains as the eye really sees them.

In all this you make judgments as an independent observer, not as the third vice president of a corporation or as an assistant deputy district attorney. Many dangers naturally attach to this position of independent observer, not the least of which are the pain and indignation that come with clear sight.

There are cynical artists who withhold the truth from their art in order to gain an audience and to make money, just as there are cynical clergy who preach while neither loving nor believing, and these cynical artists are often among the most successful, since they are very attuned to the kinds of lies audiences love. But I am guessing — and hoping — that you prefer to live seriously.

Other artists will tell only a fraction of what they know to be true or will alter or subvert the truth, because of self-censorship, a longing to be popular, or a desire not to offend. As the French writer Jean Cocteau put it, "After you have written a thing and you reread it, there is always the temptation to remove its poison, to blunt its sting." Elmore Leonard, the popular mystery writer, said, "I leave out the parts that people skip." Both of these practices are manifestations of the impulse to have and keep an audience, an impulse every salesperson understands.

But, as visual artist Les Levine put it, "Artists are going to die like anyone else — do they want to leave behind a lot of work they don't believe in?" Every artist internally debates this issue. Should she sing a jingle or a hymn? Should she sing in harmony or protest injustice? Should he tell the dark truth about the alcoholism in his family or entertain his fans with his command of language?

As Martha Rosler, a visual artist, explained, "The main effort of most of mass media is to get you to succumb to magic and lose your critical ability. I want the work to be more of an irritant." If truth is an irritant, however, how is the truth-telling artist to survive? You may never frame the question to yourself in so many words, but you must nevertheless address it your whole career.

The artist who most keenly feels the need to tell the truth will make the fewest concessions, will resist falsification the most, and may, like a scorned prophet, find herself vilified and misunderstood. The artist who is more accommodating, however, who more willingly embraces the commercial and the false, may himself be embraced but may wonder if he is squandering his precious time on earth.

EMPATHY

One actor does not cry on the stage, yet he makes the audience cry. Another actor is bathed in bitter tears, but the audience does not respond.

— MICHAEL SHCHEPETKIN

While the powerful artist is also the self-centered artist, it is not paradoxical to suggest that he is also more empathic than the next person. This is not to say that artists are necessarily compassionate or sympathetic. They may be, for the ability to empathize makes it easier to sympathize. But empathy is not compassion. It is, rather, a certain kind of insight, an ability to correctly identify the thoughts and feelings — even the whole inner reality — of another person.

The artist less able to empathize is perhaps better equipped to maintain a single-minded and self-serving stance with regard to her career. She may feel comfortable writing formulaic fiction, because the one-dimensionality required of her characters suits her perfectly. She may, in her business negotiations, take good care of her interests, feeling content to remain in her own shoes. She may also recognize, however, that her art does not run deep.

While the artist who empathizes least is challenged to act decently, the artist who empathizes most is challenged to maintain sufficient boundaries between himself and others. Then he can dare to experience another's reality without drowning in it.

SELF-CENTEREDNESS

Of course, to start with, I love all my pupils. Then I find the talented ones. They are always the most arrogant.

— ALEXANDRA DANILOVA

One of the more troubling paradoxes of the artist's personality is that artists, champions of human values and heroic in their journeys, able to admire and to analyze, are nevertheless often arrogant creatures. Perhaps the simple explanation for this is that the self-trust and self-direction that artists require, amounting to a healthy respect for their visions and values, equal a powerful self-centeredness. They demand of themselves that they remain firmly in their own shoes, even at the expense of others. As the writer Susan Braudy put it, "I'm basically a treacherous person with no sense of loyalty. I'd write openly about my sainted mother's sex life for art."

The artist not equipped with this necessary arrogance will be repeatedly sidetracked or subverted by others' agendas. He will lack a sufficient sense of purpose, will frequently stall and block, and will bring a nagging passivity to his art career. His resolve to make great art may remain a potent idea only, a kind of unexpended force in his body. He is likely to accomplish much less than he otherwise might, support others rather than find support for himself, attempt the small rather than the large, and rebound less well from rejection.

The self-centered artist, conversely, is challenged to remember that she is a human being with limitations. She hasn't the time to turn every idea into a book, the ability to top each work with a greater one, the energy to toil ceaselessly at her art, or the right to trample others as she pursues her goals. If she mistakes or oversteps these limits, she risks burnout, depression and the angry complaints of those whose rights she has cavalierly trampled.

SELF-DIRECTION

Anybody who makes public art has to invent the territory as he or she walks through it.

— MARY MISS

Just as the restless, committed, curious, and perhaps obsessed explorer follows the river from bend to bend, shooting rapids and pulling himself out of the water, so the self-directed artist launches himself on an exploratory art journey. He judges which fork in the river he will take, when he will rest and when he will push on, and whom he will take with him, if anyone. While he doesn't possess unlimited freedom as he journeys, bound as he is by the demands of his personality, by his time and place, and by circumstances beyond his control, he does possess unrestricted inner permission to explore every available avenue.

The contemporary artist must especially direct and trust himself, because he lives in a constantly changing art environment. The performance piece, the installation piece, the wrapped building, the computer artwork are all aspects of an art vocabulary that resembles no previous one. As Pablo Picasso put it, "Beginning with Van Gogh, we are all, in a measure, autodidacts. Painters no longer live within a tradition, and so each of us must re-create an entire language."

The artist who insufficiently directs and trusts herself will likely fail to find her voice. This failure is particularly dangerous in an era lacking the safety net of tradition. The less self-directing artist is probably best characterized as ambivalent. She finds it hard to choose among her projects, has trouble settling on one medium or one style, finds it hard to choose between tackling commercial art or personal art. She may block at every turn.

If she will not choose which fork in the river to take, who will do it for her? From where will the message come? Will it be found at a workshop? She may attend many. Will it be found at the foot of a mentor? She may search for a teacher, a spiritual leader, a motivator. Will it be found in group wisdom? She may join a church or a movement to receive guidance.

The supremely self-directed artist, however, may find himself unable to countenance other people's opinions and feedback. This intolerance causes him great loneliness and joylessness, the terrible fruits of this particular existential stance. He possesses tremendous passion for art-making, and he understands his medium as well as anyone can, for he has really explored it. But he is likely to be haunted by what he has not explored, perhaps love and intimacy especially. As one composer exclaimed bitterly about himself: "Beethoven can write music, thank God — but he can do nothing else on earth."

ASSERTIVENESS

When a new man faces the orchestra — from the way he walks up the steps to the podium and opens his score — before he even picks up his baton — we know whether he is the master or we.

— FRANZ STRAUSS

Some traits in the artist's personality may lead to a certain sort of passivity (like productive daydreaming) and others to a certain aggressiveness that logically flows from his passion, self-centeredness, and self-direction. This assertiveness is part of the necessary arrogance of the artist.

If asserting yourself makes you feel anxious, frightened, or guilty, you will hesitate to argue with the director who's cut your best monologue or take to task the editor who's failed to deliver on her promise to champion your new book. You will be unable to aggressively forge new art. If, however, you're especially eager to assert yourself, you may discover that your power is not always welcome in relationships; it may make them feel as abrasive as sandpaper. You may even regularly alienate everyone around you.

Related to assertiveness is an ability to take risks. Every medium is risky, and a certain fearlessness, which may or may not be in evidence elsewhere in your life, is required as you leap across the stage, allow your watercolors to drip perilously down the expensive paper, or determine to spend the next three years working on a novel about whales.

The more fearful and conforming you are, the more you'll see danger as you approach art-making. If, however, you're willing to take any risk, you're in danger of manifesting too great a heroism. To take one example, you may ignore the demands of the marketplace and produce mighty work that no one wants. Your epic poem, heroically created, may remain forever in a corner of your drawer. You will have asserted yourself, but to what end?

RESILIENCY

If your mind breaks because of the training, all is lost.

— PAOLO BORTOLUZZI

Artists must be survivors. They must earn a living or find enough support to stay alive. They must bounce back from their depressions and return to the fray after repeated rejections, after their shows close, after their novels are remaindered. To meet the challenges they face requires great resiliency. Everyone must bounce back from disappointments, but not everyone chooses so adventurous and challenging a life. Checks for the civil servant and the tenured teacher arrive each month. The peacetime soldier and the shop clerk may spend months engaged in routine tasks. But the artist runs risks at every turn.

As the writer James Dickey explained, "We have always had a tradition in America of hounding our artists to death. The best poets of my generation are all suicides." Sinclair Lewis wrote, "Every compulsion is put on writers to become safe, polite, obedient, and sterile." Whether the challenges come from without, as Dickey and Lewis propose, or from within, the artist must pray that she is elastic enough to bounce back from each jarring drop to the pavement.

NONCONFORMITY

Good rock stars take drugs, molest policemen, and epitomize fun, freedom, and bullshit. Can the busiest anarchist on your block match that?

— RICHARD NEVILLE

Nonconformity is best thought of as the sum total of the ways in which artists, resolved to manifest their individuality, revolt against prevailing customs and beliefs. Both the guitar-smashing Jimi Hendrix and the reclusive Emily Dickinson epitomize that quality.

Sometimes, for instance, artists may espouse the most conservative of values, as Dostoyevsky did in arguing for a return to religious orthodoxy. Yet to call such an artist "conforming" is to make a fundamental mistake. Such artists are rebelling in their own principled ways against what Herman Melville called the "colorless, all-color atheism" of the average person, just as the angry comic or the revolutionary painter is revolting against the status quo.

We believe that powerful artists are always nonconformists and rebels, even though one may pledge allegiance to God, another to humankind, and a third to the devil. Artists who rebel the least, who are architects rather than opponents of the status quo, may fit neatly into their society but may not speak or know their minds. Artists who are entirely rebellious and nonconforming, however, are bound to upset everyone — themselves especially, since they have so much of the whirlwind within them.

STRATEGIES

Personality is a puzzle, made more puzzling by the fact that we're never able to investigate ourselves in a completely objective fashion. But as limited as we are, we nevertheless can make many inferences about ourselves by examining our thoughts and feelings, by noting and analyzing our be-haviors, by studying how people interact with us, and by reflecting on past events. There are many paths to self-understanding, personal growth, and healing. Use the following strategies as first steps on your journey of self-exploration.

Use guided writing, as described in chapter 13, to isolate core personality issues. Some of the events and dynamics in our lives are so profoundly traumatic that if we fail to address and recover from them, as best we can, we risk leading severely impaired lives. The wounds left from having parents who were alcoholic; abusive emotionally, physically, or sexually; mentally disturbed; controlling; withdrawn; or unavailable rarely heal of their own accord. Use the following questions, and others that you create, to help you address these core issues:

1. Who am I? What is my real identity (or what are my many identities)? Who or what am I describing when I talk about my "self"?

2. What are my most pressing personality issues?

3. What was the single most damaging aspect of growing up in my family?

4. Was I abused as a child? How did that abuse affect me? Do I now abuse myself? Am I self-destructive or dependent on alcohol or drugs?

5. Am I in charge of my life? If not, what prevents me from taking charge?

6. How would I describe the artist's personality? Do I see it as primarily healthy or unhealthy?

7. What makes me an artist? Do I possess the qualities I think an artist needs?

8. How does my artist's personality help or hinder me in other areas of my life?

9. What do I most need to change about myself?

10. How will I investigate my personality? Is it time to start psychotherapy, intensive journaling, or a 12-step program? Should I take a

few psychology or counseling classes, begin a mindful meditation practice, or write an analytical autobiography? What specific efforts will I make to better understand myself?

Use your art medium as a tool for growth and healing. The following exercises, adapted from Evelyn Virshup's *Right Brain People in a Left Brain World*, employ visual media. Alternately, you can create exercises for yourself that make use of the art medium you know best.

VISUAL MEDIA EXERCISES

1. Close your eyes and fantasize about a chasm. Design a way of crossing that chasm, imagining that you have every means known (or unknown as yet) at your disposal. Then open your eyes and draw your solution.

   Observe your solution silently. Note the size of the chasm (the problem) and the inventiveness, efficiency, and safeness of the solution. If there is a rope bridge across it, is it tied securely? If the chasm is huge, does that represent how you feel about the problem? Did you reach the solution with little thought, or did you give it a great deal of consideration?

   Observe nonjudgmentally. See if you can reach new conclusions about crossing this chasm; see if you can come up with new, more varied ways of coping with problems.

2. Fold a large piece of paper into quarters. Silently draw on the first quarter a symbolic representation of "Where do I come from?" After a few moments, draw on the second quarter, "Where do I want to go?" Next, draw a representation of "What is in my way?" Finally, draw one of "How am I going to overcome my obstacles?"

   Grow aware of what you perceive as the obstacles confronting you and of your solutions to overcoming those obstacles.

3. Take a fantasy trip with closed eyes. Walking along a country road with a fishing pole over your shoulder, you come upon a stream.

Cast a line into the water and, after a few moments, reel in what you have caught in your fantasy. With your eyes open, draw what you have caught. Now write a story about the object at the end of the line. In a sense you will be talking about yourself and how you feel about your life at the moment. How do you see yourself?

4. Create two animals on one piece of paper. They don't have to look like anything you've ever seen. Take about ten minutes to do the drawing. Describe the animals you have drawn. Write down three adjectives that describe them. Note the animals' expressions. Can you make up something the animals might want to say to each other? Can you write free verse or fantasy about what the animals say or do?

   The second animal often has qualities that contrast to those of the first. This exercise generally reveals polarities, contrasts, or conflicts within a person; it will show different, sometimes opposing facets of personality. The absence of a mouth, for example, suggests difficulty in communicating. Observe and learn from the fantasy animals you've created.

5. Molding clay, in silence with eyes closed, is an effective way to become aware of yourself. As you feel the clay and squeeze, pound, jab, caress, or do what you wish to do to it, consider that this material is really you. Say to yourself, "This is me, this is how I am feeling now." Spend ten to fifteen minutes experiencing the power of clay with no coiled pots, ashtrays, or other goals in mind; just silently feel the clay with your eyes closed. Then study the form of the clay with open eyes, looking for new images to suggest themselves. If you intuitively become aware of a glimmer of an image, grasp it and develop it. This is your metaphoric mind speaking to you.

Examine each of the ten personality traits discussed in this chapter. Single out the one trait that feels most important for you to better understand. How does it operate in your life? Do you want more or less of it, or more of it at certain times and less of it at others? Look at two personality traits together. Would you like a slightly different balance between them? A radically different balance? In your present circumstances, for instance, is it important that you not empathize with the director, who perhaps has good reasons for taking away your solo song in the third act, working instead on assertively retaining that solo? Or, conversely, is it more appropriate that you restrain your assertiveness and practice empathy instead?

Now examine each of the ten traits in turn. Define each for yourself. Use them as subject matter for a series of paintings, collages, songs, or poems. Treat them as puzzle pieces, and familiarize yourself with the ways they interrelate and interact in your personality makeup.

Examine the concept of human limits. Do you believe that there are human limits, or do you believe that everything is attainable? What are your limits? Which of them can be stretched? How might you stretch them? Which can't be stretched?

There is much that just cannot be accomplished. Whole novels may not work. Whole years may go by with no offers of important acting work. Many challenges will confront you that you will not be able to adequately meet. This is your truth, and every other person's truth as well. Learn your limits and begin to accept them, even as you stretch them to manifest your greatness.

3 Of *Moods* and *Madness*

That many creative and performing artists are visited by severe depression remains much of a secret, even though the biographies of artists, anecdotal and clinical evidence, and recent psychological studies all speak to that truth.

Artists are certainly not alone in this. A great many people struggle with bouts of depression. Studies indicate that, worldwide, from 4 to 10 percent of adult women and from 2 to 4 percent of adult men suffer from depression at any given time. Many more are confounded by the blues. But a far higher percentage of creative and performing artists suffer from debilitating depressions. Recent studies suggest figures of 30, 40, 50 percent, and higher.

One study, by Dr. Samuel Janus, of fifty-five successful comedians concluded that "the vast majority of funny men are sad men." Dr. Janus reported that most of the comedians he studied were severely depressed off-stage. "There are numerous indications," he wrote, "that many of our top comedians, if one listens to their routines, are really crying out loud."

Dr. Nancy Andreasen conducted a study that looked first at fifteen writers associated with the University of Iowa Writers' Workshop and was later expanded to include fifteen additional writers. Dr. Andreasen concluded that 43 percent of the writers evidenced some degree of manic-depressive illness; a full 80 percent sought treatment for mood disorders; two of the thirty committed suicide.

Dr. Kay Jamison, in a study of forty-seven British artists and writers, found that 38 percent had sought treatment for mood disorders, compared to fewer than 2 percent in the general population. Half the poets in the group, and two-thirds of the playwrights, sought treatment.

These and similar studies suggest that creative and performing artists are more often challenged by depression than are people not drawn to the arts. William Styron, in his memoir about his own incapacitating depression, names some of his famous fellow sufferers: Virginia Woolf, Randall Jarrell, Sylvia Plath, Jack London, Anne Sexton, Ernest Hemingway, and Hart Crane. Among musicians we might list Rossini, Robert Schumann, and Beethoven.

Fred Cutter points out the unambiguous suicidal imagery in the works of five hundred well-known painters, among them Jackson Pollock (*Ten Ways of Killing Myself*), Andy Warhol (*The Suicide*), Edvard Munch (*The Suicide*), and Paul Klee (*Suicide on the Bridge*). It seems that the artist's mood is often black, at times so black that he or she considers suicide.

Depressive episodes often begin early in the artist's life, sometimes in childhood, more often in adolescence. Isolated, sensitive, feeling different from his peers, the artist is frequently the victim of depression as a teenager. The poet Maxine Kumin described her own youthful struggles: "I was a lonely kid, very introspective. I felt very much at odds with my environment and my culture. I was just a real loner, taking my solace in books. I think I was terribly, terribly moody as an adolescent. I had very dark moods. I was very depressed."

Is there any one reason why artists are so likely to be visited by depression? Almost certainly not. There are, first of all, too many sorts of depressions. Some are called neurotic, others existential; some are associated with mania and as such are considered part of a special cyclical disorder (called manic-depressive illness or bipolar disorder). The depressions called major, like William Styron's, are sometimes accompanied by florid psychotic episodes.

Some forms of depression may have a significant biological or genetic link, as is suspected of the depression that occurs in manic-depressive illness. Some depressions seem more rooted in fury, some in self-hatred, some in loneliness, some in sadness. Others seem triggered by envy, boredom, or hopelessness. Some seem in some sense adaptive — the depressed person conserving psychic energy, withdrawing from the pressures of the world, and taking a break from attempting to master anxieties.

In the life of an artist, the incidents that can bring on depression are too numerous to catalog: the rejection of a latest poem, the good luck of a fellow poet, a loveless visit home, the rent coming due, the loss of a new love, roaches appearing in the refrigerator. As many different self-disparaging and despairing thoughts can bring on depressions as there are stars in the sky. Indeed, the very look of the starry sky can bring on an existential depression.

We might identify a characteristic artistic personality and make the case that something in that personality is the key to this high incidence of depression — say, that artists are more introspective than the next person (which is usually the case), or that they are more open to experience and therefore more sensitive, or that they typically experienced loss or abandonment in childhood. We would still be left with too many important individual differences to draw any clear conclusions.

One artist might be more ambitious, and so more depressed if her career founders. Another artist might be more open to experience, and so more exposed to pain in the world. A third might be more intelligent, and so more prone to existential depressions. I suspect that the many personality traits we reviewed in chapter 2, which appear so often and to such a marked degree in the artist, open the artist up to the possibility of depression. Some combination of these traits may even, when taken together, turn out to be a kind of blueprint for depression.

Whatever the sources of your blue moods, you're bound, when you're depressed, to suffer from some or many of the following: sadness; boredom; fatigue; insomnia or excessive sleep; significant weight loss or gain; loss of hope; indecisiveness; diminished interest and pleasure in your usual activities, including art-making; diminished sex drive; irritability; inertia; restlessness; diminished ability to concentrate; loss of self-esteem; morbidity; recurrent thoughts of death; and suicidal ideation.

Each feature of the depressive episode challenges you. To overcome your insomnia you may begin taking sleeping pills and develop a habit. To combat your inertia you may opt for stimulants. Artists often turn to drugs to combat their depression. Singer-songwriter James Taylor, who described his bouts of severe depression as "unexplainable black moods," said, "There's a type of despair that I experience as being very deep. In the past my tendency was to crawl in a hole and poison myself, intoxicate myself."

The artist who uses drugs regularly is likely to experience depressive episodes that are then related to his or her drug use. Singer-songwriter Paul Simon described such a period in his life, while he lived in London: "It was very unsatisfying, the drug use, although I started out loving it. But at the end, it was bad. I couldn't write. It made me depressed. It made me antisocial. It brought out nastiness in me. When I'd deal with people while I was high, I'd listen to them and think, 'Boy, he's really stupid. That guy's really phony. Phony smile, phony everything.' And the same thing with me. I'd say, 'Oh, boy, you really are ridiculous. Absolutely ridiculous.'"

For a more complete discussion of the challenges faced by creative individuals with respect to depression, please take a look at *The Van Gogh Blues: The Creative Person's Path through Depression*. In it I argue that the primary depression confronting artists is existential in nature and is best remedied by the active pursuit of meaning-making: that is, you fight depression by forcing life to matter.

THE MANIC ARTIST

I had this driving ambition — I was going to be a simply smashing actor.

— SIR LAURENCE OLIVIER

Artists are regularly troubled by depression and by the ineffective or self-abusing coping mechanisms they employ to fight their depressions. But their lighter moods often prove troublesome as well, for the "up" artist is frequently manic and neither happy nor at ease in the universe.

For many artists, manic episodes or manic-edged moods, like their depressive episodes, begin early in life. The artist may experience clinical mania, characterized by pseudoeuphoria, irritability, grandiosity, a decreased need for sleep, an increased activity level, a racing mind, and sometimes hallucinations and delusions. Or he may experience hypomania, a milder and less impairing version of the disorder, which divorces the artist from reality less. Most likely, he will experience an even milder mania that will nonetheless distinctly color his moods and give him the sense that he is racing along, perhaps in decent spirits but nevertheless under real pressure to create and to succeed.

Your everyday intense, driven, and enthusiastic way of being may have a manic feel to it. This restrained mania may become one of your most characteristic moods: mind racing, hands moving, dreams vivid, art alive to you. The visual artist Patricia Tavenner explained, "My head and my hands never stop." Poet Richard Wilbur described fellow poet Theodore Roethke: "He would arrive at the door bearing cases of champagne and silver dollars for the children, and when he felt himself getting too manic he would spend an hour or more under our shower, cooling down."

Part of this manic edge is doubtless related to the fact that artists are gambling every day. You gamble that you will be spotted in your present small role and discovered, or that the right magazine will publish your story, or that you haven't made a foolish choice in pursuing poetry instead of practicing medicine. You also gamble each time you start to do your art. Art-making is one of the greatest gambles of all. As visual artist Helen Frankenthaler put it, "No matter how fine or meticulous or tortured a picture may be in execution, the risk or chance of its working or not working is always there, no matter what the method."

It is a high-stakes gamble, after all, to work with all your being on something that has so great a chance of failing. The sculptor Alberto Giacometti said, "To my terror the sculptures became smaller and smaller. Then they became so minuscule that often with a final stroke of the knife they disappeared into dust."

To face such a life of risk taking, you have to rev yourself up. In fact, some kind of mania is the predominant mood in many art communities. As visual artist Sandy Walker said of the contemporary New York art scene, "Living in New York is like living with your finger in the socket." Who can sustain such intensity in their work? Not to crash after a painting or a writing jag or a brilliant performance seems almost more unnatural than crashing. As Georges Braque said on seeing Picasso's *Les Demoiselles d'Avignon* for the first time, "After spitting fire, what is the artist to do? Sit and smile contentedly?"

Passionate when you're really working, moved by the performances you see and the books you read, aroused by color, excited by the look of your city, stirred by the possibility of applause, anxious, your nerve ends exposed, you may live manically; and therefore you may be, right at your most energized and vital, a person ready to plummet.

This alternating between intense moods, from mania to depression, from enthusiastic encounter to discouraged retreat, may be the natural way of the creative person. Michael Kalil, the architect and artist, struggling to design a scale model of his habitation module, explained, "First I got excited, then I got depressed. My background disintegrated: there was no up and down." Writer J. D. Salinger, in an autobiographical note, described himself as "alternately cynical and Polyanna-like, happy and morose, affectionate and indifferent." Another writer, E. L. Doctorow, offered up the following advertisement for manic depression: "The writer's life is a daily crisis. Very great ups and downs. I would like to qualify as a full-blown manic depressive, because any state that is really realized would be very productive for a writer."

Whether or not this fluctuation of mood is inevitable, whether it mimics manic-depressive illness or is just a distant cousin, you will be challenged to deal with it more often than you would wish — maybe even constantly.

THE ARTIST AND ANXIETY

Is it really necessary to encumber oneself with this anxiety to bring to life things that have no apparent reason for stirring?

— POL BURY

As if your manic and depressive moods weren't burdensome enough, you're also likely to experience severe anxiety. All of us must wrestle with anxious feelings and the physical and emotional consequences of anxiety, prompting psychiatrist Barry Blackwell to write, "We can predict that with the arrival of the millennium the whole of America will be taking tranquilizers."

In addition to the anxiety inherent in simply being human, as an artist you are also confronted by chronic performance anxiety. The painter and the musician, the writer and the actor, are performing. Your performances will be judged, and the specter of embarrassing failure haunts many an artist. In a 1987 survey of 2,212 professional classical musicians, for instance, 24 percent complained of experiencing severe performance anxiety. Twenty-seven percent of these sufferers used beta-blockers to help ease their anxiety.

Significant anxiety also wells up in the artist when it comes to taking care of business. Meetings with gallery owners, curators, literary agents, publishers, casting directors, and other representatives of the business end of art — because these meetings feel so momentous, matter so much, and are fraught with so much possibility — frequently terrify artists.

On top of being human, a performer, and, of necessity, a businessperson, you also possess personality attributes that invite anxiety. You accept as your stock-in-trade a sensitivity to the doings of the world — and the world can be a fearful place. Fascinated by the human condition, alive to the historical moment, you are one of our culture's witnesses. Among your goals is to speak through your art about what you witness, and witnessing makes you more vulnerable to feelings of anxiety. This is both your burden and your gift to society. As Russian American visual artists Vitaly Komar and Aleksandr Melamid put it, "It is our fate and our misfortune that we live in history. An artist who doesn't know history paints like a cow, because cows have no memory."

The artist wants to witness. If she desired that less, or if the world appreciated her witnessing more and criticized and rejected her less, she might feel less anxious. Indeed, it may be, as visual artist Louise Nevelson put it, that "all great innovations are built on rejections." But that fact does nothing to help quiet an artist's nerves or raise her spirits. That you are striving, that you have dreams and ambitions, are sources of anxiety. As Paul Klee put it, "He who strives will never enjoy this life peacefully." Willem de Kooning made the same point with a different aphorism: "Art never seems to make me peaceful or pure."

For a fuller discussion of anxiety's role in the creative process and in the lives of creative individuals, please consult *Fearless Creating: A Step-by-Step Guide to Starting and Completing Your Work of Art*. In that book I describe the sorts of anxiety that attend each stage of the creative process — for instance, the hungry-mind anxiety associated with the wish to create, the chaotic-mind anxiety of working, and the critical-mind anxiety that arises at the showing stage — and present strategies for dealing with these anxieties.

THE ANGRY ARTIST

Part of my disease is anger.

— JIM CODY

Artists often feel rageful. Anger, in fact, may be one of their dominant moods. What, exactly, do you rage against? That you are poor, unrecognized, and isolated? That art is hard to do and that you can't stop doing it? That your relationships frequently don't work; that you feel part of no community; that you are visited by depression? You may be furious at the marketplace: furious that popular movies are homogenized fairy tales, that the audience for real work is so small, and that the audience for your own brand of art is an even smaller fraction of that already small number.

You may also be angered by your critics, by academics, by theorists. Painter Pierre-Auguste Renoir once exploded, "Don't ask me whether painting ought to be subjective or objective. I don't give a damn!" The visual artist David Smith explained, "We've let anthropologists, philosophers, historians, connoisseurs, mercenaries, and everybody else tell us what art is or what it should be. I think we ought to very simply let it be what the artist says it is."

You may also rage at the same things that anger other human beings — that your grandparents died in the Holocaust, that your great-great-grandparents were kept in chains. Gender issues may infuriate you, a fury sarcastically expressed by the painters Larry Rivers and Frank O'Hara: "All we painters hate women; unless we hate men." And as the novelist Marilyn

French put it, "I think women are very, very angry. I don't think people probably have any idea how angry women are, because women are trained to be nice. Women are extremely angry. And if my books have anger in them, it's because that anger is out there in the world."

EMOTIONAL DISTURBANCES AND MADNESS

We were all a little nuts in the Dorsey band. Ziggy Elman, a great trumpet player. Joe Bushkin on piano, another nut. The Pied Pipers were all crazed, every one. Connie Haines was on the verge of becoming nuts.

— BUDDY RICH

As these anxious states grow more severe in an artist, they may constellate into certain recognizable syndromes. One artist may manifest his anxiety by experiencing severe and prolonged pain that appears to have no organic cause; this clinical syndrome is known as psychogenic pain disorder. A second artist might manifest her anxiety by engaging in repetitive behaviors, such as washing her hands a hundred times a day; this clinical syndrome is known as obsessive-compulsive disorder. A third artist may manifest his anxiety by needing to avoid crowds and public places, a clinical syndrome known as agoraphobia.

These individuals, while impaired and in pain, do not, as a rule, break with reality. But some artists do. In our exploration of the emotional well-being of artists, we must consider the matter of madness and the artist's relationship to it. The individual with the childhood history, personality, identity, aspirations, and inner makeup of the artist almost certainly is at greater risk of going mad than the next person. And since madness appears to run at the rate of about 1 percent in all cultures at all times, even if the rate were no higher for creative and performing artists, at least tens of thousands of our fellow artists would find themselves challenged to remain sane.

While it may be controversial to assert that artists are at higher risk for madness, it is nevertheless a sensible assertion. For whatever else it may be, madness is, in significant measure, a kind of intense acting-in, a departure from everyday reality to the battlefield of a stormy inner reality. The artist, self-absorbed, intense, and thriving on her inner life, regularly lives closer to such a departure than do her less introverted, less imaginative, and less agitated brothers and sisters.

Because the artist experiences such intensity in his inner life, he is at greater risk of going mad. The intensity that flows in a pattern of highs and lows — of creative effort and lassitude, enthusiasm and depression, fruitful hours and blocked hours, the birth of a project and its death, performances and the aftermath of performances — subjects the artist to disturbances and disorders of mood. When that intensity grows so great that it cannot be discharged in any usual way, then the artist begins to resemble a boiler about to explode.

This image from mechanics is not meant to seduce us into ignoring the psychology of the matter, for we are talking about human beings going mad, not boilers exploding. The image may remind us, though, of how tumultuous are the forces within the person we call mad. Even the person who descends slowly into madness — declining a little each year, growing a little more eccentric, less capable, and less communicative — begins the descent with a roiling storm blowing through him, overpowering his limited human ability to remain sane.

What Is Madness?

I am one individual, imprisoned in myself, hanged and condemned to solitary confinement in my own ego for life.

— JEAN TINGUELY

It seems appropriate to continue this discussion of the artist's relationship to madness with a sensible definition of madness — or, in clinical language, of psychosis. But it's a bit of folly to define something we do not understand. We do not understand whether, and in what measure, the individual contributes with his thoughts and feelings to that state of deterioration, personality disorganization, disordered thinking, or regression we call psychosis. We do not know whether the psychotic is visited by madness, as one is unexpectedly visited by relatives; or whether he makes his own madness, as one contributes to one's own high blood pressure by failing to handle stress effectively; or whether he invites his own madness, as one invites a friend to dinner. We do not know what part of madness is hereditary, what part environmental. We do not know if brain irregularities cause schizophrenia or are the result of schizophrenia.

What we do know is that the insane person can sometimes maintain knowledgeable contact with the world, can make rational and subtle calculations with respect to that outside world, even while he appears to be manifestly insane. This fact, derived from retrospective reports of the formerly insane and from studies concluding that madmen can act sane in order to get the institutional benefits and privileges they want, suggest that the madman is more in contact with the world than he lets on or than we might think. His madness, terrible to behold, is perhaps more like a screen than a wall, or more like a wall with chinks in it. It may be that the psychotic has not so much disintegrated as retreated into his psychotic state; retreated, as the psychiatrist Malcolm Bowers put it, from sanity.

From that place of retreat he still observes the world. One may, for instance, burn a catatonic schizophrenic's fingers without him flinching. But later, if he's so inclined, he can report on every nuance of every gesture made by the one who burned him. This hardly means that the madman is playing a wild charade. Rather, it means that we must wonder where he is and what he is doing, how he got there, and if his wires are crossed or his soul disturbed.

We understand madness so little that clinicians define it by how it looks rather than by what it is. If you looked a certain way — if you laughed inappropriately, coined new words, complained of a dull thud in your chest, failed a mental-status exam, and hoarded food — you, too, would be called mad. If, especially, you demonstrated one of the hallmark signs of madness — delusions or hallucinations — and couldn't point to a drug trip or to specific brain damage to explain your communications with Mars, you could count on acquiring that label.

To repeat, we know precious little about madness. With that enormous disclaimer, let us take a stab at one view of it. Even if only partly true, this view would help explain why the artist and the mad person face the similar grave danger of an unplanned departure into virulent acting-in.

A View of Madness

I didn't know what was expected of me. I was a dummy. I thought perhaps I was on the wrong planet. My teachers could have been speaking Russian or Chinese as far as I was concerned. I would sit perplexed, drinking ink.

— ANTHONY HOPKINS

It is quite possible that a special inner intensity characterizes the everyday experience of the person who goes mad. In the child this intensity is likely to manifest itself in restlessness, irritability, and an inability to concentrate rather than in a clear withdrawal from the world. Whether this intensity and subsequent acting-in stem from hereditary or environmental factors, or an interaction of the two, remains an open question. For the moment we will assume that madness has a psychological component and that it is not simply a defect in the brain's machinery.

This point of view is reinforced by a pair of special cases of madness: battle fatigue and the brief reactive psychosis sometimes seen in newcomers to a foreign land. The incidence of psychosis is considerably higher both in the trenches and among refugees and new arrivals in foreign places than it is in the general population. These particularly stressful situations, in which the individual comes to feel profoundly powerless and abnormally isolated, are no doubt initially met by the individual's first line of ego defenses.

For example, psychically leaving the scene — dissociating — is a common temporary defense of children who are molested and abused. It is also implicated in the strange cases of psychogenic fugues and amnesias, in which the individual disappears from his New York law partnership one day and resurfaces a year later as a short-order cook in a small town in Kansas, with no memory of, and blissfully unconcerned about, his past. In mild forms it is an everyday defense, a staple in the repertoire of ways we protect ourselves.

But for some significant number of soldiers experiencing weeks of constant bombardment, and for some significant number of refugees experiencing the wild disruption of fleeing their homelands, these everyday defenses prove inadequate. Hearing their own voices only, in an ever-stranger dialogue with themselves, they finally break; they go mad. They retreat from or are forced to flee sanity. Even if they were predisposed to madness (the genetic link), we nevertheless intuitively understand that we, too, might break under such conditions. Anyone might. In that case we are forced to admit that each of us is susceptible to the onslaughts of madness.

In this view, the person who will go mad experiences life as if she were a stranger in a strange land or as if she were under constant bombardment. For her the normal range of ego defenses proves inadequate. More and more she disengages from the world and retreats into her acting-in world. In the characteristic fashion of madness, these pressurized feelings and thoughts are transformed and embodied, and a war begins between the forces of good and evil in the madwoman's mind.

If psychic intensity is one hallmark of the madwoman, and severe isolation a second, a special kind of internal splitting is a third. Something in the makeup and experiences of these individuals causes them to hold in warring opposition two extreme positions: one of power, omnipotence, and godlikeness on the one hand, and one of loathsomeness, insignificance, and pained injury on the other. These positions are extreme forms of positive and negative inflation. The individual, at once grandiose and abased, simultaneously maintains a subjective sense of godlikeness and a subjective sense of victimization. We might call this her *god-bug* sense of herself.

These extreme antithetical positions are regularly evidenced in madness. As Edward Edinger, a Jungian analyst, pointed out in *Ego and Archetype*, "Taking on oneself too much of anything is indicative of inflation because it transcends human limits. Too much humility as well as too much arrogance, too much love and altruism as well as too much power striving and selfishness, are all symptoms of inflation."

As a child and young adult, before he goes mad, the individual rarely splits off and embodies his thoughts and feelings in so radical a fashion. Yet the process of positive and negative inflation probably begins early on. The child, perhaps initially distancing himself from his parents and perhaps needing that distance to survive, begins to feel different from other people. Understanding himself to be different, he likely also thinks of himself as special. He feels a little uncanny in his growing envelope of isolation; his language and jokes become private, his preoccupations obsessional, his connection with the world more tenuous. In growing isolation, with terrors and pressures mounting around him, he grows more abject and small and becomes at once grandiose and a little pathetic.

Our candidate for a psychotic break may be the hard-to-reach child, the impatient child, the agitated, preoccupied, moody, strange, or withdrawn child. If he is relatively less injured and relatively more competent, he may look healthy enough until he breaks suddenly in young adulthood. This is the path of the reactive psychotic. If, however, he is relatively more injured and less competent, his decline into strangeness may begin early on and may proceed rather undramatically toward complete disintegration. This is the path of the process psychotic.

Whichever the case, the young person, although already acting-in, hasn't yet split. She doesn't really feel like a god — she feels less potent than that. And she doesn't really feel like a bug — she feels more significant than that. At the outset she possesses an existential understanding of her own humanness and at least a confused idea of the nature of human limits. But the disputes between her contradictory feelings, waged in the dream arena of her mind, percolate. They begin to erupt as bizarre behaviors and obsessive episodes — the compulsive hunt for a flawless nectarine or for positive proof of Shakespeare's identity. These are the opening salvos of the full-fledged war to come.

When will this inner turmoil erupt into full warfare? Most typically in late adolescence or early adulthood, when the young person attempts to enter into a first intimate relationship or break away from home. Such moments bring the hurt and haughty youth's extreme and unregulated self-identifications into collision with one another and with the world. Is he a god to his first girlfriend — or a worm? Is he omnipotent in his college dormitory — or impotent? The strain of facing the special terrors of relationship sends the youth further inward. There the battle intensifies.

The first psychotic episode, perhaps following a painful rejection or a stressful altercation, likely commences with a prodromal period lasting hours, days, weeks, or months. During this time the youth appears to be growing stranger and to be deteriorating. He becomes more eccentric, more absent, more self-referential, less able to take care of himself. He is likely to sleep little, to make phone calls at three in the morning, to begin to talk to himself on buses. He begins to preach the gospel or curse and rage in public. The world sees him as someone to avoid.

To the youth, however, this may seem like a time of great energy, great sensory awareness, and great import or moment. He may feel frightened or ecstatic; at any rate, everything is fraught with meaning, intensified. Everyone is speaking about him, looking at him. Nothing can be overlooked. He begins to see visions, to hear voices. Great, portentous events are on the horizon.

In his book *Retreat from Sanity*, Malcolm Bowers reports on the experiences of a twenty-year-old visual artist: "He describes a mystic or 'cryptic' state during which the solutions to various problems seem obvious. In these states he feels capable of bringing together the arts and sciences, his separated parents, and himself into harmonious 'oscillation' with the world. Going without sleep heightens the mystic state and improves his 'freedom and vision' in painting. In this state he cannot tell whether he is thrilled, frightened, pained, or anxious — they are all the same."

One thirty-eight-year-old music teacher reported on his growing madness: "God actually touched my heart. The next day was horror and ecstasy. I began to feel that I might be the agent of some spiritual reawakening. The emotional experience became overpowering."

We may wonder, as many have wondered, if this prodromal period doesn't represent a valiant attempt on the person's part to make sense of his warring feelings by, in effect, inviting them to come forward and do battle openly and plainly. If it is indeed a kind of invitation, then it is easy to understand how feelings of ecstasy and expectation might accompany the invitation, along with the dread that approaching the brink produces.

R. D. Laing, during the period when he believed (along with many other radical psychiatrists) that madness was a quest on the mad person's part to break free and grow, quoted one patient's understanding of his psychosis in an article in *The Psychedelic Review*: "I believe I caused the illness myself. In my attempt to penetrate the other world I met its natural guardians, the embodiment of my own weaknesses and faults. I had forced untimely access to the 'source of life,' and the curse of the 'gods' descended on me. Then came illumination. A new life began for me and from then on I felt different from other people."

The central feature of a budding psychotic episode is that the individual cannot or will not turn off her obsessive intensity. Perhaps she can't help herself; perhaps the battle is a desperate attempt to bring peace through warfare, a violent effort at synthesis or reorganization. When Shakespeare announced that "the lunatic, the lover, and the poet are of imagination all compact," he underlined their common bond: their "seething brains." The madwoman is besieged by her own thoughts. If her language grows loose and if she coins new words, it is probably because her way of speaking begins to reflect the complex, conflict-driven inner dialogue in which she is participating. Her new, odd language is certainly not meaningless. The psychiatrist Harry Stack Sullivan, for one, called the mad person's linguistic efforts "very high order abstractions."

If we do not understand the madwoman, it is perhaps because we are not up to doing the work that would be required to understand her, just as we may not be up to doing the work required to understand *Finnegans Wake*, James Joyce's protracted dialogue with his mad daughter, or the cantos of the occasionally mad poet Ezra Pound.

Madness as a Human Experience

Everything is a burden. Is there anything that does not weigh on me?

— EUGENE IONESCO

The madman's experience appears to be a very human one. He believes that he is worth something, and this worth is magnified as his brain relentlessly seethes. He also feels injured and misunderstood, and these feelings are intensified as his mind reels, until they produce a fantastic inner landscape.

We intuitively understand how Ivan, the middle son in Dostoyevsky's *The Brothers Karamazov*, grows mad as he broods on the painful existential questions that torment him. We intuitively understand how someone whose eyes seem to bleed as he stares at the landscape with his brush poised — as Cézanne described his sensations while painting — harbors within himself the possibility of madness.

To further underscore this humanness, we may look in another direction.

The Minnesota Multiphasic Personality Inventory, or MMPI, is one of the most widely used personality inventories. It is an empirically normed test, which means that rather than being theory driven, its questions were selected according to their ability to distinguish between two populations, one hospitalized in psychiatric institutions and the other not. If, for instance, both groups answered yes the same number of times to a given question, that question was discarded, since it possessed no ability to discriminate. If, however, one group answered yes or no more often than the other group, that question was retained.

Several scales were developed in the course of analyzing the data. One was called the Schizophrenia Scale. If an individual managed a significantly high score on this scale, on the order of two standard deviations above the mean, and the other scales had a certain characteristic look to them, then the subject had responded in a manner closely resembling the responses of those hospitalized individuals labeled as schizophrenic.

Let's ponder for a moment the sorts of questions that distinguished between the two groups and the sorts of answers these schizophrenic patients typically gave. Asked if they preferred daydreaming to doing anything else, they tended to answer yes. Asked if they felt understood, they tended to answer no. Asked if they thought they'd often been unfairly punished, they tended to answer yes. Asked if they thought they got all the sympathy they ought to get, they tended to answer no. Asked if they'd ever been in love with anyone, they tended to answer no. Asked if almost every day something happened to frighten them, they tended to answer yes.

These are only a few of the items on the Schizophrenia Scale. Among the remaining questions are ones that probe for eccentricities, hallucinations, delusions, and the like. The mad person seems, in this analysis, to be a hurt, lonely, fearful, misunderstood, and introspective individual who also demonstrates certain signs of madness. It does not surprise us to find that artists, according to the psychologist Frank Barron's MMPI studies, tend to show slight elevations on the Schizophrenia Scale. For the artist is intensely involved enough with her own thoughts, and misunderstood, injured, and isolated enough to begin to climb that scale.

Treating Madness

What is most real for me are the illusions I create with my paintings.
Everything else is quicksand.

— EUGÈNE DELACROIX

How can madness be treated? Many would argue that medication is the treatment of choice, the only treatment, really. Others argue that drugs simply quell the organism, that they are no more a treatment than a tranquilizer dart fired at a raging rhino is. But if mad people aren't to be tranquilized, how are they to be helped in turning off their intensity? How are they to allay their anxieties? How can they find peace, rather than wage war?

The story of the Belgian colony of Gheel may provide us with some important clues. Legend has it that an Irish king, after the death of his wife, was persuaded by the devil to propose marriage to his own daughter. The terrified and outraged girl fled to Belgium, where her father found and killed her. In the *Handbook of Psychiatry*, K. J. Karnosh and E. M. Zucker described what happened next:

> In the night the angels came, recapitated the body and concealed it in the forest near the village of Gheel. Years later five lunatics chained together spent the night with their keepers at a small wayside shrine near the Belgian village. Overnight all the victims recovered. In the 15th century, pilgrimages to Gheel from every part of the civilized world were organized for the mentally sick. Many of the pilgrims remained in Gheel with the inhabitants of the locality, and in the passing years it became the natural thing to accept them into the homes; thus the first "colony" was formed and for that matter the only one which had been consistently successful.

Our previous discussion suggests that the madman must persuade himself that he is neither a god nor a loathsome creature. If he can do that, he may relieve himself of both burdensome self-identifications. He must also find safe ways of escaping his self-protective cocoon of isolation as he begins to engage and accept the world, neutralize his intense self-consciousness, and escape from his brooding thoughts.

It may be that the effectiveness of a milieu like the colony of Gheel is rooted in its ability to help the madman accomplish just these necessary goals, by accepting him and offering him a normalizing routine and simple work. This is not to say that one can't go mad or remain mad in the company of cows. But digging in the earth may be more therapeutic than electroshock therapy or antipsychotic medication, especially if that digging is not a "therapeutic task" in a hospital garden but a piece of natural work in a functioning environment.

Let's end this brief discussion by asserting that madness, as the painter Jim Dine said about his own intensity, is not the least bit funny. Nevertheless, it may be as human a reaction to the perils of living as the anxieties, depressions, and addictions that plague so many of us.

Few of us will find ourselves the Napoleon or the Virgin Mary of the locked ward. Few of us will need, as a consequence of our inner preoccupations, to lend our minds out to the visiting forces of good and evil. But if we are artists, we perhaps understand that we have a certain affinity with madmen and madwomen. It is not that we crave, worship, or respect madness. Nor do we take our eccentricities and obsessions to be tokens of our family resemblance. Rather, we understand in what measure we share with our afflicted brothers and sisters an intensity that sometimes threatens to crack the walls of our living vessel.

This excursion into a theory of madness has value because it suggests that a life lived deep in an envelope of isolation is potentially hazardous to mental health. Artists who live in self-imposed isolation, bound up with their own thoughts and processes, must find ways to regularly break out into the sun and shadow of everyday reality if they are to remain well.

Paul Klee exclaimed in his diary, "Am I God? I have accumulated so many great things in me!" But we also remember these other words of Klee's, quoted earlier: "He who strives will never enjoy this life peacefully." The lucky artist may be the one who, while in human measure a god, has nevertheless found satisfactory ways of escaping the relentless firing of his or her synapses.

STRATEGIES

The following section includes both self-help strategies and information about professional resources. Many of the challenges discussed in this chapter call for professional consultation, with respect both to diagnosis and to treatment. The following strategies focus on ameliorating depression and anxiety; for information on the diagnosis and treatment of psychosis, please consult the National Alliance on Mental Illness (www.nami.org).

Deciding If You Need Help

Answers to the following questions offer diagnostic clues in the assessment of depression. They are not offered to help you make a formal self-diagnosis, but rather to alert you to the signs of depression. A yes answer may be suggestive of depression; or, in context, it may be suggestive of some other condition. Please consult a licensed or certified mental-health professional if you suspect that you are suffering from depression.

1. Have you experienced a depressed mood (dysphoria) for at least two weeks?

2. Have you experienced a diminished interest or diminished pleasure (anhedonia) in your usual activities for at least two weeks?

3. Have you recently experienced a significant weight loss, weight gain, or a change in your appetite?

4. Are you sleeping more than usual (hypersomnia), do you have significant difficulty getting to sleep, or do you awake early in the morning and find it difficult or impossible to get back to sleep?

5. Do you experience a significant amount of fatigue, or are you in a persistent state of low energy?

6. Are you experiencing a diminished sex drive or menstrual disturbances or irregularities?

7. Are you having severe trouble with memory lapses, concentration, or decision making?

8. Do you think about death and/or suicide? Do you have a plan to commit suicide?

9. Do you experience feelings of worthlessness, guilt, helplessness, and/or hopelessness?

10. Do you experience a good deal of tension or irritability or find yourself often worrying about relatively minor matters?

Treating Depression

A comprehensive treatment plan for depression includes most or all of the following elements. You should also contact your personal physician and/or the Depression and Bipolar Disorder Alliance (www.dbsalliance.org).

As a first step in the treatment of depression, seek a medical work-up. Obtain a diagnosis of and treatment for any medical problems that may be implicated in your depression. If, for instance, you have undiagnosed diabetes, which renders you impotent, that impotence may bring on a depression.

Examine the role prescription drugs may be playing in your depression. Stopping or changing medications may be indicated.

Stop the use of easily abused substances. These include alcohol, marijuana, and cocaine.

Consider taking antidepressants. Some people benefit greatly from antidepressant medications such as MAO inhibitors and tricyclics; some benefit only minimally. For others, such drugs appear to have no effect at all. Similarly, some people more easily tolerate the side effects of antidepressants than others. Including antidepressant medications as part of your treatment program is a choice that you should make in an informed manner, in consultation with a physician. Educate yourself about the possible benefits and likely side effects.

Do family-of-origin work. Insight therapy can help you better understand how the dynamics of your childhood formed and perhaps scarred you. Low self-esteem, a self-critical nature, undiluted rage at a parent, long-term reactions to childhood loss and abandonment, and other crucial residues of growing up can precipitate depressions. You can tackle this family-of-origin work by yourself, with the help of workbooks and self-help books, or in individual or group psychotherapy.

If you tackle this work by yourself, with the help of the guided writing practice described in chapter 13, consider using the following questions to focus your thoughts:

- Did a depressed atmosphere pervade my childhood home?

- Did my parents seem defeated?

- Where my parents pessimists?

- What part of my upbringing might be contributing to my depression?

- Does some issue between my father and me need to be aired or cleared up before this depression will lift?

- Does some issue between my mother and me need to be aired or cleared up before this depression will lift?

- Is my depression related (even after all these years) to my parents' divorce, the loss of one or both of my parents, or their emotional abandonment of me?

- Does depression seem to run in my family? If so, to what do I attribute that pattern?

Focus on the expression of feelings, insights into feelings, and acceptance of feelings. Much depression is rooted in unexpressed and unexamined feelings. For you, as an artist, it's important to ventilate feelings associated with the challenges outlined in this book. You may feel sorrowful that you're not sufficiently recognized, guilty about spending too little time at your art, rageful at a marketplace that is uninterested in or antagonistic to your art products, or envious of your fellow artists. These feelings, as long as they remain unexpressed and unacknowledged, knot your depression in place.

Do cognitive work. The way you habitually speak to yourself can depress you. Examining your array of negative self-statements and beginning to alter them (the central processes of cognitive therapy) are important steps in your battle plan to fight depression.

Do existential work. Family-of-origin work looks backward. Existential work focuses on you as you are this minute. Will you take responsibility for your own well-being? Will you commit to making the changes you deem necessary? Will you reinvest meaning in your art and write or audition again? Will you rehearse and get ready for your concert? Will you do battle with your excuses, your lassitude, your disinclination to work? Will you come up with your own reasons for living? Meeting these challenges of "authentic living" reduces depression.

Examine your interpersonal dynamics. Daily interactions with the people in your life can make you anxious and depressed. Look at the different relationships that form your interpersonal life. We'll examine this more closely in part 3, but for now ask yourself: Is a particular relationship disturbing me? A lack of relationship? Actively address your relationship issues, remembering that, while there are limits to what you can accomplish interpersonally, such limits can be stretched significantly.

Learn stress management. Stress-management techniques include meditation, yogic and other deep-breathing practices, regular exercise, biofeedback and autogenic training, and the use of visualizations and progressive relaxation techniques. They also include taking time-outs for yourself, growing assertive, decreasing your sense of learned helplessness, and extinguishing inappropriate thoughts. Include in your program of stress management whatever soothes you and releases tension — a soak in the tub, a massage, browsing in a bookstore or museum. Treat yourself to something relaxing every day.

Treating Anxiety

As with depression, anxiety is typically treated with medication, talk therapy, or both. The approach just described also serves as an anxiety-reduction program, with the same proviso that a medical work-up be included as a first step in managing your anxiety.

Other Personal Responsibility Strategies

Take charge of your energy. When the performance ends and you're too wound up to relax, it's up to you to find ways of draining your battery that don't harm you. You're the one in charge of accepting or refusing the speed, cocaine, heroin, marijuana, or alcohol. You're the one who says yes or no to joining the group after the show, the one too wired to go home, the one full of barely contained energy while waiting for your book to be published. How will you manage your energy? Find the active or meditative techniques that work for you, master them, and use them.

Accept that you are a live wire coursing with electricity. Your dramas, your lustiness, your fantastic irrationalities, your passions are likely to shock and dismay you. Sometimes you'll experience high-voltage despair and disappointment. Sometimes you'll rage out of all proportion to the events in your life. These outsized feelings are you with your insulation off, awash in a shower of emotional electrical sparks. Become your own master electrician and learn to control that energy.

Take charge of your moods. If your mania or depression is so gripping that only medication will touch it, you are in charge of seeking out and accepting medication. It is up to you to manage the anxiety that prevents you from doing business effectively, that hinders your ability to perform or audition, that causes you to block. Beer, speed, cocaine, heroin, or champagne is not a long-term answer. Cutting yourself with a razor so that the pain will bring you back to life is not a long-term answer. Compulsive eating is not a long-term answer. Sleeping around is not a long-term answer. Inside you know better. Look for healthy answers and commit yourself to the courageous effort required to put your new answers into practice.

Explore mental-health counseling. Treatment for depression and anxiety-related ailments is available in hospital and clinic settings and from psychiatrists, psychologists, and certified or licensed mental-health counselors (including family therapists and clinical social workers). Psychiatrists, who are medical doctors, can prescribe medications, including antidepressants, tranquilizers, and antipsychotic drugs, and may also employ talk therapy. Other mental-health practitioners engage in one form or another of talk therapy, supplemented sometimes by art therapy or psychodrama techniques.

Some hospital clinics or freestanding clinics specialize in the treatment of depression and/or anxiety-related conditions. Many use behavioral or cognitive approaches; others employ antidepressant or antianxiety medications as the basis of treatment. Some specialize in work with certain issues, like assertiveness, or with certain populations, like survivors of incest or abuse. Often the lowest-cost psychotherapy is available through college and university counselor-training programs, where clients are seen by interns and trainees. These interns are not necessarily too young or too inexperienced to help.

Ask yourself the following questions as you begin work with a new therapist: Does the therapist seem particularly ignorant about the realities of the artist's life? Does he or she want to glamorize or romanticize the artist's life, on the one hand, or dismiss or devalue art, on the other? Does the therapist seem to imply that you should grow up? Does he or she look up to you or down on you? Is he or she cold, smug, controlling, or abusive? If you find yourself answering any of these questions in the affirmative, you may want to ask yourself if that therapist is right for you.

Use appropriate medical services. Artists frequently experience special medical problems associated with their particular discipline. The musician and the dancer, like the athlete, often play with pain. The glazes that potters use include hazardous chemicals, as do some of the materials used by printmakers, painters, and other visual artists. These special health needs have begun to be addressed as the specialty of arts medicine has grown. For more information please visit the Performing Arts Medicine Association's website, www.artsmed.org.

4   *Obscurity* and *Stardom*

*Any writer who says he doesn't worry about fame, who says he has never,
from time to time, gauged his success against that of other writers,
is lying.*

— SEAN ELDER

Most artists desire recognition, and the persistent lack of it may be a bitter pill to swallow. The artist who is too soon recognized, as Norman Mailer felt himself to be, might argue that early fame is harder on the artist than years of obscurity. But the composer with a score for a powerful symphony locked away in his drawer and the actress who has never found her way into a great drama would be hard-pressed to agree with Mailer. Similarly, the painter who has her entire output of paintings to enjoy because she cannot sell them may praise her fortitude and applaud her accomplishments but still experience great sadness.

If you are not honored with real, appropriate recognition, you struggle not to consider yourself a failure. Though you may argue that it is the world that has failed you, it is hard to take comfort in that knowledge. You need recognition more than you need an accurate understanding of why recognition has eluded you. During your years in the trenches, as you deal with what may turn out to be a maddeningly insufficient lack of recognition, you are challenged to find ways of maintaining your faith, courage, good cheer, and emotional equilibrium.

RECOGNITION AND GOOD WORK

I decided that my painting would never be the equivalent of that
pseudo-Cuban music for nightclubs. I refused to paint cha-cha-cha.

— WILFREDO LAM

The artist wants to be recognized for the quality of her work. It will not do, emotionally speaking, to gain fame for the mediocrity of your art, for your publicity stunts or drinking habits, for your affairs or your parties with celebrities. All that may earn you fame, but your goal is to do work that matters and to be recognized for that work.

Take, for instance, the case of Jean Cocteau, the fabulously notorious French playwright, novelist, filmmaker, and artist. No man could hope to achieve greater fame than did Cocteau, whose career was likened in its brilliance to that of Merlin. But Cocteau complained bitterly that he was never really recognized. He called himself "the most invisible of poets and the most visible of men." He saw that he possessed celebrity, not real recognition. Others saw that, too. Jean Genet, Cocteau's protégé, charged his mentor with "having done nothing but be a star for ten years." Cocteau, stung by his sense that recognition had eluded him, wrote in his diary: "My fame derives from a legend consisting of gossip and carelessness. No author is so known, so unknown, so misunderstood as I am."

The contemporary star, even more than Cocteau, is caught in a great blizzard of publicity, gossip, and myth making, so that it becomes nearly impossible for Christo to know if his wrapped bridges and buildings are bringing him recognition or notoriety; nearly impossible for painter R. C. Gorman to know if his reputation is based on his stylized paintings of Indians or on the fact that celebrities like Elizabeth Taylor regularly visit him in

Taos; nearly impossible for Cher to know if she is respected as an actress and performer or held in ridicule as the embodiment of low culture.

In order to warm the artist's heart, the praise that she receives needs to connect to a felt sense that she is doing good work. Random or wrongheaded praise won't do the trick; that will only exacerbate her feeling that she is unseen and misunderstood.

RECOGNITION, CRITICISM, AND REJECTION

How seldom do we meet with a proper amount of sympathy, knowledge, honesty, and courage in a critic.

— C. P. E. BACH

Even left-handed praise is the exception rather than the rule in the artist's search for recognition. More often than not your recognition will consist of criticism, not praise. You may be criticized for not attempting work you have no desire to attempt, for pandering to mass taste, for working too exotically or too narrowly, for not sounding like Luciano Pavarotti, Willie Nelson, or Aretha Franklin — or for sounding like Luciano Pavarotti, Willie Nelson, or Aretha Franklin. You may be criticized for being too parochial or too catholic, for being out of fashion or for being in fashion. You may be attacked in a review that purports to praise you. In short, you may be criticized for everything and anything under the sun.

Can you escape this criticism as you struggle for recognition? No. The journalist Elbert Hubbard said, "To escape criticism, do nothing, say nothing, be nothing." You simply can't escape the "venomous serpents that delight in hissing," as writer W. B. Daniel called them, or the "drooling, driveling, doleful, depressing, dropsical drips," as the conductor Sir Thomas Beecham characterized his critics. You can't escape criticism, you can't tame your critics. You may not even be able to rid your dreams of them. Igor Stravinsky wrote: "I had another dream about music critics. They were small and rodent-like with padlocked ears, as if they had stepped out of a painting by Goya."

The artist will be criticized as an individual; his whole group, once he is considered part of a group, will also be criticized. Whether the criticism is directed at French surrealist poets, New Age musicians, Soviet realist painters, performance artists, African American filmmakers, photographers who work large, watercolorists who work small, too-handsome actors, or tuba players, the artist discovers that he must defend himself against criticism leveled not directly at him but at artists whom he is told are his comrades.

It is disheartening to hear that only postmodernist writers are worth reading, or that only Japanese prints are worth collecting, or that only European filmmakers are really doing art. You may find yourself, in addition to cultivating and protecting your own reputation, needing to protect the whole genre, style, or idiom in which you are working. George Inness, the nineteenth-century American artist, for example, felt compelled to write: "Nothing is considered good without a foreign name on it. When one of our biggest dealers on Fifth Avenue was asked to procure for a gentleman two American pictures for one thousand dollars each, he said he could not take the order because there was not a picture produced in America worth one thousand dollars!"

When you must also fight to have your genre — be it modern dance, poetry, live theater — recognized, an extra burden falls on you, one you don't want to shoulder but can't avoid. Nor do you possess many effective ways of responding to criticism. If your mother shudders as she views your latest work and wonders aloud why you persist in painting screams, what can you say in defense? If your mate, viewing your latest work, finds herself without a response, how will you address what feels like her silent criticism? Can you cry out and demand, "Say you love it, damn it!"? You may not even know if you love it yourself, and your doubts are magnified by the shudders and silences around you.

Writhing in pain at all this internal and external criticism, you may make some retaliatory gesture, as did the writer who rented an airplane to buzz over the office of an editor who'd rejected his manuscript. If you have the money, time, and inclination to do battle, you may counterattack, as Broadway producer David Merrick regularly did. Merrick placed a full-page ad in the *New York Herald Tribune* peppered with raves for his latest show from people with the same names as the critics who'd panned it.

Another time he offered up ads with references to his critics' love lives. Is such revenge sweet, or is it futile and embarrassing?

As often as the artist is criticized, he's probably more often rejected. If you produce a product for which there is only a limited demand, if you ignore the requirements of the marketplace, if you're unlucky and lack connections, if you do work that is objectively inferior to the work of other artists in your territory, if you venture into new territory, if your message isn't a bland one, then you are more likely to experience rejection. The producer Don Simpson described life as a production executive at Paramount: "You're tired all the time, and you're never in a great mood because you have to say no to 200 people a week. Ninety percent of your judgments are no. You offend people, you hurt people, you may damage people."

In the lives of artists there are a thousand varieties of criticism, much of it implied, and there are also a thousand varieties of rejection, much of it covert. The writer's novel is published, but in a small and careless printing. The dancer moves from the corps de ballet and debuts as a soloist, but the next time the ballet is performed she is back in the corps. The actress or musician who has been steadily — and heroically — working is asked in an interview, "Where have you been all these years?"

The playwright's play is booed off the stage opening night and cancelled after five performances, as Chekhov's *The Seagull* was. The composer's concerto is rejected by every famous soloist, as Tchaikovsky's violin concerto was at first, then finally performed, only to be castigated in the manner of Edward Hanslick's review: "The violin was yanked about, torn asunder, beaten black and blue. Tchaikovsky's violin concerto brings us for the first time to the horrid idea that there may be music that stinks in the ear."

The artist may be criticized and rejected in tragicomic ways. The following news item came from Derby, England: "Seven metal sculptures, representing one year's labor by artist Denis O'Connor, were sold as scrap for $16 by his landlord while he was on vacation, the artist told a civil court hearing this week." The landlord told the court that he thought the sculptures were junk. Perhaps he did think that. Or perhaps he had merely found the perfect expression of his antipathy toward the artist. How better to reject the sculptor and cast him in a ridiculous light than by mistaking his images of birds and trains for junk?

For a more complete discussion of the ways that an artist — or anyone — can handle the criticism she is bound to receive, please consult *Toxic Criticism*. In that book I describe tactics like writing "dear critic" letters that you use to ventilate your feelings and other strategies for becoming less affected by the criticism you receive.

RIVALRIES AND ENVY

Competition is for horses, not artists.

— BÉLA BARTÓK

In this highly charged force field, in which each artist secretly longs for recognition, attempts but only sometimes accomplishes excellent work, and is battered by criticism and rejection, terrible antipathies between artists, and between artists and players in the marketplace, smolder and sometimes erupt.

Truman Capote, himself only wanting to be praised, characterized Jack Kerouac's work as "typing, not writing." One poet stated in an open letter in *Small Press Review*, "I am often puzzled how someone could write all those highly sympathetic poetic biographies and be so vicious in his criticism of his fellow writers." Painter Mary Cassatt criticized all the paintings she viewed at a visit to Gertrude Stein's — and all the people there as well. The dancer Igor Markevitch described ballet impresario Diaghilev's sadistic glee in humiliating Prokofiev: "One day, I visited Diaghilev in his hotel. As I entered the lobby, I met a man who had just been to see him. The man was in tears. When I saw Diaghilev minutes later, I asked him who that poor fellow was. He smiled diabolically, and said, 'Oh, that was Prokofiev. He burst into tears because I asked him to change the finale of his score for *Le Fils Prodigue*. It was the third time I requested the change.' Diaghilev seemed to take a sadistic pleasure in making his artists suffer."

Take, as a last example of the genre, the following item, reported by San Francisco columnist Herb Caen: "The literary roundtable that meets at Trader Vic's includes such illuminati as Arthur Hailey, Paul Erdman, Oakley Hall, Henry Carlisle, Barnaby Conrad, Herb Gold, Blair Fuller and

Martin Cruz Smith. Among the very few women writers ever invited, rather condescendingly, was Miss Danielle Steel, who looked around the table and said sweetly, 'Y'know, I've sold more books than all of you put together.' A simple fact that caused a terrible silence to fall over the distinguished group."

The psychologist Peter Salovey explained this dynamic: "Everyone feels some envy or jealousy, but only in those domains that matter the most for his own view of himself. You feel envy or jealousy in those areas where you stake your reputation and pride."

Even real but limited recognition is likely to feel insufficient to the artist who invests his whole being in his reputation as an artist. Not only is such an artist challenged to live without the recognition he craves and to experience his fellow artists as something other than rivals, he's also challenged to master what may turn out to be his own insatiable appetite for recognition.

OBSCURITY AND INJURY

In the arts there are no A's awarded for effort.

— JOHN BRAINE

Who emerges from this picture of rejection, criticism, and envy? An artist who feels herself unfairly treated. Forty years down the road he may receive the Nobel Prize for literature and still complain bitterly, as Saul Bellow did, that the award took too long in coming. One writer had this to say in *Small Press Review*: "I've been writing now for nearly twenty years. The first half of that time I didn't get published at all, and for the second half my appearance in print has been limited to little magazines that pay in copies and self-published broadsides, open letters, pamphlets, and full-length books. Obscurity doesn't build character. It feeds resentment, envy, anger, and fear."

The novelist does not start out expecting to go unpublished or to be the underpublicized mid-list author of a big press. The poet does not start out expecting to self-publish. The pianist does not start out expecting to play at weddings and bar mitzvahs. The actress does not start out expecting to see door after door close in her face. The realization that this has happened comes gradually. It may take years in coming. Sometimes the artist will feel closer to realizing his dream, sometimes farther away. For a few, a full measure of recognition will come one day. As columnist and novelist Anna Quindlen, on tour with her first novel, put it, "One of the best parts is when people say, 'Oh, you must get so tired of signing books.' On the contrary, I've been waiting all my life to do that!"

WHEN SUCCESS COMES

A ballerina's life can be glorious. But it does not get any easier. I don't think anyone must ever think about it getting easier.

— ALICIA MARKOVA

Few artists achieve the success they dream of. Even the artist with several gallery shows, mid-list novels, or records to his credit likely neither reaps rich rewards nor feels singularly successful. And yet it may be an even greater challenge for the artist who achieves immense success to survive his own stardom. As the singer Pat Benatar explained, "I wasn't prepared for stardom. I wasn't prepared for everyone wanting a little piece of me, literally and figuratively. The first year was so hard, going from being a nobody to a somebody."

The artist who isn't a star laughs at such problems. "Just give me stardom!" he cries. "I'll try my hand at it!" But stardom can and often does injure the celebrity artist. Actor Charlton Heston said, "Celebrity is a corrosive condition. Fame literally destroys actors. It has crippled a score or more and it has left none unmarked. You can't be a celebrity and remain a normal person."

Once the artist wins a little approval from the world, once he becomes even a little known and acquires even a little audience, certain challenges come into play. At the extremity of stardom, failing to negotiate them isolates the artist, overwhelms him, or causes him to change in disturbing ways. Why should this be the case? Consider the following.

The Freeze-Frame Reaction

*I can't stand to sing the same song the same way two nights in succession,
let alone two years or ten years. If you can, then it ain't music; it's
close-order drill or exercise or yodeling or something, not music.*

— BILLIE HOLIDAY

Once an artist becomes successful, her audience typically expects a certain
kind of work from her. She has little permission to grow or change. She's
supposed to remain frozen in the position they met her in and in which
they presume they like her best. Bandleader Artie Shaw put it well: "In
1938, I was the highest-paid bandleader in America, and yet I was belea-
guered. The audience would not support me if I did what I wanted to do.
I had to do what they wanted me to do. Music to order. How do you do
the same tune every night the same way? How many years can you play
'Begin the Beguine' without getting a little vomity? I got to a place where
they said, 'Stop, don't grow anymore.' That's like telling a pregnant woman,
'Stop, don't get more pregnant.'"

Singer-songwriter Paul Simon described his own predicament: "Having
a track record to live up to and the history of success had become a hindrance. It becomes harder to break out of what people expect you to do.
Nobody encouraged me to break with Art Garfunkel. Everybody said,
'What the hell's wrong? Why don't they stay together?'"

Stravinsky complained: "I cannot compose what they want from me,
which would be to repeat myself. That is the way people write themselves
out." To expect that the artist doesn't want to grow once she has become
successful is to think of her as mercenary, in it only for the money and tangible rewards. But a desire for riches is not usually the real motive in an
artist's heart. In love with her medium and believing herself to be full of
astounding possibilities, she wants to grow, to experiment, to stretch limits. Repeating herself bores and frustrates her. But her audience is unwilling even to permit her fictional detective to start smoking a pipe, let alone
get married or move to Tangiers.

The artist is therefore challenged to find ways to make fame less stifling than it can easily become. For instance, some artists have announced early on to their fans: "Love me, love my changes." Some have done two kinds of work, one of which remains familiar and unchanging and one of which is less formulaic. The Belgian writer Georges Simenon, for example, produced an array of comfortable Inspector Maigret mysteries but also a number of psychological novels not restricted by a recurring character. Film stars return to the stage, sitcom actors stretch by going against type in film, and rock musicians, tired of electrification and drum machines, join together to play acoustic music.

Deceitful Compromises

I can definitely recognize greed. I know when a man is playing for money.

— COLEMAN HAWKINS

The path to stardom may involve the artist in significantly compromising situations. Compromise is a well-nigh inevitable component of doing business in the arts or anywhere else. But some compromises are more likely than others to deflect artists from their original intentions and creative aspirations, to diminish their self-esteem and sense of moral worth, and to injure them.

Among the worst compromises are such deceits as the desperate or cynical writer who has his books ghostwritten, the artist who allows others to paint his paintings, or "singing" groups who are actually lip-syncing, such as Milli Vanilli. These practices, because they are outright frauds, may strike us as the worst sorts of compromises. But these flagrant deceits, like the sitcom laugh track, are perhaps only the loudest examples of industry-wide moral lapses.

How much must you compromise? What will you do to secure and maintain your popularity and your income? Consider, in this regard, the case of Sir Arthur Conan Doyle, the creator of Sherlock Holmes. Coming to hate the fact that his historical novels, such as *The White Company*, could not compete with his immensely popular Sherlock Holmes stories,

Doyle killed Holmes off. Outraged, Doyle's public and his publishers put intense pressure on him to resurrect his fictional detective. Wishing Holmes dead but under pressure to revive him, Doyle made what we may suppose was the painful decision to bring Holmes back from purgatory. He maintained, however, that the detective would have only a brief second coming.

We might dub this particular solution the compromise of the limited sequel. Like the "freeze-frame" phenomenon, it speaks to the fact that the successful artist, like the successful retailer, has customers whose expectations she fails to meet only at great peril to her career. That peril is not only to the artist herself but also to her family and her "stockholders" — her publishers, agents, producers, collectors, dealers, and all the rest who depend on her. She may expect pressure to be exerted from all sides as she mulls over a decision, pressure to keep doing the popular and lucrative thing until the public tires of her sequels.

Plateauing

What I found myself writing, after the success of my first book, was a second book based on what I thought various people wanted — something fairy tale–like, or exotic, or cerebral, or cultural, or historical, or poetic, or simple, or complex.

— AMY TAN

Often the successful artist harbors the sentiment, as did Doyle, that the work that has made him famous isn't his best work. Even the most heroic, iconoclastic artist can find himself trapped by his own image, popularity, and fame, so that he comes to feel that his work has stagnated, plateaued, and never had the chance to mature. Pablo Picasso put it this way: "Today I am famous and very rich. But when I am completely honest with myself, I haven't the nerve to consider myself an artist in the great and ancient sense of the word. I am a public entertainer who has understood his times. This is a bitter confession, more painful indeed than it may seem, but it has the merit of being sincere."

The Bursting-Balloons Syndrome

Every year there's a whole new crop of performers.

— SHERRY EAKER

The successful artist may also worry about how fragile a commodity is his fame. Will his balloon burst at any second? Memories of the toughness of his journey to success, along with an appreciation of the realities of the world, may conspire to make him live in fear of losing his fame. As the singer John Cougar Mellencamp put it, "Somehow I always think that the record company is going to drop me next week, that the next record is going to come out and sell five copies, and I'll be back to pouring concrete."

The artist is not wrong to fear the possibility of such loss — it is a realistic apprehension. The public may turn away from him; tastes may change; his drinking may begin to lose him roles. The artist may be a Bach, but history shows that Bach fell into obscurity. The artist may be a Faulkner, but history shows that Faulkner fell into obscurity. Fame can be fleeting. Few artists manage to spend a lifetime in the public eye; few acquire the sort of name recognition that persists from year to year and decade to decade. Writing a bestseller or winning an Academy Award guarantees no lasting fame. Even the artist whose name we instantly recognize may be out of work for longer stretches than he would like us to know.

The artist may also harbor the irrational fear that she will be exposed as a fraud. Or she may simply not *feel* successful, doubting her success at a gut level. As the actor Jack Lemmon put it, "Success is always someone else's opinion, not your opinion." She may fear that fashions will change and that something new will win the hearts of collectors or of the few patrons of live dance or theater. The marketplace will exert its special brand of tyranny, and suddenly raw work, which was thought to be so beautiful, will now be considered ugly; or subtle work, which was thought to be so profound, will now be considered insipid. As the German artist Hermann Albert put it, "People used to demand beauty, grandeur, and such-like from works of art. Later they wanted the opposite, and that's a form of dictatorship, too."

If the artist's medium demands that she race against the clock, she may also fear her balloon bursting as she grows older. The dancer, like the athlete, is especially confronted by the specter of a time-bound career. Age also alters the standing of the leading man or woman and the rock musician. When will the rock singer finally look too silly breaking his guitar over his knee or cavorting as the last angry old man? As singer Grace Slick put it, "There's nothing more ridiculous than old people on the stage."

The artist may also fear that she herself will prick the balloon. The successful artist has almost too many chances for self-sabotage, considering that her perch is precarious, that her art is difficult to do, and that she faces enormous pressures. As a result she frequently does burst her balloon herself. Pianist Claudio Arrau described this dynamic well: "We artists suddenly fall sick before major appearances. We create frightful emotional upsets, we risk losing what we hold dearest. We fall and break an arm. We have car accidents. Singers suddenly become hoarse, can't make their high notes, and often tighten their neck muscles into such a vise that it is amazing that their vocal cords function at all. Instrumentalists suddenly lose the use of some fingers or suddenly can't play the simplest (or the most difficult) passages."

In this regard we must remember that the successful artist, like his less famous brothers and sisters, is confronted by all the personality challenges discussed earlier, including disorders of mood. The artist who salutes his audience with a big smile and a clenched fist as he is applauded may in fact be severely depressed before, after, and even during his performance. The following newspaper account captures some of this reality: "The dramatic intensity of Rachmaninoff's 'Third Piano Concerto' took an unexpected turn at UCLA when soloist Norberto Capone suddenly stopped in the middle of a solo passage, rose to his feet, and announced that he would play no more. As a stunned Mehli Mehta looked on from the podium, the 34-year-old pianist calmly told the hushed crowd Sunday night, 'This is a crisis I've been dealing with. I don't want to play in public anymore. I'm sorry.'"

In part owing to insecurity, the newly crowned star also loathes saying no. He may try to please everybody. Having waited years for his art to bring him recognition and now suddenly surrounded by apparent well-wishers, he is challenged to remain true to himself, to refuse some invitations, to carefully examine all the contracts he signs. A poet friend warned the painter Marc Chagall: "Do you realize that you are famous here? Just the same, don't count on the money Walden owes you. He won't pay you, for he maintains that the glory is enough for you!"

Cult of Personality

If a man be without the virtues proper to humanity, what has he to do with music?

— CONFUCIUS

The star is hard-pressed, once he achieves stardom, to feel like a normal person, to act like a normal person, or to be treated like a normal person. Stardom brings with it such a pervasive air of unreality, and it so changes the artist's relationship with other human beings and with himself, that he may wonder if he'll ever be able to get his feet back on the ground.

Especially during the first months and years of stardom, a loss of inner tranquility can easily occur. This sudden and severe disequilibrium can disorient, upset, and block the newly famous artist. Some artists seem never to recover and to recapture the qualities of absorption out of which their art flowed. Naguib Mahfouz, the Egyptian Nobel Prize–winning author, upon tasting worldwide fame for the first time at the ripe age of seventy-seven, lamented: "I can tackle small things as far as my health condition permits. But even for this I do not have the psychological tranquility."

Tennessee Williams wrote an eloquent essay called "The Catastrophe of Success," which first appeared in the *New York Times* and was later used as an introduction in the New Classics edition of his play *The Glass Menagerie*. Here is an excerpt:

[After the great success of *The Glass Menagerie*] I was snatched out of virtual oblivion and thrust into sudden prominence, and from the precarious tenancy of furnished rooms about the country I was removed to a suite in a first-class Manhattan hotel. [After some time] I found myself becoming indifferent to people. A well of cynicism rose in me. Sincerity and kindliness seemed to have gone out of my friends' voices. I got so sick of hearing people say, "I loved your play!" that I could not say thank you anymore. I was walking around dead in my shoes and I knew it.

The artist is both pleased and disturbed by the new attention he receives. He feels internal pressure to make instant decisions. He feels pressured to lock up the next giant role, to quickly capitalize on his fame, to secure the next big book contract. Who will he let interview him, and at which openings will he appear? How will he invest or spend his money? Will he move from his small apartment behind a factory to a grand house on the hill?

In making these quick decisions he may alter his life, perhaps without improving it. He may find himself madly on the go, a party animal and performing seal, the recipient of designer drugs and a participant in sexual adventures. He may find himself living in a town he had never even meant to visit, in an enormous house with servants and guard dogs, more isolated than he ever was as an aspiring artist. Singer-songwriter Johnny Cash reflected on his own situation: "I still don't know why I ever moved to California. I like it there, had worked out there quite a bit and thought I'd love living there. But I didn't really belong out there. I never really felt at home there."

Life in solitude is no longer the same, and life out in public is even more transformed. The newly famous artist is noticed, pawed, and scrutinized. His former anonymity, from which he had been able to view and study the world and which he thought he would willingly give up for recognition, begins to feel like too great a commodity to have lost. Actress Meryl Streep expressed her dilemma: "The soul, the source of what I do, is observation. But since I became famous I can't watch people — because they're watching me."

A pimple on the cheek of an unknown artist is a pimple. On the celebrity's cheek it becomes a stigma. The unknown artist need possess no arsenal of witticisms or pat responses with which to fend off interviewers. But the celebrity will look foolish or aloof if he doesn't respond glibly. The unknown artist need take relatively little care of what she says or how she says it. But the celebrity will be quoted, and a few quotes will go a long way toward defining for all time how the world thinks of him.

The celebrity's utterances suddenly have value — as do his underwear and his garbage. He becomes in no time both a symbol of the great riches that elude the many and an entrée into that world of wealth. No aspiring actor can forget that the celebrity director across the room can change her life overnight. No aspiring writer can forget that the celebrity writer is deep inside the castle, while she remains outside. Contact with the star feels both dreadful and wonderful — two words that together form a definition of awe.

The star is easily experienced as a kind of god, not because of who he is, but because of what he possesses and what he represents. At the same time, many in the artist's sphere rebel at this deification of him. So the artist will find himself surrounded by a gleeful multitude who are happy to notice that he has gotten fat, that his last picture was a stinker, or that his wife has run off.

The star — loved, feared, despised for succeeding, wooed, envied, seduced, and invisible as a real human being — is on everybody's trophy list and on everyone's target list. Metaphorically and sometimes literally, he is marked for destruction. As Truman Capote put it, "The people simply cannot endure success over too long a period of time. It has to be destroyed."

The artist who becomes a cult figure, who carries the burden of a public mythology, can grow angry with his audience and the world. He may, at the same time, feel embarrassed by his own bellyaching, because he understands as well as anyone what a statistical rarity his success represents. He may work hard to quell his feelings of anger, believing them unseemly. But the feelings are likely to persist and to finally leak out, as they leaked out of singer James Taylor's lips: "They don't want to see an album cover without my face on it, the record company says. They want *Sweet Baby James*. And the audiences may want *Sweet Baby James*, too. So I thought, the next cover I make, I'll get someone with an airbrush; I'll get a tan on my ass, and I'll get someone to photograph it with one of those lights that makes a halo around you, and I'll call it *James Taylor — Like You Like Him*."

The artist isn't glad that he appears sour and ungrateful. But when he finds himself trapped by an alien, false, or inhuman public image — as a ladies' man when he is gay, as a sex god when he is simply human, as a sweet young man when he is angry and unruly inside — he can't help but despair at the discrepancy between his cult image and his real self. It is no easier in this regard to be James Dean or Beaver Cleaver. The writer Joel Selvin made these observations about the singer Ricky Nelson: "I discovered a deeply troubled young man who hated the TV show that had made him famous. He acted out his resentment in every way he could — drugs, motorcycle gangs, car crashes, music — but he couldn't stop what made him Ricky Nelson, which was the very TV image his father had created."

The Misuse of Power

If my father [Otto Preminger] didn't get his own way, he'd throw the same kind of temper tantrum he'd thrown as a 3-year-old. For the person on the receiving end, these explosive outbursts were a horrible, devastating experience.

— ERIK LEE PREMINGER

If the artist sometimes experiences her success as terrible and burdensome, she may also experience it as a special and wonderful kind of arrival. At those dizzying heights she may fulfill all her material ambitions, hobnob with royalty and billionaires, wield interpersonal power, and seduce and conquer. In partaking of that magic she is challenged not to grow tyrannical.

The editor William Feather wrote, "Success makes us intolerant of failure, and failure makes us intolerant of success." Just as the unrecognized artist may despise all stars, the star may come to despise all unrecognized artists. She may begin to deny her own failures and become the one whom no one can criticize — not her stockholders, for whom she is making money, and not her fans, for whom she is a cult figure. This regal, lofty, and icy insulation distances the celebrity artist, who, like the queen, is challenged not to grow corrupt as she rules her kingdom. Erik Bruhn, the dancer, explained: "When you become a box-office name, nobody dares to tell you anything. They don't realize that sometimes there is a need to be told that something is still working or that something is bad. You hear neither. I'm sure Rudolf Nureyev never heard any criticism from anybody. The point is, fellow dancers are afraid to say anything. Even more so, directors and managers never say anything — as long as the house is full."

It is in the arena of interpersonal relations that the star can especially abuse her power. The tyrannical director, the dictatorial conductor, the star in any art discipline wields undeniable power. The choreographer George Balanchine, for instance, demanded that his dancers not marry. He defended his position in the following way: "For a female dancer, marriage means the end of her individuality. Men don't lose this individuality. Take a promising eighteen-year-old girl. She is beautiful. She dances like a dream. She becomes a star. Suddenly, from being a star she becomes Mrs. So-and-So, married to a doctor. She runs around like mad being a dancer and being a wife — and, of course, it's all over. I say dancers should have romances, love affairs, but not marriages."

In no other legal line of work could a man exercise the supreme control that Balanchine exercised over the twelve- and thirteen-year-old girls whom he selected to teach. While admonishing them not to marry, and firing them if they did, *he* felt entitled to marry them. He married four of his star ballerinas and lived with a fifth. It is not the least bit far-fetched to suppose that Balanchine desired to possess all his female dancers, soul and body. His position of power and prestige provided him with the means to that end.

Dancer Sallie Wilson described studying as a young girl with the choreographer and dancer Anthony Tudor: "He was an inspiration, but he tinkered with people. He liked to get into their hearts and break them, thinking that made you a better person or a better dancer. He toyed with people's emotions — anyone he was interested in. He told me when it was time for me to lose my virginity. I set about doing that. I told him when I had done it and he gave a dinner party for me."

For all artists, stardom brings with it a new round of control, authority, and dependency issues. One artist may discover that she is suddenly dependent on invitations from the rich and experience her stardom as a new kind of slavery. Another may discover in stardom the potential to control others, score victories, and practically fulfill the fantasy of becoming God.

Albert Camus wrote, "When he is recognized as a talent, the creator's great suffering begins." This may sound like a self-serving lie or a romantic exaggeration, yet it's clearly the case that many of our celebrity artists appear ravaged and done in by their fame. We must suppose that fame really is as dangerous as it is thrilling. The wise celebrity artist will take precautions against burning himself to a cinder in the great glow of his long-awaited stardom.

STRATEGIES

Dealing with a Lack of Recognition

Use self-assessment and guided writing, as described in chapter 13. Try to determine why you haven't gained the recognition you desire. Consider the following questions in connection with point 7 of your guided writing practice.

- Am I ambivalent about gaining recognition? What do I see as the dangers or drawbacks of being recognized?

- Am I uncompromising? Am I locked into one path or one product? Am I locked in opposition to the marketplace?

- Am I producing a product that is not wanted? Are my business strategies poor? Is my lack of recognition related more to my personality or to my product?

- Do I need to do better work? Have I been working too superficially or uncreatively? Do I do too much of my work in my head and not enough in my sketchbook or in the practice room?

- How have I defined recognition? How will I know that I'm recognized "enough"? What do I consider an acceptable level of recognition, given the sort of art I do?

Test your willingness. If and when you come up with strategies to increase your chances of success, the question will remain as to whether you want to make changes. Do you want to continue doing your most personal, important art, even though you've calculated that a turn to the commercial will offer better chances of gaining recognition? Will you make a compromise today that was anathema to you yesterday?

Test your willingness, and if you're willing, engage in new business practices, produce new products, self-promote, make and consult your business action plan (as described in chapter 8), and try everything you can. Work harder at realizing your art and at marketing it. Challenge your unwillingness to make changes. If, finally, you remain unwilling, accept and honor your decision.

Engage in detachment training. While you remain unrecognized, and even after you gain recognition, it's extremely valuable to learn how to balance a healthy disinterest against your ambition and need for recognition. It is not an act of renunciation to acknowledge the unfathomable whimsy at work all around us — that the role you're auditioning for may be earmarked for the producer's cousin, that the orchestra seat you're trying out for may be reserved for a student of the conductor's old violin teacher. In the face of such realities, it's crucial that you learn the art of detachment. Be as ambitious as you like, but do not attach to outcomes.

Get a life. It's imperative that you maintain a life outside your art that is rich in meaning and rich in relationships. Consult the discussion on "parallel-life work" at the end of chapter 9 for a fuller description of this point.

Be realistic about the recognition you can achieve. Artists envision themselves in different roles — as artists but also as teachers, activists, rebels, entertainers, classicists, recluses. What may feel like too small an audience to a popular singer may seem like an excellent audience to a singer striving to keep the madrigal alive. Try to evaluate what constitutes a reasonable amount of recognition, given the role or roles you've chosen for yourself. If, say, you want to stretch limits, solve artistic problems, uphold a cultural tradition, or manifest your spiritual nature, isn't it wise to revel in the audience you acquire and not expect to be as well-known as a movie star?

Find joy in the process as well as in the product. The issue of recognition is in part the issue of process versus outcome. Insofar as the process brings you joy, insofar as constructing a paragraph, painting shafts of sunlight, or playing a passage fills you with delight, for that hour the issue of recognition vanishes. Insofar as the effort to construct that paragraph or to master that passage is a heartfelt struggle, welling up from deep sources, for that hour the issue of recognition vanishes. Notice the joy you take in the work, to remind yourself why you embarked on this journey in the first place.

Define success for yourself and redefine it as necessary. What would make for a successful day, week, or month? Having the opportunity to write? Producing one excellent story? Producing important fragments of one story? Pleasing yourself with your efforts? However you define short-term success, invest meaning in your definition and work to achieve it in that time frame.

Strive to gain a small audience — even an audience of one. Has someone responded to your work? Has someone advocated your work and sought to advance you? Reestablish and maintain contact with those important people. Invite them to a private showing of your new work or to hear your new polonaise. Cultivate a relationship with, and make time for, anyone who respects your work.

Engage in inner work to mitigate the pain caused by a lack of recognition. Try to accept your feelings. Strive to reconstruct your life so that your emotional well-being does not depend on whether and to what extent you are recognized by the world. Learn to recognize yourself and to appreciate and respect your own efforts.

Consider a different commitment. If it hurts too much for too long to go unrecognized, or if you decide that it's in your best interests to make a drastic change, entertain the idea of making a transition to another commitment. You may be able to manifest your creativity, remain true to your sense of mission, and satisfy your needs to be recognized and respected in a hitherto undreamed-of career. For a fuller explanation of this point, please consult chapter 15.

Dealing with Success

Use guided writing. Consider the following questions in conjunction with point 7 of the guided writing practice described in chapter 13.

- What new challenges have arisen now that I've become successful? Is one particular challenge the most pressing?

- Can I create a tactic to handle each new challenge? How, for instance, will I choose among the many projects being offered me? What plan or procedure will I use to help me choose? (One client, a writer, visualized an "ideal" shelf full of her books, past and future, and determined not to write a book unless it appeared on that shelf. In this way she kept alive the idea that she was producing a body of work she could love and respect.)

- What previous challenges have still not disappeared in the aftermath of success? How will I handle them?

- Do I feel successful? How high must I rise in order to actually *feel* successful? Can I do work that I love, or must I only do work that will make me *more* successful?

- Am I losing *me* as I gain more recognition? Am I remaining true to myself? Am I more frightened than ever, more full of myself, phonier? Is personality integration an even greater issue than it was before?

Go slowly. Success is a kind of energy field. You vibrate in it like a charged particle. There are new demands on your time and talents, new interview requests and business questions, new possibilities and opportunities. In this context, when you have a free half hour you may continue spinning like a top. Walk, breathe, stretch, meditate. Do the mundane: scrape a carrot, sweep the patio. Calm down.

Manage your money. You may not have paydays like this again. Study a book on money management, or talk to a reputable financial advisor. Learn your options. Think before you hire a full-time personal trainer or buy a car that corners tightly at a hundred miles an hour. Think before you find yourself in the position of needing to earn millions in order to cover expenses and feed your vast retinue.

Protect your privacy. Begin to calculate how public and how accessible you want to be. Learn how not to give yourself away. Learn to say "thank you" and "I don't have an answer to that question." Have an interview persona and a public persona. At the same time, be able to access your humanity.

Watch your impulses. You may feel a powerful urge to give money away, to indulge in the excesses suddenly available to you, to accept the drugs and sexual opportunities offered you, to gamble for high stakes, to wield your new power carelessly and tyrannically. Practice impulse control.

Manage your opportunities. What will you do next, and why will you do it? How will you choose your next movie, your next book, your next tour?

Count to a hundred before committing to anything, even though you may be experiencing the powerful desire to strike while the iron is hot each time an opportunity is offered. Express your excitement, but don't commit until you've engaged yourself in real dialogue.

Build and maintain your professional support team. Engage, as necessary, an entertainment lawyer, accountant, business manager, publicist, investment specialist. Keep up cordial contact with peers and business associates. Send a card to the editor with whom you no longer work, the gallery owner who no longer represents you, the director who directed you in your first film.

Guard against feeling like an imposter. You may have persistent doubts — that you're really a marvelous director or writer, that you really can create powerful sculpture or memorable music, that you're as stunningly beautiful, sexy, or talented as your publicist claims. Having doubts, even legitimate ones, does not make you a fraud. Accept that you're not your publicist's fantasy creation or the projection of your producer's wildest dreams, but an entirely human being.

Manage your anxiety. New stresses exist in your life. More is expected of you. The ante on each project has been upped. Success is not a magic pill that allays anxieties. Embark on a full-fledged anxiety-management program.

Expect setbacks. The next book you write after your bestseller may disappoint you, your publisher, and/or your readers. The movie you direct after your blockbuster may bomb. But even if your stock is lowered in the eyes of the world, it need not sink in your eyes. Virtually no artist experiences one success after another. Determine to come back. If doors have closed to you, consult your business action plan and analyze ways to reopen them. Demonstrate your courage all over again.

Guard against the internal pressure to continually top yourself. Watch that you don't grow insatiable. How high must you rise? So high that no one in your field can consider herself your equal? So high that no one sells more albums or more books than you do? No feast is so sumptuous that an insatiable appetite won't find it wanting.

Guard against existential discomfort, despair, and depression. After half a million people have come to hear you perform, what will your new goals be? Will one million fans satisfy you next time? It may be more important to play for a few close friends in the warmth of your living room. Having approached or achieved your goals, what will matter next? Redefine your future, allowing for the possibility that new meaning will reside in unexpected places.

Remain human. Decline to become a stereotype or a frozen icon. Be more than the bad-boy rock singer, the sex goddess, the reclusive dancer, the brilliant violin virtuoso. Remember that you have a heart and a mind as well as a reputation.

The Artist's Personality

In the introduction I defined the successful artist as one who is self-aware and who understands herself, her life as an artist, and the world in which she lives. The exercises that follow, and those that appear at the ends of part 2 and part 3 and that make up the lion's share of part 4, will help you gain that understanding and are meant to be used in conjunction with your guided writing program, as described in chapter 13.

EXERCISE 1. SELF-DOUBT

Artists are regularly plagued by doubts. These doubts may be small and gnawing or large and pervasive. The artist may doubt herself as an artist or as a person. These doubts can prevent artists from working and are surprisingly powerful obstacles, for who would think that a sudden, perhaps objectively baseless doubt could incapacitate a person? And yet such doubts derail careers and disrupt lives.

How do these doubts affect artists? Claude Monet scrutinized his last paintings and burnt a great many of them. Pierre-Auguste Renoir, at the height of his career, suddenly doubted that he could draw and decided to travel to Italy to practice sketching. Albert Camus, doubting his work, ironically disparaged his novels by calling them "slim." Thomas Hardy, worried that as a self-taught man he wasn't the equal of Oxford and Cambridge graduates, obsessed on that theme in one of his great last novels, *Jude the Obscure*.

But what exactly is a *doubt*? To define the word doubt personally and to gauge its importance in your life are the goals of this exercise. In *Webster's New World Dictionary*, *doubt* is defined in all the following ways. Use your journal (as described in chapter 13) to record your reactions to these definitions and to the questions that follow:

TO DOUBT (THE VERB):

1. "To be uncertain in opinion or belief."

    - Are you uncertain about the direction or quality of the artwork you're presently doing?

    - Are you uncertain about the reception your work will receive?

    - Are you uncertain about the goodness of your past work?

    - Are you uncertain about how to meet or manage the marketplace?

2. "To be inclined to disbelief."

    - Are you inclined to disbelieve that you have the ability, talent, creative resources, skills, or general wherewithal to do your artwork effectively?

    - Are you *often* inclined to disbelieve, *regularly* so inclined, or only *sometimes* so inclined?

3. "To hesitate."

    - Just as you approach the canvas, computer screen, script, or instrument, do you hesitate?

    - What doubt enters your mind at that moment? Can you describe it?

4. "To be skeptical of."

    - Are you skeptical about your chances of succeeding in the art marketplace because you aren't well connected or don't seem to possess a seller's personality?

- Are you skeptical of the public's taste?
- Does that skepticism sap your motivational juices?

A DOUBT (THE NOUN):

1. "A wavering of opinion or belief."
   - When the idea for a story comes to you, do you waver in your opinion about its potential goodness rather than embarking on writing it?
   - When the desire comes over you to paint in a new idiom, do you waver in your opinion about the smartness of moving in a new direction rather than wasting, at worst, a few feet of canvas?
   - Do you make up your mind to audition for a part and then waver in your opinion that you're the right person for the role?

2. "A lack of conviction."
   - Are you convinced that you're an artist?
   - Do you have the courage of your convictions?

3. "A condition of uncertainty."
   - As you travel your path, are you regularly uncertain about which road to take?
   - Are you more confronted by a confusion of choices than by stretches of continuous work?

4. "A lack of trust or confidence."
   - Do you trust yourself?
   - Do you feel self-confident?

Consider these many definitions, for much that prevents you from thriving as a person and as an artist may be located in them. Now comment on the following:

1. Even if I'm uncertain about the work that I'm doing, it's better to do the work, mistakes and all, than to procrastinate and block.

2. It's better to obsess about the *work* than about my *doubts* about the work.

3. When a doubt strikes, I know what I'll do to combat it: (list your strategies for combating doubt).

EXERCISE 2. COMPULSION

Productive artists, the kind who appear almost incapable of not creating, frequently speak of being driven by an inner compulsion to work. What is this inner compulsion? Can you acquire it if you don't already have it? Would a person desiring some sort of "normal life" even want to acquire it? Comment on the following:

1. You're either born with this inner compulsion to create, or you're not.

2. This inner compulsion must flow from a conviction that you're special and have something important to contribute. I'm not sure I feel that special.

3. All people do things to help relieve themselves of their anxieties. The compulsion to create is one anxiety-reduction mechanism in human beings.

4. If I honor this inner compulsion, which indeed I feel, I would become a compulsive person.

5. I recognize this inner compulsion in myself, but I don't trust it and don't want to entertain it.

6. This inner compulsion is just another name for the life force. I mean to nurture it and manifest it, even if many internal and external blocks impede me.

7. To manifest this vitality or life force, I think I must take more risks, show more courage, and be truer to myself.

8. I do not recognize this crying need in myself, and perhaps that means that I should strive for an artful life and an art-filled life, but not an art-committed life.

EXERCISE 3. THE AVANT-GARDE ARTIST

Often artists feel it imperative to create or perform work that is unfamiliar, idiosyncratic, and inaccessible. They do this to express themselves in ways that are unavailable through conventional means. The Kafkaesque in literature, postmodern deconstructive imagery in rock videos, and repetition in minimalist music are each rooted in this need. One variation of this idea is expressed in Russian by the word *ostranenie*: art as defamiliarization, art that makes familiar perceptions seem strange.

But do artists expressing this need and working in this fashion grow alienated and place extra stress on their emotional well-being? Answer the following questions:

1. Do you produce work that is difficult and inaccessible?

2. Do you defamiliarize your art?

3. Does this way of working help you or harm you as a person?

4. Does this way of working isolate you from others?

5. Does the act of creating difficult art further distance you from this time and place?

6. Can you move in your life (if not in your art) from deconstruction to reconstruction, from alienation to involvement? Do you think you might want to?

EXERCISE 4. OBSTACLES TO SELF-KNOWING

The notion that each of us possesses blind spots is at once provocative and upsetting. Is it really true that we are prevented, or that we prevent ourselves, from knowing ourselves? Comment on any of the following statements that ring true for you:

1. I realize that in certain areas of my life I refuse to know myself very well.

2. Like everyone, I have my defenses.

3. I've had many troubling experiences that I refuse to think about.

4. I would not like the me I would see if I saw myself too clearly.

5. I can defend myself from the attacks of others, but only if I consider them "bad" or "wrong" and me "good" or "right."

6. Who has the time to look for blind spots?

7. I am already too nearly my own worst enemy to dare poking around, looking for other blemishes and weaknesses in myself.

8. Criticism hurts, especially self-criticism.

9. Rejection hurts, especially self-rejection.

10. If I began to see in those areas where I am now blind, I would have to make radical, scary changes in my life.

How might you begin to see what you are now blind to? Comment on each of the following:

1. I have certain recurrent troubling thoughts and feelings, or I engage in certain recurrent troubling behaviors that I avoid really thinking about.

2. I can learn about my blind spots by asking other people to report on the ones they observe in me.

3. I can learn about my blind spots by willing myself to remember what I already know about them.

4. I can interrogate myself (perhaps by using guided writing).

EXERCISE 5. GROUP ASSOCIATIONS AND PERSONALITY

Every artist possesses important group associations and identifications that affect her identity and personality. An artist will be, besides an artist, an

African American, a woman, a single mother, a middle-aged ex-wife with ancestors who came from Africa, Trinidad, and Baton Rouge, and so on. Who is she first of all? Who is she second of all?

She may experience herself as a woman first; that is, as a person alert to the ways in which she is addressed and treated as a woman and the ways in which she reacts as a woman. Or she may experience herself as an African American first; that is, as a person alert to the ways in which she is addressed and treated as an African American and the ways in which she reacts as an African American.

It matters with which group or groups an artist identifies. If she identifies herself as a writer first, she may sit comfortably around a table with other writers, half of whom are men: but if she identifies herself as a feminist writer, she may or may not want to keep such company. Each self-identification affects how any artist will feel in a certain group, whether the group is made up of mothers at a playground or art collectors at a party. Beyond that, it will affect how she feels about all issues and thereby will profoundly affect her work.

With which groups do you identify? What are your primary identifications? How is your answer to the question "Who are you?" affected by your group identifications? Comment on the following statements. Which apply to you?

1. At this point in my life, I seem to be identifying with one group in particular.

2. I experience both positive and negative consequences of identifying so strongly with this group.

3. Because I identify with this group, I find myself at odds with other groups and even identify them as the "enemy."

4. Along with this primary identification, I also identify myself with several other groups, including...

5. Possessing several group identifications leads to certain challenges and conflicts.

6. To stop identifying myself with a certain group or groups may have positive consequences.

7. To stop identifying myself with a certain group or groups may have negative consequences.

8. Whether or not I find it burdensome, it is natural and even inevitable that I possess many group identifications.

EXERCISE 6. ANXIOUS SITUATIONS

Think for a minute about the sorts of places that, because of your personality, principles, or upbringing, you would never venture into. Invent a character with the sort of personality traits, principles, or upbringing that would allow him or her to venture into one of those places. Follow that character there. Describe the setting in some detail, and indicate why the character is successful or comfortable in that setting and why, by contrast, you are not.

EXERCISE 7. THE CHALLENGE
OF MULTIPLE ARTIST IDENTITIES

Every creative person has multiple ways of identifying himself and "holding" his connection to his art and his reasons for creating in that discipline. For example, all the following identities are available to the visual artist:

- The Beautifier
- The Channel
- The Innovator
- The Amateur Hobbyist
- The Alchemist
- The Bohemian
- The Master
- The Crafter
- The Entertainer
- The Intellectual
- The Decorator
- The Fabricator
- The Servant
- The Communicator
- The Activist
- The Genius
- The Problem Solver
- The Trickster

- The Leader
- The Eccentric
- The Conservator
- The Witness
- The Technician
- The Child at Play
- The Ethicist
- The Savior
- The Careerist
- The Shaman
- The Apprentice

- The Outsider
- The Guild Worker
- The Naïf
- The Energizer
- The Meditator
- The Natural
- The Humanist
- The Arbiter of Meaning
- The Expressive
- The Materialist
- The Artist

You can hear these many different "takes" on the artist's identity whenever artists speak:

- HOLMAN HUNT: "Art is love."

- EDGAR DEGAS: "Art is really a battle."

- MARISOL: "Art is about mystery."

- ROBERT HENRI: "Art is an outsider, a gypsy over the face of the earth."

- PAUL GAUGUIN: "Art = a mad search for individualism."

- MARCEL DUCHAMP: "If 'art' comes from Sanskrit, as I've heard, it signifies 'making.' "

- CLAES OLDENBURG: "I am for an art that is political-erotic-mystical, that does something more than sit on its ass in a museum."

- ALICE NEEL: "Art is about being completely and utterly yourself."

- GINO SEVERINI: "Art is nothing but humanized science."

- ERIC FISCHL: "[Art] has served to reinforce our relationship to each other."

- LOUISE BOURGEOIS: "Art is a way of recognizing yourself."

- WAYNE THIEBAUD: "Art has to be stolen from Mount Olympus."

Is this a blessing or a curse, this amazing welter of ways to "see yourself" as an artist? Quite possibly it is more on the order of a curse — or at least an enduring source of difficulty. Because so many identities are possible, and because each can be internally questioned and disputed, it is common for an individual to feel on thin ice with her identity choices.

She may feel like a genius; but when she paints, nothing great arises; so she says to herself, "At least let me treat this as a meditation"; but that identity piece fails to sustain her as she flounders about searching for subject matter and enthusiasm; so she changes her mind and says, "Well, let me at least do some decorative work; I can make some things to decorate my environment and the environment of my friends"; but that makes her feel like an amateur, a word that holds negative connotations, and in addition she feels the vast gulf between "decorating" and serving her spiritual needs; so she says to herself, "Let me channel something deep and natural," but all that emerges is something decorative; and so on. In a matter of minutes she has cycled through the identities of Genius, Meditator, Decorator, Amateur, Channel, and more, unsettling herself every step of the way.

Virtually no artist is spared this profound problem of too many available identities, each with its own shadow side and its own potential for meaning failure. Picasso the Trickster/Innovator begins to fear that he has become an Entertainer and has failed miserably at his Shamanic/Humanist duties. Rothko the Meditator doubts that his meditations are as powerful or as meaningful as he intended them to be. Tamara de Lempicka feels real as an Outsider and less real as the fashionable Entertainer she becomes. Van Gogh is torn between his Servant and his Savior identity, torn between humility and grandeur. This abstract artist feels like a Shaman but not enough of a Humanist, that representational artist feels like a Humanist but also too much like a Decorator. Even strong, self-directing artists are not immune to these identity conflicts and meaning difficulties, since these troubles come with the territory.

Any significant change in the world around the artist only exacerbates this problem. Consider how the following external events would affect these visual artists' identities:

- A traditional potter learns that tourists will soon be arriving to buy wares in her village.

- A mid-nineteenth-century painter sees his first photograph.

- A graffiti artist who belongs to a gang is discovered by a Chelsea art dealer and becomes the darling of collectors.

- An object that formerly only a master craftsperson could produce is now mass produced.

- An artist who has always worked in wood discovers that the wood he loves has become endangered.

- An artist becomes a parent, and suddenly a larger income becomes a priority.

Try your hand at completing the following:

1. I can see that the issue of multiple artist identities, each with its own shadow side and meaning hazards, provides me with the following challenges: _____.

2. I think that I would like to choose one identity as my primary one, because I believe it really is my preferred, richest, most meaningful identity. I will organize my life and my art-making around the demands of that particular identity.

   - The artist identity I choose is _____.

   - By this I mean _____.

   - The personal consequences of choosing this particular identity are _____.

   - I am in danger of doubting this identity if and when _____.

   - When a meaning crisis or identity conflict occurs and I begin to doubt the value or rightness of this identity, I will

     _____.

3. I see that, instead of being able to choose just one artist identity, I am obliged to juggle several.

   - These include _____.

- I can successfully juggle them if I _____.

- The biggest danger in trying to juggle these multiple identities is _____.

- If I were forced to choose one identity only, it would be _____.

- I would choose this one because _____.

EXERCISE 8. METAPHORS FOR TRANSFORMATION

In the *Journal of Transpersonal Psychology*, psychologist Ralph Metzner describes "ten classical metaphors of self-transformation": "In prior periods in the mystical and religious literature of East and West, and in the secret oral traditions of esoteric, spiritual schools, the teachers have resorted to myths, parables, similes, symbols, and metaphors to allude to that strange process that changes *us*, our *selves*."

Metaphorically speaking, how would you like to change? Do any of the following ten metaphors pique your interest? What concrete steps must you take to implement the changes you want?

1. The movement from sleepwalking to awakening.

2. The movement from illusion to reality.

3. The movement from darkness to enlightenment.

4. The movement from imprisonment to liberation.

5. The movement from fragmentation to wholeness.

6. The movement from separation to oneness.

7. The movement from being on a journey to arriving at the destination.

8. The movement from being in exile to coming home.

9. The movement from seed to flowering tree.

10. The movement from death to rebirth.

PART 2

The Challenges of the Work

5

Craft

Be a good craftsman; it won't stop you from being a genius.

— PIERRE-AUGUSTE RENOIR

To create is to *do*. It is to have an idea for a painting and then to actually paint it. It is to go to the pottery wheel and let the pot emerge under your fingers. It is to dream mathematics and then go to the blackboard or computer and do the math. In an art-committed life, there is art to make, not just art to wish into existence.

You create by working at some particular craft. *Craft* is a large word that holds everything you do as a creative person. To learn your craft means to learn how to compose a photograph, to play with the correct fingering, to plot a novel, to test a hypothesis; but it also means learning how to be open, resilient, and imaginative. To say that you are "learning the craft of acting" means much more than saying that you are learning your lines: it means that you are learning how to be present, how to listen, how to access your emotions. *Craft* encompasses not only what you do as a creative person as you pursue excellence but also how you organize your personality in pursuit of that excellence.

ACTUALLY DOING

To say yes, you have to sweat and roll up your sleeves and plunge both hands into life up to the elbows.

— JEAN ANOUILH

Craft is doing. You learn to write by writing, you learn to paint by painting. The creative life comes with a lifelong apprenticeship that begins with "first paintings" and "first drawings" and continues throughout an artist's career, as each new piece poses its questions and makes its demands. You learn your craft by doing: there is no substitute for getting to the work.

Leslie, a visual artist, described her process:

I tend to do a lot of thinking — and tend to think that I can get a lot *done* by thinking. But I am beginning to understand that creating happens by doing something, not by thinking about it. What I want to do is improve the relationship between my thinking and my doing, to get more of a balance. For me this means less thinking and more doing. To focus more on doing, I need to stop being so cautious and to make creating less a special activity and more an everyday activity.

We want to think about our creative work, about what it should be and what it needs to succeed, but we also want to get our thinking and our doing in balance. You think about a visual composition; then, sooner rather than later, you test out your idea in the crucible of reality, on a canvas. You think about what it might need; but then, sooner rather than later, you give it what it needs and learn whether or not you were right in your prediction. You step back; but then you step forward.

It is fine to give credence to the idea that we must incubate work and that therefore there will be times when we are not actually working. But we must give at least as much credence to the idea that without doing a ton of work we won't have a clue what we're doing.

CREATING IN BOUNDS

At a certain point, you have to go to the edge of the cliff and jump —
put your ideas into a form, share that form with others.

— MEREDITH MONK

Craft requires form. You are painting a two-foot square painting, making a watercolor on a certain kind of paper, sculpting with a new type of marble. You learn how to paint a mural on a wall by painting a mural on a wall, not by painting other sorts of things. You can't hone your craft until you accept the necessity and legitimacy of form. Until you choose a container into which to pour your thoughts and feelings — a container with a name like fabricated sculpture, landscape painting, site-specific installation, collage, and so on — craft can't really begin.

Ronnie, a writer, described her struggles with finding a form:

A craft problem in the piece I'm currently writing is that I have lots of bits and pieces, but no sense of the whole, so no container, no sense of where the joins go and no way to begin making them. The project I'm working on now is the largest piece I've ever written. It's time to begin crafting its shape, but I'm daunted. I've not been working well in the past few weeks, because I feel that I need to sit down with all the bits and pieces for several hours, see what I have, and really ask hard questions about shape. I haven't had or made those several hours, so I've ended up completely stuck.

To would-be creators, form can feel like a loss of freedom. They don't want to be constrained by something with the "limitations" of a novel, say, but prefer to do a novel–symphony–collage–epic poem–something. What they discover is that they are engaged in fantasy and avoidance. They are dreaming of some superintegration, the way others dream of world peace. An art-committed creator knows that she must make choices in the territory of form and that her choices (like framing her painting, not framing her painting, or having the painting extend onto the frame) are part of her art. You can rebel against the sonnet, the symphony, the short story, or any form you can name, but once you've enjoyed the momentary thrill of rebellion, you will still need to find a form and a container.

CREATING DEEPLY

It is not hard work which is dreary; it is superficial work.

— EDITH HAMILTON

It is possible to create without engaging your mind or your feelings. People create from that superficial place all the time. Their art shows it. Craft begins when you quiet your mind and go beneath the surface to the place where art resides. A noisy mind electing to do superficial work produces art that fails to resonate. A quiet mind interested in diving deep comes back with poetry.

Barry, a visual artist, explained his struggles with this concept:

I think that "not going deep" is an important factor in why I am not staying with my work. I get started on a piece, but I don't lose myself in the process. One day I did some meditation before working, and it was amazing the flow that I was getting. But I couldn't stay in that state very long because soon I began judging my work. I began to feel that I couldn't possibly get the piece done the way I wanted to get it done; those thoughts began to dominate my mind, and going deep became impossible.

To eliminate fear from the process and to provide yourself with the opportunity to work deeply, conceptualize the creative act as a meditation whose goal is to quiet the mind. The kind of meditation that will benefit you as an artist is not some arcane practice but just a way to quiet your mind in a few seconds by taking a few deep breaths and accompanying them with a thought like "I am perfectly fine," "I am ready," or "I am ready to work." This simple procedure makes all the difference between going deep and staying on the surface. The intentional quieting of self as preparation for entering the trance of working is the answer to the question, "How can I go deep?"

CREATING IMAGINATIVELY

A bit of thread can set a world in motion. I start from something considered dead and arrive at a world. And when I put a title on it, it becomes even more alive.

— JOAN MIRÓ

Dullness breeds dullness. Curiosity, liveliness, and playfulness produce original ideas and fresh imagery. Paintings come alive not because the artist is "talented" or "capable" but because she is soaring through the universe in her imagination and bringing back souvenirs. We all know that dreamy state — the exact opposite of the tight, controlling, demanding, dull state that a fear of failure produces — where our birds have extra wings and our castles jeweled moats. To create is just to dream like this.

Marcia, a creativity coach, told me about a client's experience with imagination:

One client had tremendous difficulty creating imaginatively. She was convinced that she had to have a precise, detailed plan of her work before she could begin. I offered a number of approaches that she couldn't commit to. She struggled with this issue for a long time. I found myself running out of ideas. Finally, I asked her to play with her tools for thirty minutes every day for a week with absolutely no plan in mind. She asked for more direction. I told her there were no directions. This was so far out of her comfort zone that it must have been pure agony. But she did play; and she had a breakthrough. Without a plan in mind, she created a piece that she liked. This success must have resonated with her, because she listed working more spontaneously as her primary artistic goal for this year.

Although art isn't play per se, it is a kind of play, the kind that combines enjoyment, spontaneity, and mental relaxation without precluding either seriousness or concentration. It is a special sort of play that allows for a smile and a furrowed brow to exist simultaneously. It is the kind of play that characterized Beethoven's greatest work, the work that is nowhere recorded, those fantastic piano pieces that he would improvise at parties. At the piano, playing, he was divinity. This is not play as prank, play as game, play as amusement, or play as relaxation: it is play as a total immersion in imagination.

CREATING HONORABLY

You approach both a new work and a revival with the same amount of integrity and hard work.

— PAMELA REED

Artists often dodge the work, take shortcuts, skip the hard parts, flee from the work too soon, get caught up in micromassaging a corner of the canvas, and in countless other ways refrain from asking the only real question: "What does the work need?" The more you honorably face the demands of the work, the better the work will be. You will look like a fine craftsperson by virtue of the fact that you stayed put and did what your art needed you to do.

This is what Jack, a writer, had to say about this dynamic:

I am afraid of writing dialogue. I know the basic rules but feel incredibly insecure, so instead of trying my hand at writing lots of dialogue, I look for suggestions in books and take "dialogue writing" workshops. Every time I open one of those books or show up at one of those workshops a voice inside me says, "You should be working on your novel and learning about dialogue by writing! Can't you just *stop* this frightened search for magic rules and principles?" The answer looks to be no. Dialogue still stops me — and I'm signed up for another workshop.

When we don't know what to do with our piece, we tend to do something other than work it out by trial-and-error experimentation. The only way to learn how to write effective dialogue is to write dialogue, read what you've written, and, if it isn't good yet, to make it better or delete it. Every creator should pledge to "write honorably" or to "honor what my painting needs" or to "honor my filmmaking" and, in service of that pledge, be honest about what is required, including more hours, more attention, more fight, more diligence — whatever is the truth of the matter. Personal integrity comes from one place and from one place only.

CREATING REGULARLY

I am so full of my work, I can't stop to eat or sleep, or for anything but a daily run.

— LOUISA MAY ALCOTT

In an art-committed life there are only a few good reasons not to create today: because you finished a suite of paintings yesterday and are giving your brain a one-day vacation, because you have a temperature of 103, because your daughter is getting married this afternoon (though you could still write a little in the morning). Maybe thirty days a year fall into this category. On the other 330-plus days, you honor your commitments and you hone your craft by working.

Sandy, a creativity coach, described how one of her clients was getting in his own way:

> My client doesn't have his own pottery studio but has a friend who invited him to use his. Scheduling conflicts kept interfering with my client's ability to make use of that invitation. He was dying to work regularly, he said, and felt completely stymied and depressed. It so happens that he is also a pottery instructor at a private studio. I wondered if it was possible for him to make use of that private studio, and he agreed that it was. For someone who claimed to want to work regularly, how was it that such an obvious solution hadn't popped into his head? You have to wonder.

If you are embarked on an art-committed life, working every day is the way. No roles for you? Write your own play. No concerts for two weeks?

Practice; and also compose. No brilliant ideas percolating in your brain? Quiet your mind and allow a brilliant idea in. If you hear yourself saying, "I wish I were creating today but...," get out a pair of scissors and cut that "but" right out of the picture. Would you like your heart to beat only on Sundays or your lungs to work only occasionally? Treat *regular* and *routine* as key words in your liturgy.

MAKING CHOICES

My slow painting, I tell myself, is like life; you don't know how it's going to end. But that doesn't release you from choosing from moment to moment, from point to point.

— ANDREW FORGE

Creating is the act of making one choice after another. You applied some red to the canvas. Now what? You put in two birds. Now what? Craft is the act of choosing, the art of choosing, and, most important, the willingness to embrace the challenging reality that choosing is a never-ending requirement. Until you embrace that reality, you leave the door open to completely misunderstanding the creative process and allow yourself the luxurious dodge of supposing that "it will come when it comes." Yes, it will come when it comes, but that in no way lets you off the hook from making a billion choices.

Sherri, a painter, had this to say:

This week's painting sessions have been centered around the idea of making definite choices, especially during the middle and late stages of a given painting. I have honored this weekly goal for my painting process, and as a result have experienced renewed anxiety while painting. Despite the anxiety, I have also made progress on my paintings by just being definite about choices. The commitment to keep improving looks to be stronger than the desire to avoid making choices. I am willing to pay the price of anxiety.

Everything an artist does amounts to a choice, which helps explain why artists are so prone to procrastination and flight. Who really wants to do that much choosing? Who wants to look out at a wild landscape full of far too much visual data and choose which elements to select for the canvas? Who wants to consider the infinite number of ways he might begin his novel and make a definite choice from among that infinity? These are more intricate and more taxing decisions than choosing what to have for lunch or what to watch after dinner. Every artist who hopes to succeed at his art must embrace the idea that, like it or not, incessant choosing is his lot.

MAKING SKILLFUL JOINS

I use brushes of diminishing sizes that are gradually reduced to the smallest sable point. What takes forever is closing in on the minutest detail and still have it be part of the whole.

— CATHERINE MURPHY

Art-making is not like carpentry, except when it is. There will be times when you are required to find a way to get from this part of the composition to that other part in a way that doesn't excite you but that you know is necessary. One important aspect of craft is nailing together all your beautiful bits and creating the extra contrivances and incidental music your piece requires.

Max, a sculptor, explained his challenges:

> What I struggle with is skillful joining. I am often missing basic skills, basic mechanical skills that I must learn in order to pull off the look that I want. The work gets delayed, I get frustrated, and it's difficult then to recapture any excitement after I've finished learning how to handle a new drill or after I've finished reading up on nontoxic glues. What I am trying to do is build my skill set by planning ahead and taking needed workshops. If I prep in this way I think my joining will go much more smoothly, and I'll experience far less anxiety.

Even if something doesn't come easily to us, we can learn how to accomplish it with honest perseverance and a willingness to look at what we are doing. If we need to improve our drawing skills, we make an effort to improve our drawing skills. If we need to learn the correct format for our screenplay, we learn the correct format. If we need an extra number for our musical, we compose an extra number. It is wonderful when some things come easily, but it is not a tragedy if some things are trying and taxing. To master those things, we simply roll up our sleeves a little higher.

VIEWING

Only when the object exists can I think clearly about it.

— MARY FRANK

As we create, we must lovingly but firmly appraise what we are creating. We want to know if it works, if it has come alive, which parts have succeeded and which parts haven't, which areas have their small troubles and which their large. The object comes into existence; then we can think more clearly about it. We look at the object from the perspective of both architect and building inspector, of someone with an investment in this piece, even a love of this piece, but also of someone with the task of ensuring that every aspect of the piece is up to code. There was craft in the doing; now there needs to be craft in the appraising.

John, a composer, put it this way:

> No one can tell me what to make, although others may have opinions about the quality and relevance of my work. It is my responsibility to determine what I say and to determine when I have said it as well as I am able to say it. It is my responsibility to continue to challenge myself and improve as an artist and to work with integrity, telling my truth and doing what is difficult when my work calls for it. These are the aspects of making meaning that ring most loudly for me. To accomplish all this, I have to look my work squarely in the eye, without flinching.

You have two goals as you view the work you're bringing into existence, and the second is as important as the first. The first is to keep the work on track and to make it good. The second is not to let its problems and faults provide you with a handy excuse to stop working and stop creating. There is nothing easier — and ultimately more disappointing — than noticing a large problem, throwing up your hands, and exclaiming that you aren't suited to, equal to, or deserving of an art-committed life. Don't permit yourself to do this. Love your work and examine it carefully, not to find a reason to quit but to make it better.

REVISING

Teach yourself by your own mistakes.

— WILLIAM FAULKNER

Revising encompasses everything from toiling over a square inch of a painting until it is right to repainting whole sections. It involves taking things out, putting things in, making small changes, and making enormous changes. Revising is to art as evolution is to creating: if, in the fire of creating, you made a creature that can't reach the leaves at the top of the trees, in the revision process you give it a longer neck and call it a giraffe. There is no less imagination, soul, or craft required at this stage of the process — but there are also many real problems to solve.

Joanne, a novelist, explained why she put off revising her work:

Some writers seem to love the revision process, or so they say. I don't. I love inhabiting my novel, living it, and finding my way to the end — and then I want to feel finished. I don't want to reread it, I don't want to see the mistakes I've made, I don't want to have to struggle to make it better. I know that I have to revise, but I find it so exhausting and distasteful that, while it may take me six months to write the draft, it can take me another year or two to find the will to take the next step. I guess that I have to change this relationship, but I don't find revising getting any easier even with three novels under my belt.

Coming up with a new, elegant scientific theory can be an ecstatic experience — but then it must be tested and, quite likely, revised. Nor may one revision, no matter how thorough, prove enough. The changes we made the first time through, as good as they may have been, can produce new problems or highlight areas of weakness. A craftsperson continues forthrightly revising until her artwork is as good as she can make it.

GETTING TO THE END

Finishing a painting demands a heart of steel: everything requires a decision, and I find difficulties where I least expected them.

— EUGÈNE DELACROIX

Until we get to the end of a piece, it is hard to know what we have exactly — a fact that can act as a powerful motivator not to reach the end. Fearing that the piece may prove weak, fearing our ability to adequately revise it, not wanting to look its problem parts in the eye, we avoid getting to the end by taking months off while claiming not to know how to end it; or we decide to putter endlessly around the periphery, refusing to come to a decisive conclusion. Getting to the end is an act of courage; it is also the only the way to experience a sense of completion.

Charlie, a writer, confessed this:

I have come to understand that I don't start stories because I dread finishing them and being confronted by having to judge them worthy or unworthy. I know this is an act of cowardice and completely prevents me from learning whether I have any good stories in me, but the thought of having to call a story "done" — and then having to send it out, since it is "done" — petrifies me. Sometimes I think that if I could get permission from myself to just work on a story without worrying at all about completing it, that would get me started; but I can't get the "completion thing" out of my head.

Completing is a dynamic decision that is forced on the artist, who must announce to himself and to the world that, for now at least, he will not add more paint, introduce another character, or do anything else to the work in front of him. He may have left a lot of the canvas showing through; nevertheless, he reckons it complete. He may have produced so quiet an ending that readers are left wondering where the "real ending" is; nevertheless, he reckons it complete. He may not be able to prove his theory empirically; nevertheless, he reckons it complete. He makes his decision; then he makes his announcement.

WORKING IMPERFECTLY

The aim of the creative act is to have something coalesce: a novel, a scientific theory, an invention, a painting, a character on the stage. We hope that what coalesces is something that we can call good, even great. What we do not aspire to is an unreal, inhuman, impossible perfection, that mistake-free ideal that only exists in the minds and vocabulary of cruel parents.

Janice, a painter, confessed,

I'm a perfectionist, and I want my artwork to be perfect. This prevents me from getting started on new projects or, if I manage to start one, from finishing it. I think to myself: If it's not going to be the very best, why do it at all? I have no idea how to move past this.

One way to better accept yourself as a human being is to move from a merely intellectual understanding that messes are part of the creative process to a visceral understanding of that truth.

Every artist knows intellectually that a percentage of her work will prove less than stellar, especially if she happens to be taking risks with subject matter or technique. But acceptance of that hard truth on a deep feeling level eludes many of us. Do you understand in your heart of hearts that messes and mistakes are not only okay but part of the creative process and *crucial* to the process? They are not the goal — the goal is excellent work. But our mistakes are as integral to the process as falling down is integral to learning how to walk.

An infant would never think, "I will not walk until I can walk perfectly." Only adults think such inhuman, antiprocess, paralyzing thoughts. If an infant wants to get to the toy across the room she will crawl, walk, tumble, or fly. She will do whatever it takes — because she actually wants that toy. Make yourself that beautiful vehicle of vitality and desire, and fall as many times as necessary as you strive to get from here to there.

When I begin a book — and I've written between forty and fifty — I am excited to see what will emerge. Maybe something beautiful will appear on the first try, maybe the book will need two complete overhauls and three additional revisions, maybe it will never come to life and need to be abandoned. Maybe I will make a complete hash of it. I am easy with all those outcomes, including the last. If I were not, I would be asking the creative process to be something that it cannot be: a guarantee that if I show up, excellent things will happen. The showing up is the main thing; the excellence, if it comes, is an added, and only an occasional, blessing.

STRATEGIES

A Craft Checklist

Using craft as a nicely large word to hold everything you do as a creative person in your discipline, employ the following craft checklist to remind yourself of your tasks. You can hang this list above your computer or tack it to your studio wall.

1. Am I creating? Am I actually doing the work?

2. Am I creating a piece with requisite form? Am I creating "in bounds"?

3. Am I getting quiet and going deep?

4. Am I engaging my imagination?

5. Am I creating honorably and avoiding illegitimate shortcuts?

6. Am I creating regularly, every day or almost every day?

7. Am I making the choices that need to be made?

8. Am I integrating the parts of the piece into a seamless whole? Am I skillfully making all the necessary joins?

9. Am I lovingly but unflinchingly appraising what I've created?

10. Am I honorably revising?

11. Am I completing my work? Am I getting to the end of things in a timely and appropriate way?

6

Blocks

What can ruin a first-rate writer? Booze, pot, too much sex, too much
failure in one's private life, too much attrition, too much recognition, too
little recognition, frustration. Nearly everything in the scheme of things
works to dull a first-rate talent. But the worst probably is cowardice.

— NORMAN MAILER

Blocking is only in part about not producing. Creative blocks also provide information about your moods, the messages you received in childhood, your environment, your vitality or lack thereof, and much more.

All human beings are regularly blocked. It is one characteristic of being
human that we regularly fail to actualize our potential. Not only do we procrastinate, avoid challenges, take the easy path, and leap to the television or
to the bottle to avoid the muses, but we generally live more dully than we
might, blocked off from beauty and from our own wisdom.

Who wouldn't create — sing, make pictures, tell stories — if he weren't
constrained not to? Who wouldn't try her hand at a hundred different art
forms, from drumming to potting, from folk dancing to filmmaking, if she
weren't constrained not to? But these constraints, the blocks to our creativity,

are practically numberless. There is the constraint of too little time. There is the constraint of having to make a living. There are the constraints of fear: fear that your voice will crack or that the audience will find your story boring. There are the constraints of belief: the belief that art is frivolous or useless, that you are untalented, that forgoing art is a sign of stability or sanity. There are the constraints of personality: the inhibitions, doubts, and anxieties, the characteristic style that each of us settles into, with its paranoid, depressed, shy, or antic edge.

You'd like to accomplish more, defuse inhibiting fears, and procrastinate less — but so would all people. You are sometimes, perhaps often, blocked and resistant to doing the work you want or need to do — but so are all people. Blocks are the constraints put on all of us by nature and by circumstances. It is in this context that we will look at blocks in this chapter.

SOURCES OF BLOCKS

The cognitive therapist tends to see creative blockage as the result of the maladaptive self-talk and rigid or inappropriate work rules that the artist adapts for himself. In this view, the artist is blocked because he is saying the wrong things to himself. The psychoanalyst tends to see creative blockage as the result of self-censorship and the repression of the id. In this view, the artist is blocked because of inner conflicts. Other psychologists have equated blocks with the artist's stupidity, laziness, or lack of talent. The psychologist Edmund Bergler, for instance, argued that creative blocks were nothing more than "euphemisms for sterility of production."

Ultimately, yes, there is one source of blockage: being human. Having said that, I think it's crucial for the artist to sort out the various causes of blockage in her life, even if only in a tentative way. It is hard to remove constraints if we don't know what they are, what they feel like, and something about where they come from.

It's important, after all, for an actress to know if she has stopped auditioning because she is tired of rejection, plagued by the introjected critical voice of her father, angry at the lack of strong roles available to her, or disillusioned with the art form of acting. It's important for the poet to know if

Creativity for *Life*

he has stopped writing poetry because he happened on a poem by another poet that he found too good, because his drinking has gotten the better of him, or because his outstanding debts are weighing too heavily on his mind.

I offer the following twenty blocks (in no particular order) as a prod to your imagination. If you recognize your blocks here, you can begin the work of reducing them to manageable size or eliminating them altogether. They are:

1. Blocks from parental voices
2. Personality blocks
3. Personality trait blocks
4. Self-censorship
5. Self-criticism
6. World-criticism
7. World-wariness
8. Existential blocks
9. Conflicts between life and art
10. Fatigue
11. Pressure paralysis
12. Environmental blocks
13. Social blocks
14. Situational blocks
15. Skill deficits
16. Myths and idealizations
17. Self-abuse
18. Anxieties
19. Depression
20. Incubation and fallow periods

Let's examine these in some detail.

Blocks from Parental Voices

As a child, you may have been told repeatedly that you were stupid, lazy, unworthy, untalented, or unimaginative. Now, at your easel or your computer screen, you hear your mother's or father's terrible voice and sit paralyzed. Or you no longer hear that hurtful voice but have introjected it; the label has taken hold. It is no longer your parent's voice but your own that tells you that you're untalented or stupid.

As a child, you may have felt that nothing you did was ever quite good enough. You couldn't please your parents; you couldn't begin to figure out what might please them. The resultant confusion, shame, anger, and self-doubt are bound to produce ambivalence that saps your motivational strength and makes you doubt that you have the wherewithal to proceed. You remember and are burdened by the message sent by your parents: that they did not love you enough, respect you enough, or care enough.

Personality Blocks

Affected by our experiences, raised in a certain family, living in a certain culture at a certain time, acting and being acted on, the product of certain chromosomes, each of us ends up with a personality that seems — especially if we would like to make changes in it — all too immutable. You may come to possess a personality style, for instance, that is rigid, harshly self-critical, obsessive, or fearful. The fearful artist may effectively accomplish detail work but may block when faced with the task of approaching a blank canvas. The paranoid artist may function well enough in isolation, producing fiction or practicing music, but may block at performing in public.

You've also acquired your own defensive structure, built around those defenses that were appropriate or valuable in childhood. Dissociation, for instance, may have helped you deal with an abusive or otherwise crazy-making family. But now you may dissociate owing to the stress of producing art or of dealing with the marketplace, with the result that you forget what you intended to photograph or what you meant to say to your agent.

Personality Trait Blocks

In chapter 2, we examined the artist's personality in terms of the traits an artist appears to need in order to create. Persistent blocking can occur if one or several of these traits are relatively absent. Assertiveness, for instance, which is extremely valuable to the working artist and which can be thought of as the artist's necessary arrogance, is a quality that many talented, imaginative, but often-blocked artists possess insufficiently. An artist may be just a shade too passive, and that passivity can have far-reaching consequences. As the psychiatrist Lawrence Hatterer explained, "An aggressive artist will make the most of a minor talent, while a more brilliant passive artist can easily be lost to the world."

Self-Censorship

Blockage can occur because you can't or won't let out dangerous or disowned psychic material, such as memories of childhood molestation or life with an alcoholic parent. Freud pinpointed this source of blockage, and it's the one that has most interested psychoanalytic investigators. Creative and performing artists do indeed have difficulty when their work puts them in touch with psychological material they would prefer not to explore.

One client, who sang and acted, wanted very much to put together her own one-woman performance piece, but she found that she couldn't begin. She seemed to be prevented from writing about men and women in relationships, the intended subject of her show, by the fact that her brothers had tormented and humiliated her as a girl, a grievance that she remembered but had never addressed or redressed.

Intransigent blocks are often related to this interior guardedness. It is a special act of courage, in a context of danger, for an artist with such a block to proceed with his or her art.

Self-Criticism

Artists frequently criticize their art products and their marketing efforts. These judgments, which may be accurate but are harsh and self-punishing, lower the artist's morale and may ultimately paralyze him. The artist who begins to believe, standing before a blank canvas, that his first stroke will doom the painting, or the actor who decides after unsuccessful auditions that he is bound to botch every future audition out of nervousness, is hard-pressed to proceed with his art.

After years of this self-criticism, you may finally judge yourself unequal to the task of creating or performing. Your image of yourself as an artist loses more and more of its luster. You begin to doubt both the quality of the specific work or performance at hand and your ultimate worth as an artist. This dual charge can render you artistically impotent.

World-Criticism

Blockage can occur if you decide, on a conscious or unconscious level, that the world is too sick, difficult, unresponsive, alienating, stupid, or bourgeois a place in which to do art. In a manner of speaking you judge the world a fraud or a failure. This judgment is often tied to your feeling unrecognized, unrewarded, rejected, and embattled. But the judgment may arise independently of your personal frustrations, independent of the cattle-call auditions you endure or the embarrassing smallness of the roles you win. It may come upon you simply because you chanced to watch the news.

It is easy to grow cynical but harder to realize that such cynicism can become a source of blockage. The artist, angered or saddened by the world, may not understand that her blockage is actually her refusal to bring art products into a world that she does not love.

World-Wariness

You can easily become paranoid as you pursue your art-making, experience criticism and rejection, and learn the hard lessons of the marketplace. You may come to mistrust others and approach the world warily. You may begin to expect that your performances will be negatively evaluated or that your peers will keep their contacts and connections secret from you. Feeling as if you're negotiating a minefield, you may remain continually alert and wary of the hidden agendas of others.

The artist wary of the world is less likely to want to put his products or his person out into it. Criticized enough, rejected enough, he may, like Melville after the poor reception of *Moby-Dick*, not write for another thirty years. Criticized enough, the actress may stop performing, as Anjelica Huston did for six years after critics attacked her performance in *A Walk with Love and Death*.

The actor may be unable to face another audition; the writer, another editorial comment; the classical composer, another mixed review. The artist can grow so wary of these negative aspects of human contact that growing vegetables or sleeping seems like an excellent alternative to making art.

Existential Blocks

The artist who becomes disillusioned and stops believing in the worth of his art, or in the intrinsic value of art, may experience the leakage of meaning from his art-making or performing. Albert Camus wrote, "I have seen many people die because life for them was not worth living. From this I conclude that the question of life's meaning is the most urgent question of all." While firefighters may only rarely question the intrinsic value of firefighting or bakers the intrinsic value of baking, artists very often question the intrinsic value of making art.

The actress who derives her income from making commercials may experience her life as depressing and empty. The writer who began with the intention of creating serious drama and who now makes a fine living writing soap operas may experience a similar meaning loss. Both may look successful on the outside but feel dejected on the inside. A client, a young actor whose father was a successful television writer, described how such an air of disappointment and defeat hung in the air of his childhood home. His father masked his existential depression with cynicism and worldly intellectualizations, but the pessimistic message nevertheless got communicated to the son, who was battling his own depression.

What the unproductive artist describes as his failure of will or insufficient motivation may rather be a lack of belief in the meaningfulness of art or of the art-making he's presently pursuing. The most salient difference between the regularly blocked artist and the regularly productive artist may not be the greater talent of the latter, but the fact that the productive artist possesses and retains his missionary zeal.

Carlos Santana likened artists to "warriors in the trenches who have the vision of saving us from going over the edge." The artist who possesses this vision will pursue her art even if she sometimes blocks. The artist who is less certain about the meaningfulness of his profession or the value of his work is harder-pressed to battle for art's sake.

Conflicts between Life and Art

Severe conflicts arise for the artist as she attempts to apportion time and mind space between the regular demands of life and the regular demands of doing art. The artist is often convinced that she can't have a life and also devote herself to art. She believes that if she wants, at the end of the workday, to relax over a drink, visit with friends, or put her feet up, then there will be no time left for art.

All the pressures that we human beings face — familial and financial needs, inner compulsions, leaky faucets, sex drives, illnesses — conspire to throw us off course and make it seem that we need to choose between attending to life or attending to art. Often we begin to feel that this decision must be an either/or one. If, consciously or not, we choose to attend to life, then our subsequent stabs at art-making are likely to be met with strong internal resistance.

Fatigue

You may block because you are drained from your creative efforts, your marketing efforts, or both. You may simply be too tired after wrestling with the plot of your novel or the making of a hundred pounds of new clay to write query letters to agents or locate markets for your art pottery. Each step of the way is taxing and can exhaust energy needed for the next step.

It may sometimes feel joyous and effortless to write, paint, rehearse, or go out on tour, but sometimes it feels like nothing but grueling work. It may sometimes feel like an exciting challenge to promote your novel, interest reviewers in your book, set up interviews and be interviewed, supply your publisher with a useful mailing list, and cajole a book-signing evening out of your local bookstore. But just as often you may find yourself feeling tired before you even begin.

Much of creating or performing is unglamorous, arduous, and sometimes maddeningly repetitious work. A symphony musician who plays more or less the same pieces for thirty years is typically burned out and can sometimes only be provoked into really making music by a charismatic visiting guest conductor. Here blockage involves the artist subtly disconnecting from his art, practicing less, caring less, loving less. Real estate speculation becomes more attractive than music-making. The artist has not consciously disowned his art, but when he thinks about it he finds himself yawning.

Fatigue and accompanying blockage also come with leading the sort of marginal life that artists often lead. The effort required to put food on the table, to deal with an illness without benefit of a hospital plan, to pay the rent, to get a toothache treated, to attend to the needs of a spouse or children can tire out even the most passionate and dedicated artist.

Pressure Paralysis

How you perceive the importance of a given task or performance can easily cause you to block. A particularly crucial audition, book deadline, concert, or gallery show can induce the kind of anxiety that leads to total paralysis. As one client put it, "Every one of my performances seems to come with three exclamation points attached!" One flutist, appearing in her first major solo performance at Carnegie Hall, blocked on the first piece, left the stage, and left professional performing for good. Although she remained an amateur musician, she no longer dared aspire to a career as a concert soloist. That one terrible moment of performance anxiety altered the course of her life.

This kind of paralysis may not strike only in the actual moment of execution. Artists with an important event looming on the horizon can, out of mounting anxiety, fail to rehearse, write, or paint. Sometimes, after a long period of procrastination and blockage, they manage to avert disaster through last-minute heroics — the manuscript delivered on time, the part memorized, the piece rehearsed. These artists can even convince themselves that they need or like deadlines and the feeling of last-minute pressure. Nevertheless they know that the period before the heroics commence is one of frustration, depression, and self-criticism.

If an artist holds every one of her products or performances as desperately important, she may find this cycle of procrastination and feverish last-minute heroics becoming a way of life. She may then succumb to a stress-induced illness and burnout, or contrive to limit her opportunities in order to avoid the accompanying anxiety.

Environmental Blocks

An artist often finds himself living in a noisy, chaotic, or uproarious environment. Because he lives marginally, he may have roommates. Because he lives in New York or Los Angeles, his cousins from the Midwest will want to visit, just when he feels ripe to paint. Or because he works so often in isolation in the country, he may desire a trip into town as an antidote to that isolation, at the very moment when he might write a short story instead.

Often the lives of artists are busily sexual, filled with considerable partying, drug-using, and much internal and external noise. In such a lively environment the artist encounters difficulty writing, painting, or rehearsing. If you spend too much time in such chaos you may begin to experience solitude as intolerable and find moments of hard-won silence deafening and maddening.

Social Blocks

Many of us grow up learning social, cultural, or familial rules that can end up inhibiting creative work. The female artist who learned rules about politeness and femininity may now find it difficult to adopt an appropriately assertive stance. She may defer to men and dislike herself for doing so, run errands and clean up rather than do her art, and in many ways play out stereotypical female roles. The male artist, for his part, may have been told that art was a feminine pursuit, unsuitable work for a man.

Or the artist may have grown up in a cultural environment in which hard work was not particularly valued, in which working at art was not prized, or in which the demands for conformity were overwhelming. The artist may have been encouraged to play an instrument, for instance, but in a context of great cultural conformity, so that practicing came easily as long as there were clear directions and strict teachers. When such an artist enters a conservatory, where he must structure his own time and make his own decisions, he may falter.

Criticism and rejection are twin demons in the world of social evaluation. It takes courage and a persistent dismissal of the evaluative powers of others for the writer to resubmit his manuscript after a dozen agents have panned it, for the painter to send out slides of her paintings one more time after a hundred gallery owners have returned them, for the dancer to continue in a dance company even though every day the director calls him fat.

Sometimes what fails the artist is not his courage but his ability to keep these critical evaluations from getting under his skin. He may begin to believe that he really is too fat, or that his paintings really are too red, or that his novel really is too quiet, not because he's come to that judgment himself but because others have told him so too many times.

Situational Blocks

The productive artist who rarely blocks will nevertheless sometimes feel stymied when she finds herself unable to answer the particular artistic, technical, or practical question that confronts her.

A sculptor may face a commission larger in scale and more ambitious than anything he's tackled before. The novelist, having boxed herself into a corner with a new idea, may have no idea how to end her story. The violinist, examining the score of a rigorous competition piece he's planning to add to his repertoire, may see that he's chosen something at the outer limits of his virtuosity. The painter, deciding on an intellectual level to make a move from gestural abstract Expressionism to figurative abstract Expressionism, may not know how to translate that intent into art. The actor, used to bravely auditioning for any contemporary part under the sun, may flee from an offer to play an Elizabethan role, fearing that the British accent the part calls for is beyond him.

Since the work facing artists is regularly challenging, and sometimes fiercely so, artists frequently block as they attempt to meet the challenge inherent in a particularly taxing situation. Proceeding up a rock wall just as sheer as the ones they have tackled before, only a little sheerer, and plagued by the extra anxiety that the extra sheerness provokes, they will sometimes dangle there, a thousand feet above the valley, without the wherewithal to get up or down.

Skill Deficits

You may have an idea of what you wish to create, but you may lack the technical skills necessary to get the job done. Until you acquire those skills through training and practice, or until you let go of the idea of doing that particular creative piece, blockage will occur. The difference between this block and the one described above is that in the former case the artist likely had the skills necessary to do the work — to tackle the large sculpture, the difficult violin piece, or the British accent. It was fear, doubt, inexperience, confusion, and a lack of self-confidence that prevented him from proceeding. In the present case proceeding is literally impossible, unless and until a certain skill is acquired.

Vincent van Gogh, for example, deciding at the age of twenty-eight not to commit suicide but rather to retire as a preacher and begin life anew as a painter, knew that he lacked the drawing skills necessary to paint at the level to which he aspired. Instead of blocking, he determined to spend the next two years teaching himself to draw. A less honest, rigorous, and dedicated artist would surely have ended up perplexed at his inability to paint to his liking and frustrated at his failure to realize his artistic vision.

Myths and Idealizations

Myths about creativity, the creative process, the artist's personality, and the artist's life can all contribute to blockage. The artist who waits to be inspired before beginning work may wait a very long time. The artist who goes out searching for community, dreaming of finding a modern-day Paris of the twenties, may wander endlessly. The artist who romanticizes his drinking, his self-abuse, or his eccentricities may lead himself down paths he comes to despise — and that those around him despise as well.

Artists who idealize stardom, who believe they can't live without it, may block if stardom eludes them. Naturally, any artist is hard-pressed not to crave fame. Attaining it is often the only way you can make a living at art.

Our culture, for its part, encourages the idea that one is either a star or a failure. Consciously or not, you begin to label even your significant successes as failures, if those successes don't bring you stardom. Even a string of successes may not warm your heart much. Thus the thought may intrude on you, even as you're working well on a short story, that the story won't make you famous — and you stop writing. Or you realize that by accepting a certain orchestra position you are "dooming yourself to obscurity," experience a panic attack, and refuse to write your letter of acceptance.

On the other side of the coin, the famous artist who had dreamed of fame and gotten it may, in turn, find fame an empty commodity. Tolstoy, who achieved enormous fame by age forty as the most revered writer in Russia, began to disparage the stardom he had always desired. He complained bitterly: "Well, what if I should be more famous than Gogol, Pushkin, Shakespeare, Molière — than all the writers of the world — well, and what then? I could find no reply. Such questions demand an immediate answer; without one it is impossible to live. Yet answer there was none."

Tolstoy wrote very little fiction for the next forty years of his life.

Self-Abuse

To deal with your artistic anxiety and your existential difficulties, you may abuse speed, alcohol, cocaine, heroin, or some other drug, including tranquilizers, sleeping pills, and codeine. Or you may engage in other ritualistic, compulsive, time-consuming, and self-damaging behaviors that thrill you or quell your anxiety but that also leave you blocked and injured. One client, a musician, stopped on his way to his coaching session to sell his instrument and buy heroin. Another client, a performer, came to her first appointments jacked up on speed. Sometimes the artist is too busy scoring, too busy maintaining a drug habit, or too busy recovering from his excesses to even entertain the notion of working creatively.

Anxieties

Anxiety is the most prominent feature of all creative blocks. Our anxieties — our nerves, doubts, worries, fears, sweats, panics — constrain us much of the time. If the anxiety is generalized, the artist may feel troubled and unsafe everywhere: at his desk and on his way to his desk, at his easel and away from it, in the wings before a performance, at the cast party and at the supermarket. One client, for instance, who complained of being too anxious to audition, also doubted that she could control her car and safely drive to my office.

The anxieties that plague artists and prevent them from working are quite often realistic ones. You may worry that your mate, who is unhappy at her job, will stop supporting you. You may fear that playing a certain role will typecast you. You may wonder whether your violent visual imagery will fly in the marketplace. You may wonder if it would be wiser to do graphics, which have a chance of selling, rather than your large-scale paintings, which rarely sell. You may worry that the chemicals you use in your artmaking are toxic. You may have a hunch that it's too dangerous to write a book that ridicules Islam. Such rational doubts and worries naturally arise in your life; and with them comes blockage.

Moral anxieties may also confront you. As one contemporary writer put it, "I said to myself that if *People* magazine ever interviewed me, I'd fight to maintain my dignity. I'd refuse to let them photograph me sitting on the roof of my house, the way they like to photograph celebrities. Well, here's the photograph they took of me perched up in a tree." You're often asked to do things, or decide it prudent or necessary to do things, that disturb you. For example, your editor suggests that your novel would be much more readable if you added a kidnapping. While struggling to decide whether modifying the plot in that way is or isn't acceptable to you, you may find it impossible to proceed. If you opt not to make the change, you experience the realistic anxiety that your editor will not like the book. If you opt to make the change, you may experience pangs of self-disgust. In either case, your deadline may be threatened as you anxiously pace your studio.

An artist with a fertile imagination and a wealth of ideas, or an artist with several simultaneous work opportunities, may find her anxiety level rise as she attempts to choose among the possibilities before her. Such anxiety can produce the kind of blockage that prevents her from fully choosing, either rationally or intuitively, a course of action. Instead she may let her agent or best friend make the decision; or she may spend the next two years of her life working on one novel rather than another simply because her penny came up heads. When, blinded by anxiety, you make decisions in this fashion, it is easy to later block as you try to execute your plan — a plan that came, after all, from nowhere except a coin toss.

Depression

Depression, like anxiety, can prevent you from working. Like anxiety, depression is probably present in most cases of creative blockage. A depressive episode can stop even the most productive artist in his tracks. Depression has stopped artists as fiercely creative as Van Gogh and Beethoven. A depressed mood may envelop the artist, preventing him from working. Or his inability to work, arising from some other source, may bring on a depressed mood. In either case, the artist is confounded by his case of the blues and has little energy left to make art, to meet the marketplace, or to face life in general.

Incubation and Fallow Periods

If you're honorably wrestling with artistic questions subconsciously, that is, if you're doing the work of writing or painting but without pen or brush in hand, you may still consciously feel blocked and frustrated. Ideas in art often must incubate, just as ideas in science often must incubate; but neither the artist nor the scientist feels fully content as he lets his unconscious do its work. Still, you must sometimes wait. You may be in the minority and have symphonies come to you whole, as they came to Mozart. But even then you must wait, as Mozart did, for the propitious carriage ride during which the symphony courses through you. Or you may be in the majority, in which case you must sometimes wait on a given piece for days, weeks, years, or even decades, as Beethoven sometimes waited for his musical bits and scraps to come together as symphonies.

THE MIRACLE OF THE CREATIVE ACT

Human beings are challenged to be creative, for dullness and blockage come much more easily than creativity. A multitude of constraints prevents us from making exceptional art. You're challenged to make basic decisions about your art — whether to paint large or small, realistically or abstractly, with gouache on paper or oil on canvas. You're challenged to rethink those decisions when your art seems out of focus. You're challenged to deal with the small and with the often enormous blocks that prevent you from working well or working at all.

It does seem a wonder that anyone manages to produce excellent art. Carefully made and deeply felt art products and performances are, after all, miracles: gifts given against great odds. But it is also an incontrovertible fact that creative and performing artists regularly do break through their blocks and produce that long-bottled-up novel, that suite of photographs, that collage, that song, that performance piece. The challenges are great, but a healthy number of miracles do nevertheless occur.

STRATEGIES

Isolate the block that affects you and create a plan to eliminate it. If more than one block confronts you, prepare different plans of action to combat each. A participant in one of my writing workshops said, "I was surprised how helpful it was to identify and 'domesticate' the blocks. The biggest step for me was owning my blocks. That galvanized me into working up a second draft on the piece I've been writing, which I thought was never going to happen."

Identifying and owning your blocks can produce important, human-sized miracles. To neutralize or combat each block, choose strategies from the following blockbusting menu. Experiment and trust that your honorable trial-and-error efforts will help you determine which strategies work best for you.

Blockbusting Menu

Use guided writing. Working on point 7 of the guided writing program described in chapter 13, begin to zero in on the block or blocks that affect you. You may effectively narrow your focus by finding a word that captures the essence of your particular block. For one client, who was trying to write songs, that word turned out to be *embarrassment*. She was embarrassed to learn that the songs emerging from her were country-and-western songs, whereas she'd thought that she was meant to do more "sophisticated" work than that. For another client the word was *fear*. For him making sculptures was like standing too near the edge of a chasm. To help break through this block he decided to visit the Grand Canyon and actually stand at the edge of a great chasm, to feel the fear and confront the block.

Make a list of the twenty types of blocks described in this chapter. Work on numbering and ordering them, until you have a good idea of their relative place in your creative life. Isolate the blocks that appear most troublesome — the top half-dozen, say — and create one tactic to overcome each. If self-criticism heads the list, for instance, you might decide to meet with your inner critic. Seat him in the chair opposite you. What are his charges? That you're untalented? That you're too big a bundle of nerves to ever audition again? Listen to his charges. Think about them. Respond to them in writing — this is the very essence of guided writing work. As you engage in this written dialogue, see if your inner critic can be transformed from a mean-spirited opponent with only complaints to lodge into a collaborator with advice to offer.

By proceeding in this fashion you can address each block in turn and also continue the personality integration work outlined in chapter 2. The ultimate goals are to eliminate the block of the moment and also to become the sort of person who only rarely blocks.

Here are some other guided writing questions to consider:

- Is the source of my blockage something other than the twenty described in this chapter? How would I characterize my block?

- Is my problem a certain recurrent combination of blocks? Can I tease the combination apart and work on each block separately, or does it make more sense to work on them all together?

- Do I block only on certain work? Is rewriting easier than writing, performing easier than auditioning, a face-to-face meeting with an agent easier than a telephone conversation?

- Do I block only in certain places? Can I write songs on the road but not at home? Though I could paint in the larger studio I used to have, do I have trouble painting in my present cramped work space?

- Do I block only at certain times of the day? Are there a certain few hours of each day during which time I am almost invariably alert and creative?

- Do I block seasonally? Am I regularly unproductive in the spring, summer, fall, or winter?

- Is the blockage recent? What has changed in my life? Have my feelings about art changed? My feelings about the future? My feelings about myself? Has some event or series of events precipitated the blockage?

- What is the one thing I can do to tackle my blocks? What is another thing I can do? Can I generate a whole list of things I can do?

Learn anxiety- and stress-reduction techniques. For example, combat pressure paralysis by learning to hold on to the importance *and* the unimportance of the task before you. If an audition is coming up, practice balancing these two positions by holding your palms outstretched and weighing the importance of the audition in your left palm and its unimportance in your right. Is all the weight in your left palm? Learn to transfer some weight to your right — and to detach a little. Practice meditation, learn progressive relaxation techniques, begin an exercise program, do whatever it takes to get a handle on your persistent or incapacitating anxiety.

Change your behavior. Introduce new habits and rituals into your life. Change your work environment, your routines, your customary practice times. Make schedules and honor them. Do art first thing Sunday morning, before you read the paper. Set goals and limits. A significant behavioral change — say, working four hours at your writing, instead of one — is the exact equivalent of block elimination.

Use cognitive restructuring. Change how you think about yourself. Consider yourself capable rather than incapable. Consider yourself talented rather than untalented. Refuse to allow negative self-talk to control how you think about yourself and your work. Actively dispute negative thoughts and consciously replace them with positive ones.

Use affirmations and visualizations. Visualize your goals. Affirm that you are able to work. Affirm that you can succeed and that success does not frighten you. Create simple affirmations that resonate for you, affirmations as simple as "I can do this" or "It's time."

Build a support system. Join or form a writers' group. Have lunch with your agent and brainstorm ideas. Collaborate with other actors on a project. Collaborate with other writers on a book. Invite an art buddy over for tea and generate excitement for your latest painting plans. Share an idea with your class. Ask your teacher for help. Assign your children the task of gently reminding you that a deadline is approaching.

Make meaning. Construct and integrate into your belief system the adaptive illusion that your work is valuable. Reinvest meaning in your art-making and your vocation as an artist. Make challenges out of problems. Recast your beliefs so that your work looks more inviting to tackle. Weave your own meaning web, taking charge of the individual strands of meaning and the completed existential fabric.

Educate yourself. Gather blockbusting techniques from books. Take a class to erase a skill deficit. Attend marketing workshops. Learn how to inoculate yourself against unwanted thoughts. Take an assertiveness-training course and defeat your passivity. Educate yourself about your personality and about the marketplace. Learn what resources are available to you, and make use of them.

7 *Resistance*

The following distinction may serve you as you conceptualize how to do your creative work in a regular way. *Blockage*, the subject of the last chapter, is a function of a particular problem or issue, like our doubts about our novel, our disappointment about not having sold any of our recent paintings, or our perfectionistic streak that prevents us from feeling free to make mistakes and messes. *Resistance*, the subject of this chapter, is our everyday tissue-thin but remarkably stubborn disinclination to do the work of creating. Particular blocks come and go, but resistance, until we master it, is always with us. You might think of it as the difference between some stumbling block at work and work itself feeling like a stumbling block.

In this chapter I want to focus on a single tactic for overcoming this everyday resistance and to share with you what artists learn about the nature of resistance when they employ (or find that they can't employ) this tactic.

CRACKING AN EGG

Creative people and would-be creative people find it hard to do the thing that in the abstract sounds relatively easy to do: create and keep creating. What is at the core of the problem? For example, a novelist might write twenty novels in ten years: that's a mere two pages a day for those ten years. Even if we threw out one of every two of those pages, that would leave ten novels completed in that period. But what writer actually writes ten novels during a ten-year period? Except for the occasional romance writer, not a one. What's much more common is for a writer to write a draft of one novel and half a draft of another novel in those ten years — and to feel terribly disappointed about her output.

Two pages a day. When we're lost in the trance of writing, that's probably no more than an hour of writing. An hour of writing a day, two pages of writing a day: isn't it amazing that it should turn out to be so hard to accomplish this simple-sounding daily work? If you are a writer, remember that you aren't the only one not getting this amount of work done: virtually no writer is. What could possibly be going on?

Picture an egg. If you want to crack an egg because you are baking a cake, you whack it (carefully) on the side of your bowl, it breaks, and you drop the contents of the egg into the bowl full of flour. There's nothing simpler (though it takes a little skill to break the egg so that egg shells don't get into the batter). Your grandmother did it a million times; your young daughter can do it after a few minutes of false starts and small accidents. In the service of cooking, we are not reluctant to break that egg.

But if you are not baking a cake, an egg's shell feels remarkably formidable. There is something scary about cracking an egg for no good reason, something that makes us squeamish, something that feels like a violation of the egg. Trying to crack an egg for no good reason elicits the same sort of feeling that chalk scratching on a blackboard does. It is a physical reaction, rooted in some primitive fear or anxiety.

Creating each day requires that we crack through a shell of resistance, a shell that frightens us to crack — except when we are really working on something. Then it doesn't scare us at all and we experience no negative sensation as we crack through and begin working.

What I would like you to do this week is get a dozen eggs, put out an appropriate small bowl, and begin your daily creating — whether it be a stint of writing, painting, software designing, or composing — by cracking one egg into your bowl. Drop both the contents of the egg and the shell fragments into the bowl. Experience the cracking of that egg as the cracking through of your resistance. Feel yourself exhale as you crack it, as if you had just survived something dangerous, then proceed directly to your creative work.

What exactly is this resistance that needs cracking each day? It is made up of many parts and arises both from the primitive part of our being, where we fear shadows, and from the sophisticated part of our being, where we understand too much about difficulty and failure.

Janet, a painter, recounted her experience with cracking her daily eggs:

The practice of breaking eggs reminded me of the power behind names. When we are able to name something, we are able to have power over it. This feels very similar to naming anxiety as a natural part of the creative process. This week I approached resistance just as I approach anxiety. It will always be there, it's natural, and I either give it the power to prevent me from painting by refusing to name it, by pretending it's not there, or by misnaming it as guilt or doubt, or else I simply call it by its name, accept it for what it is (and nothing more), and move into the painting process. When I name it, I take away its power and take that power back for myself.

Another reason why cracking an egg is such an effective strategy is that the artist frequently gets stuck thinking about working rather than thinking about the work itself. She thinks, "I should paint, I should paint, I'm off from work today and I should paint, darn, I really should paint, I know I'm feeling tired and maybe a little blue, but still I should paint, since tomorrow I won't get a chance to paint and squandering today will feel so disappointing." Nowhere in that monologue is an actual thought about her current painting. What is going on is a tired — and tiring — battle between desire and everyday resistance.

The practice of cracking an egg grabs your mind's attention and pulls it away from its customary harangue about whether or not you really mean to work. Because it grabs your mind's attention, even for just a second or two, an opening occurs through which a thought about the actual work can enter. Without noticing it, you begin to think about what Marjorie wants to say to John in chapter 2, not about whether or not you are a talented writer. Without noticing it, you begin to think about the cadmium red that you love rather than about the paintings piled up in your basement. Because you distracted yourself with that egg-cracking ruse, you quieted your mind just enough to allow the trance of working to commence.

It is also impossible to run old tapes about what egg cracking signifies or about its chances for success, since it doesn't resemble anything you've attempted before. Marvin, a composer, put it this way:

> I think the egg routine works because you can't attach a story to it. There's no story behind cracking the egg. You simply do it and move on. You can't attach a story like, "I should have been cracking eggs years ago! I'm not good enough to crack this egg! Everyone else is better at cracking eggs than I am!" In fact, it's virtually impossible to drag this act out without lapsing into absurdity.
>
> Even if you try to crack the egg slowly rather than in one stroke, the liquid will start to seep through very soon. You begin to see how fragile this resistance really is and how absurd it is *not* to break through. You begin to see that all it takes is the tiniest crack in your own armor to let what's ready to pour through come out naturally. It can't help itself. Once the opening is there, it's going to come flooding out. Just name it for what it is and simply deal with it!

Try this egg-cracking exercise today. Pick a time to create and, if you like, make it a time when you usually don't create, maybe because the house is too noisy or it doesn't feel like a big enough window of time even to bother. That is, choose a time that, day in and day out, gets squandered. When the appointed time arrives, get out your egg and your bowl, crack the egg, and drop it, shell and all, into the bowl. Then commence working.

OUR RESISTANCE TO STAYING PUT

A second profound area of resistance, in addition to our resistance to beginning, is our resistance to staying put. We write some, hit a hard patch, and abandon our work for the day (or the month). You can use the egg routine to help with this brand of resistance, too. Whenever you stop creating because you have encountered some trouble spot and don't feel like continuing, take a spoon and vigorously stir the egg-and-shell mixture in your bowl. Stir it and say in a meditative way, "I don't mind messes," "I haven't worked enough yet," "I'm not leaving, I'm just starting," or whatever mantra you like. Try out various phrases. Your goal is not to leave your creating just because you feel like leaving.

Joanne, a writer, described her experience with trying out this tactic:

I'm halfway through my novel, and as I come closer to the climax my resistance grows worse and worse. Today I told myself that I wouldn't leave my desk until I had done some meaningful work. When I cracked the egg I imagined I was cracking the sensation in my stomach. I felt relieved for a while and could do some writing. Then, suddenly, I felt confused as to what should come next and had this urge to finish for the day. I always do that. As soon as the writing gets hard, I want to leave. Instead of standing up, I stirred the egg and tried to remain calm. I tried dropping my need to know what was supposed to come next and my fear of making a big mistake. After a few seconds of stirring, I found that I could resume writing.

Because we feel resistant to starting and resistant to continuing, we tend to generate excuses meant to let us off the hook. We hardly ever say, "I feel resistant to starting." What we tell ourselves is that it is surprisingly chilly and that our brain doesn't work well in the cold, that our emails have piled up and must be attended to, or that our mate will be upset if we don't accompany him to the company softball game. Indeed it is chilly, our emails have piled up, and so on, so we have told the truth — but only the partial truth, and actually more lie than truth. The real truth is that we feel resistant and not inclined to work.

Since our excuses have a ring of truth to them, they allow us to avoid our work without generating a lot of guilt. Still, the guilt begins to accumulate, because in a corner of consciousness we know what we are doing. Despite the accumulating guilt, however, we tend not to come clean and say something honest and brave like, "I have made a lot of excuses because I feel resistant to creating, and now I am going to stop all my excuse making and deal with the resistance." We find it easier to live with the accumulated guilt, as bad as that feels, than to crack through our resistance. Our everyday resistance, even in the face of mounting — and painful — guilt, still wins.

Cracking that egg can make a difference here, too. By naming resistance as the problem and tackling it head-on using the loony device of egg cracking, your excuse-making nature may suddenly become clear to you. Robin, a writer, explained this dynamic:

Until trying this egg-cracking exercise, I never uttered aloud all the excuses that I use not to write. Suddenly they became clear to me.

1. "I need to live more of my journey before I write it. I am in the midst of figuring out the solution — how can I possibly write about it yet?"

2. "I keep on writing the same thing over and over — I'm just wasting time. I'm using writing as an excuse not to get other things done."

3. "I need to just journal and free myself before writing anything real."

4. "I need to be fresh. Then I'll work half the time and get twice as much done."

5. "It will all come together. I just need to wait."

6. "I'll write when I'm free. Right now I want to take opportunities to do fun things, but when I have more free time I'll write."

7. "I have so many notes and ideas that I feel overwhelmed and confused. I need to take care of myself and give myself a break."

Thinking about resistance and about cracking that egg brought all my excuses out into the open. So, what do I want to do now? Keep cracking eggs! Keep noticing — and disputing! — the excuses I seem to endlessly make. And commit to the writing process. For me, cracking the egg signifies that commitment. I can hear the crack of the whip as I crack my egg.

I am not claiming that egg cracking is guaranteed to help you break through resistance and create regularly. Remember that you may be blocked as well as resistant: that is, something other than everyday resistance may be preventing you from creating. You may need access to information without which you can't proceed, you may be incubating a project that isn't available to you yet, you may be so bitterly disappointed about the fact that none of your novels has sold that you simply can't begin a new one. However, it pays to act as if everyday resistance is the culprit. Start with that hypothesis. Rather than saying to yourself, "I am profoundly blocked and no egg-cracking exercise could possibly make a difference!" or "My problems are so special, large, and intractable that they require something like a complete life change!" say, "Maybe I'm just resistant" and give showing up and egg cracking a chance.

Of course, you may remain resistant to naming resistance as the problem. See if you can fight that. See if you can muster the courage to face the possibility that you are really very close to working — with all that implies, including the possibility of some sweating and heavy lifting.

Leslie, a writer, talked about her resistance to the egg exercise:

I have been puzzled by the sensations I experience when I sit down to write, feelings of physical constraint. The egg exercise felt like more of the same, something burdensome and unpleasant to do. I thought, "Oh dear, another stupid thing I have to do!" At first I couldn't crack my egg. I hit it. I hit it again. Finally I smashed it into the bowl. I did manage to write two pages, but instead of feeling strong and successful I felt somehow pathetic. The following day I managed a paragraph. The whole week went that way, and I

ended up feeling exhausted. I felt like a failure, and my body re-
acted with a sore throat.

Yesterday, however, I had a mini epiphany. Something shifted,
and I stopped blaming the egg, the exercise... or anything. I sat
down and gave myself a goal of writing a thousand words. I cracked
the egg; I wrote; and when my mind wandered I took my spoon and
stirred the egg. My body felt freer. For once, I felt I was the one in
charge. When I wanted to get up, I stirred the egg and told myself,
"I am not going anywhere." I wrote for two hours and wrote well
over a thousand words. I think I am beginning to see how I can take
my writing life back from all this inertia and resistance.

Give this exercise a decent chance — a week or two, or, say, an egg car-
ton's worth. If you can't, please pay attention to your stubborn resistance
to dealing with your everyday resistance. Of course, if you are working
deeply and well every day, there is no need for the exercise or for any self-
examination. But if you are only accomplishing a fraction of the creative
work you dream of tackling and *still* won't give egg cracking a try, be brave
and consider why.

Marcy, a writer, described her avoidance:

I could not bring myself to break an egg for the sake of my writing. It isn't that it didn't seem like a good idea. Reading about the
exercise, I thought, "I get it. Starting, allowing myself to start writing, is like cracking a shell." I even put "crack egg" on my calendar.
But still I made excuses: I don't need an egg, I don't need a ritual,
eggs are for eating, if I stop on the way to writing to get an egg
I won't actually start writing, and so on. All plausible... and all
irrelevant.

What is truly relevant is that I know that I would have written
more, and with more focus, and perhaps even with more of a sense
of sacredness and satisfaction, if I had cracked eggs. Why was I not
willing to take that chance? Because I am very resistant to moving
forward as a writer... maybe because I don't feel that I deserve it. I
can be amazingly stingy with my writing self, telling myself that
I will do without the extra creative boost, the extra help, the protected

writing time, with whatever I actually need if I were serious. Not cracking an egg signified all that. It was exactly like not really trying, which I am damned tired of as my standard way of operating.

Stiffening the resistance of many creative people and most would-be creative people is the fear that whatever they manage to produce is not going to matter to anyone, themselves included. They want their work to matter, they dream about it mattering, but a voice inside tells them that it doesn't: that, first, it won't turn out well; second, that even if it did, no one would take an interest in it; and third, that even if it were wanted, it wouldn't make any real difference in the world. Why bother, then? Why not sit back and watch some television? As a result of this profound doubt, they don't find their work important enough even to waste an egg on.

This war between believing in the creative act and not believing in it, between believing that your creative efforts matter and discounting those efforts as a waste of time, thickens the veneer of resistance that is already a feature of the process. It can also become a constant background noise that prevents you from accessing your good ideas and that leaves you feeling too distracted to create. Suddenly you are not just walled off from your creative work; you are walled off from it in a prison filled with chattering monkeys.

Barbara, a writer, described how this experience can play itself out:

What a week! I hate to admit it, but there's been a "war" going on in Boston, and it's taking place right inside the gut of *me*. What could be so hard about "cracking an egg" and then putting pen to paper? The egg cracks sooooo easily. Thoughts start to materialize. Then the phone rings. Ignore it. The husband, adult child, and/or one of the aging parents needs a document, some money, some attention, or just some stroking. The dog howls for food or relief. I glance at the clock. *What* time is it!? The long list of time-sensitive job demands starts to gnaw at my insides. Dare I continue "stealing" time for this writing gig?

I realize that "writing" never appears on my to-do list, while everything else does. Aha! I see that my writing place is dishonored by unopened mail, papers to be filed, and sundries belonging to the other bodies who inhabit this dwelling. I reflect that I'm trying to fit my writing into my crazy busy days instead of writing first, then moving on with the day. I know what I need to do to change this: I need to put "writing" as the first entry on my to-do list, I need to enlist my family's cooperation, I need to silence the electronic distractions, but first of all, I have to change something fundamental, something in my belief system. I have to believe — rather than just mouth the words — that my writing matters.

Cracking an egg makes a statement: I matter. I matter enough to waste an egg. I matter enough to make this nonsensical mess, both with the egg and with my work. I opt for this absurd choice, to create, rather than for any of the easier choices, like drinking with my friends, catching up on world affairs, or getting the garden in shape. I crack my egg because that represents my task, to crack through my resistance, and because it is an absurd action, exactly like trying to matter.

STRATEGIES

There are other tactics and strategies you might employ to crack through your resistance. You might (paradoxically and lightheartedly) scream at the top of your lungs, "I will not do this work!" Screaming ventilates anxiety and shatters resistance. Scream, laugh, and get to work. You might say to yourself, "I will not go the bathroom until I start my screenplay!" Starting your screenplay will soon seem easier than not going to the bathroom.

I'm sure you get the idea. By naming resistance as the problem and by engaging in some left-field tactic that, by its oddity and absurdity, takes your mind off your everyday doubts and disinclinations, you give yourself the chance to create. Try the egg exercise for a week; or create your own resistance-busting tactic and give it a try. Resistance is a given: your willingness to break through everyday resistance remains up for grabs.

8 | *Business* as *Work*

An artist after many phone calls got an appointment with a local art dealer. The dealer kept him waiting for an hour, looked through his portfolio, and told him, "Come back when you're dead."

— SAM PROVENZANO

Do you realize what would happen if Moses were alive today? He'd go up to Mount Sinai, come back with the Ten Commandments, and spend the next eight years trying to get published.

— ROBERT ORBEN

You are talented and creative. You rarely block, and when you do block you know how to move yourself along. Your moods are not incapacitating, and you haven't stepped over into madness. Your personality is sufficiently integrated so that your necessary arrogance doesn't prevent you from having successful relationships, your nonconformity hasn't made you a pariah, and your skepticism hasn't bred in you a nihilistic darkness. You work happily in isolation but can also move into the world and have a life. You have, in short, met many of the challenges of an art-committed life.

Are you home free? No, unfortunately, not by a long shot. The next challenges you face are as great as any encountered so far. They are the multiple challenges of doing the business of art: making money, developing a career, acknowledging and making the most of your limited opportunities, living with compromise, dealing with mass taste and commercialism, negotiating the marketplace, and making personal sense of the mechanics and metaphysics of the business environment of art.

Many an artist grows bitter in this difficult arena. Many an artist flounders and fails. Many an artist succumbs to the competition. Only the rare artist sits herself down to examine these matters, consciously and carefully, for they are often painful to consider. But you have no choice but to examine them. If you are an artist, you want an audience. And if you want an audience, you must do business.

ART AND THE MARKETPLACE

The business of art requires care and a significant amount of time. Typically artists neither love this kind of work nor do it well. But if you are not your own supporter and promoter, coach, business manager, market analyst, salesperson, best business friend, and maker of luck, then you are likely to have a marginal career at best.

Many artists never admit that they are in business for themselves, even as they pursue their fiction sales or their concert bookings. Others admit that a marketplace exists but argue that it shouldn't be permitted to dictate to them. Both positions, the former a kind of denial and the latter a kind of rebellion, stem not so much from the artist's inability to do business — for in her day job she may work with a budget of millions or a staff of twenty — but from a variety of complicated factors, among them pride, anxiety, and sense of mission.

Why would your sense of mission, for instance, prevent you from doing business? For the simple reason that your mission is to do art, not commerce. The people who can promote you do commerce, not art. You know that the publisher, the gallery owner, the network executive, and the Hollywood producer are merchants. You know that the literary agent looking for a romance novel or a mystery story is looking for a certain kind of merchandise. As the painter John Baldessari put it, "For a dealer, the only reality is the rent. A lot of ambiguities about artist-dealer relationships would be cleared up if art dealers were called art merchants. That's what they do. They sell art for money. They are not messengers from god with divine knowledge about what's art and what isn't. They show you because they think they can make money from what you do."

You're also likely to believe that the public should be given what it needs, not what it wants. This vision flows from your love of your medium and your respect for traditions. You hold, in short, to a heroic ideal and a code of ethics. Zelda Fichandler, longtime manager of the District of Columbia's Arena Theater, explained: "While a theater is a public art and belongs to its public, it is an art before it is public, and so it belongs first to itself, and its first service must be self-service. A theater is part of its society. But it is a part which must remain apart since it is also chastiser, rebel, lightning rod, redeemer, and irritant."

This is the ideal; but for a regional repertory company, an orchestra, a dance company, or an individual artist, the reality remains that the audience pays the bills. In this regard Fichandler added, "The only criterion for judging a production is the power of the impression it makes on the audience."

This statement is not so much a contradiction as a recognition that two positions exist, the artistic and the commercial. Between these two positions an abiding tension persists. The eighteenth-century American painter Gilbert Stuart complained, "What a business is that of portrait painter. He is brought a potato and is expected to paint a peach." The artist learns that the public wants peaches, not potatoes. You can paint potatoes if you like, write potatoes, dance potatoes, and compose potatoes, you can with great and valiant effort communicate with some other potato eaters. In so doing you contribute to the world's reservoir of truth and beauty. But if you won't give the public peaches, you won't be paid much.

Repeatedly artists take the heroic potato position. They want their work to be good, honest, powerful — and only then successful. They want their work to be alive, not contrived and formulaic. Norwegian painter Edvard Munch declared: "No longer shall I paint interiors, and people reading, and women knitting. I shall paint living people, who breathe and feel and suffer and love."

The artist is interested in the present and has little desire to repeat old, albeit successful, formulas. As painter Jenny Holzer put it, "I could do a pretty good third-generation stripe painting, but so what?" The unexpected result of the artist's determination to do his own best art is that he is put in an adversarial relationship with the public and with those who sell to the public. In that adversarial position he comes to feel rather irrational. For what rational person would do work that's not wanted?

What rational theater director would put on plays that the public won't come to see? What rational filmmaker would make personal films no distributor will take? What rational composer would attempt a composition for a full symphony orchestra, understanding that she'll never hear it performed unless she pays an orchestra to perform it? It appears more rational to sign a vow of poverty or to run full-speed into a brick wall than to engage in such frustrating activities.

The public and players in the marketplace smile indulgently at you, the artist. They, after all, are rational; you are irrational. They comprehend the bottom line; you are dense. But you understand, perhaps outside conscious awareness, that their supposed rationality is a particular sort of lie. Todd Gitlin, a student of marketplace dynamics and the notorious bottom line in television and publishing, wrote about this putative rationality:

> Again and again, as I walked into corporate offices in Century City and environs, I was told to put aside my naïveté and recognize that television was about making money, period. But often enough the success record compiled by such ostensible geniuses of economic calculation, by their own lights, is abysmal. Just because executives intone allegiance to their peculiar version of rationality doesn't mean that they deserve to be regarded as rational. Corporate publishers are always throwing money away — on giant advances, overprinting, glitzy salaries, slush funds, and bright ideas.

You may feel stupid as you process the advice you get. For instance, Judith Applebaum and Nancy Evans, authors of *How to Get Happily Published*, advise the writer that "it is largely within your power to determine whether a publisher will buy your work and whether the public will buy it once it's released. Failures abound because hardly anybody treats getting published as if it were a rational, manageable activity — like practicing law or laying bricks — in which knowledge coupled with skill and application would suffice to ensure success."

This advice, which, like bottom-line logic, wears the mantle of supreme rationality, is almost certainly false advice for the poet, for the writer working on her version of *Ulysses*, for the painter painting in a new idiom, for the screenwriter with a serious screenplay to sell, for the actress looking for serious roles in film. It is advice that can only be translated as "write peaches, not potatoes."

Only if the writer's product is wanted in the marketplace are there rational ways of seeking a publisher and selling the work (although, as author Peter Benchley put it, the matter still rests squarely in the hands of the "gods of whimsy"). But it is largely outside the power of the writer attempting to create literature to determine whether a publisher will buy his work or whether his novel will do well in the marketplace once published. Serious fiction, like serious theater and serious music, simply sells poorly.

CAREER AND COMPROMISE

As you look around, you see that commercial art not only sells, but it even has permission to be bad. Noncommercial art not only doesn't sell, but it must be singular to have even the slightest chance. Understanding that such an enormous chasm exists between the commercial and the artistic, you frequently begin to formulate two different sets of career goals. You determine that while you would love to make money from your cherished art, you will also pursue other financial avenues. You make an agreement with yourself to attempt to do at least some commercial work.

In making this inner arrangement, you think of yourself as a professional. This is a new and frequently burdensome piece of identity to wear. The professional dancer determines to dance in anything. The professional actor determines to act in anything. The professional writer determines to write anything. You commence with commercial nonfiction or commercial fiction, audition more for commercials than for live theater, take advertising assignments and put your art photography away. In the extreme you let go of art altogether. Swing-era musician and arranger Sy Oliver described his experience: "I was a professional arranger who used to do whatever the situation called for. There are different types of musicians. There's the storybook musician, the guy who loves music and hangs around all night and jams as long as there's someone to play with. Then there's the professional musician, who is in the business to earn money, period. That's me."

Naturally you feel uncomfortable as you work out your own brand of compromise. But compromise is necessary, and you are challenged to make peace with your decisions. The cynical artist, the unimaginative artist, and the pragmatic artist have compromised from the beginning. If you agree at a late date to compromise, you are challenged to integrate that significant change into the web of your being. At the same time, you'll still long to have your best work supported, recognized, and valued, even if it can't pay its own way. Henry F. B. Gilbert, the American composer, expressed this wish as follows: "True Art seldom pays for itself; at least not for a long time. And the finer it is the less likelihood there is of its paying for itself. Money, advanced to a composer to free him from the necessity of earning it, should be regarded in the light of an investment; not as a material investment which shall eventually bring returns in kind, but as a spiritual investment which shall eventually bring rich returns of an artistic or cultural nature."

Artists regularly compromise to survive. As one screenwriter said of his life in Hollywood, "They ruin your stories. They massacre your ideas. They prostitute your art. They trample on your pride. And what do you get for it? A fortune." Visual artist Tim Rollins, describing his South Bronx neighborhood art program for learning-disabled, emotionally troubled teenagers, argued for his brand of compromise: "We at the Art and Knowledge Workshop are a little like the old Communist countries — we started out radical and ended up entrepreneurial. But I would much rather shake hands with the devil than be a martyr for some idea of purity. It's better to make certain political compromises than not pay the kids and lose them to the economy of the streets, which is mainly drug dealing."

The visual artist Sandro Chia argued that the artist, free to tackle any kind of work in the privacy of his studio, is still a slave to the system into which he is born:

> An artist is free to do whatever he likes in formulating his work,
> even the most extravagant things, but he is not allowed to say one

word against the economy because the economy will punish him in the cruelest way. It has always been like this. At one time, it was the Pope or the emperor who chose the artist and decided how much he was valued. Now, it is done by a headless entity consisting of auctions, rumors, the media, newspapers, art magazines, interviews, and so on. If you're out, you're out — you simply don't count. There is no opposition, no different opinion. Anything that happens must happen within this system.

You set limits for yourself as to how much you will compromise. But when your editor tells you that your next novel could be your breakthrough book — a real blockbuster — if only it possessed a tad more excitement, you must look at the line you've drawn in the sand and think hard about drawing it over again, nearer to mass taste, or carving it in deeper exactly where you've drawn it.

Is there a formula for compromising? Does the writer gain permission from herself to write a potboiler if she pledges to do a serious novel next? Can the successful actor keep his star in ascendancy in pop movies and still determine to make every fourth movie a significant one, even if it is a money loser? The pressure to compromise is enormous. A Pablo Picasso self-portrait sells for $47.85 million. Two books by Ken Follett are purchased for $12.3 million, and three by Jeffrey Archer are bid on at $20 million. Jack Nicholson makes a fortune on *Batman*, and Steven Spielberg makes a fortune on *E.T.* Whether these figures are generated by astounding art or by astoundingly commercial art, they send shock waves through the artist's system. And so the artist is sorely tempted to draw the line closer to mammon.

Of course it may then hurt the artist's feelings to be labeled commercial, for she understands that she is being criticized for selling out. Even an artist with the tiniest audience can find herself having to dodge this charge, even as she starves to death. As Herbie Mann, the jazz musician, put it, "If you're in jazz and more than ten people like you, you're labeled commercial."

The artist may unconsciously decide to avoid this tense business of compromising by doing art for which there is no commercial market whatsoever. He may guarantee that he will not have to deal with the world of commerce by choosing, say, to write poetry. Of course he writes poetry because, first of all, he loves it and needs to write it; but he may also harbor the understanding that his choice allows him to remain "pure." He can then play the role of uncompromising artist with a certain smugness — and a certain sense of relief.

Because the marketplace frustrates you, you may simply avoid attending to business. Because the challenges you face in taking care of business are taxing and complicated, you may feel exhausted and defeated before you begin. You know that to have a career you must negotiate a maze full of obstacles, a maze designed, it would seem, to test your courage, principles, heart, and soul. This is a dizzying prospect that you approach with a touch of vertigo.

It is true that making a dollar is hard for everyone, artists and nonartists alike. As the performance artist Eric Bogosian put it, "The artist today has it harder, but so does the truck driver and the doctor because, economically, it sucks out there." For the artist, though, the path to a dollar is particularly mystifying. Is it more important to be good, to be mediocre, to be well connected, to be white and male, to be black and female, to be lucky... or what? Even if you decide to step fully onto the path to commercial success, what exactly is that path?

Such questions confound and infuriate the artist. But you are nevertheless challenged to come to grips with the fact that the answers to these questions matter to you. You will see that your business has two sides to it: the mechanical side, which many artists' self-help and marketing books address, and the metaphysical side, which is what we'll look at next.

THE MECHANICS AND METAPHYSICS
OF ART AS BUSINESS

The mechanical and the metaphysical come together for each artist as that artist's career path. That path is a function of the artist's personality, the product she determines to sell, the goodness or appropriateness of that product, the array of compromises she is willing to make, her historical moment and cultural milieu, her group associations (as a Chinese American actor or an African American painter, for example), the decisions she makes (about teachers, mentors, and so on), and luck.

Let's look at a painter's career first. On the mechanical side, you attend an art school or a university art program, have art school shows, learn to send out slides of your paintings and to contact gallery owners. You maintain mailing lists and attempt to find fair and regular representation for your work. You frame your paintings if you can afford to. You try to become known to purchasers of art. You prepare for shows, sign contacts, garner commissions, deliver your paintings to buyers, and so forth.

On the metaphysical side lie all the following considerations: What are you painting? Is it the right moment for what you're painting? How many painters can your culture sustain, and how many painters are vying for the available slots? How does your personality help or hinder your ability to sell your art? In quelling your anxiety about the demands of the marketplace, do you rush away from contacts or toward them? In your historical moment, is it providential to be a woman painter, a Midwestern painter, a Primitive painter, or an Italian American painter? How do you think of art — as craft, decoration, entertainment, sacred product? Are your stars crossed or uncrossed?

The metaphysics of the matter combine into a prescription for failure or for success. On the one hand, you may be the wrong person doing the wrong art at the wrong time. On the other, you may be thrust by accident into a museum exhibit that becomes the hottest show of the decade. This is exactly what happened to Nathan Oliveira in 1959, when, at the age of twenty-seven, he found himself included in the Images of Man show at the Museum of Modern Art with Jackson Pollock, Willem de Kooning, and Alberto Giacometti, a fortuitous event that secured his stardom.

Because you are painting in a style, a size, and colors that are popular, you may find yourself (by accident or by design) at the forefront of a popular movement. At a certain propitious moment, your work is reviewed by the right reviewer or appears in the right show. The impact of this is not lost in the next instant but, because of your personality or connections or sheer luck, you capitalize on the opportunity. All of a sudden you matter, and your soup cans, black abstractions, or superrealistic images of cordless telephones become all the rage.

For the suddenly successful artist everything may come together in a kind of synergistic explosion that catapults him from anonymity to celebrity. Artist advocate Caroll Michels described this interactive moment: "Curator tells dealer that critic wrote an excellent review about artist. Dealer checks out artist and invites artist into gallery. Dealer tells curator that artist is now part of gallery. Curator tells museum colleagues that artist is part of gallery and has backing of critic. Curator invites artist to exhibit at museum. Curator asks critic to write introduction to exhibition catalog in which artist is included. Dealer tells clients that artist has been well reviewed and is exhibiting at museum. Clients buy."

Can this success take place only if you are calculating, only if you put yourself in the right spot at the right moment with the right product? Not necessarily. But the moment is altogether more likely to happen if you are the kind of person who will naturally think of hiring a publicist to keep your name alive, if you naturally stir up controversy, if you understand trends and fashions, if you offer up peaches, if you enlist everybody's aid in your cause.

Let's look at the novelist's path. From the mechanical point of view, you attend a creative writing program, begin to send out your first stories, and get published in your student magazine. You work on your first novel, try to interest a literary agent in it, submit clean manuscripts and appropriately stamped return envelopes. You study the market, network at writing conferences, sign contracts and meet deadlines, work with editors, publicize your work, struggle to move from your small press to a larger publisher or from the mid-list to the front of the list.

But what is your first novel about? That is a matter of first principles. Is it meant to be frankly commercial? Is it a genre piece in a popular style? If it is neither commercial nor part of an established genre, will it be lucky enough to strike that synergistic moment when agent excitement, editorial excitement, reader interest, and media hype come together in a firestorm of buzz?

For one writer, the greater part of success may be calculation. He will frankly write commercial mysteries, understand the formula and the market, give each story its own spin but not spin it away from what's expected. For another writer, success will be a matter of luck. The right agent accepts his imperfect manuscript; the right editor buys it and supports it. The story has something that ignites interest at that historical moment. Reviewers fan the flames, and the public chooses his book as the one serious novel they will read that year.

This sort of accidental good fortune is recounted too often in the biographies of well-known artists to be ignored. You may have the fortune, for instance, to have the sort of roommate Dostoyevsky had. Upon reading Dostoyevsky's first short novel, *Poor People*, his roommate literally ran with it to Russia's preeminent literary critic, Vissarion Belinsky. Belinsky read it, loved it, and single-handedly made Dostoyevsky's name.

But Dostoyevsky's good luck was not just to have that helpful roommate or to be championed by that powerful critic. It was equally to have written a naturalistic and conventional novel first. *The Double*, Dostoyevsky's second novel, was stranger, modern, existential, and psychological, and gravely disappointed Belinsky. It was too fantastic, Belinsky complained, saying that "the fantastic can have its place only in lunatic asylums, not in literature; it is the business of doctors and not of poets."

Had *The Double* come first, it would not have been championed by Belinsky, and Dostoyevsky might have had no early successes, or, possibly, any later ones. Norman Mailer confesses to this same kind of luck at the beginning of his career. By writing a conventional novel about World War II, *The Naked and the Dead*, one that could be readily accepted in the marketplace, he became famous overnight. He then had permission to write in his own voice and still be published.

The classical musician's career, taking the mechanical and the metaphysical together, revolves around her early choice of instrument, early virtuosity, early support, early teachers and successes in conservatory and at the right competitions, and her ability to carve out a concert and recording career as a soloist or to win a seat in a first-rate orchestra. It may include teaching at a university, teaching at a conservatory, or teaching private lessons and may involve the soloist in a hundred or more nights on the road each year. She may experience tremendous performance anxiety or little, learn new repertoire pieces slowly or quickly, obtain a Stradivarius, and nurse lingering wrist and elbow injuries. But, as with painters, writers, and every other artist, the metaphysical is bound to mix with the mechanical.

If, for instance, she learns from her teacher to hold her fingers and move on the piano bench like Glenn Gould, and playing in Glenn Gould's style is out, she has hurt her career. If she learns to play with flat fingers, and flat-finger playing is out, that style will hurt her at competitions. Even more important, if her teacher is influential, that connection will vitally help her career. The young musician who is the protégé of a well-connected teacher may be said to have a significant leg up on her peers. As Robert Bloom, oboist and oboe teacher, put it, "If one teacher is a little more persuasive than another, his student gets the orchestra job, and if one teacher gets a reputation for having his students get the jobs, then students go to that teacher. It is a very, very uncomfortable and commercial situation."

The career path for the actor, the metaphysical and the mechanical taken together, often has at its center what Julius Novick called the "temptations of fame and fortune, of Broadway, television, and the movies." The young actor imagines himself striking it rich. While he is attending the right classes in the right city, working in live theater and on the outskirts of film, television, and commercials, gaining agency representation, making personal and professional connections, and auditioning, his eye is fixed on the gold ring: on discovery, on breakthrough opportunities.

He may also want the opportunity to act steadily. He is then faced with the decision about where to live. Should it be New York, Los Angeles, or a city like Chicago with good regional theater? The actor who opts for regional theater may work more regularly and in more interesting pieces than his brothers in New York or Los Angeles, but he may naturally feel that he is missing his chance at stardom. Howard Witt, an actor with nine productive years in regional theater, explained: "There are certain things you have to give up when you come into a regional theater. You have to give up the idea that you're going to become famous, that you're going to become rich, that you're going to be recognized, even in the profession. I have an old saying that my mother had two sons, one joined the Foreign Legion and one went to Arena Stage, and neither was ever heard from again."

As a matter of principle, would you rather act regularly or be a star? Which decision flows more naturally from your personality? And what part of your personality do you want to access: the part that can do business or the part that prefers to have a good time? Paul McCartney explained the dilemma faced by the Beatles: "The main downfall is that we were less businessmen and more heads, which was very pleasant and very enjoyable, except there should have been the man in there who would tell us to sign bits of paper. We got a man in who started to say, come on, sign it all over to me, which was the fatal mistake."

Or consider the experience of John Hill Hewitt, the nineteenth-century American composer: "My ballads are (or rather were) well known throughout the country; for I have not published for many years. Why? For the simple reason that it does not pay the author. The publisher pockets all, and gets rich on the brains of the poor fool who is chasing *ignis fatuus*, reputation."

You can learn the rules of the game. You can learn from Rodney Gordy of Motown Records: "Knowing who needs what is the key to success." You can embrace or recoil from the advice offered to young songwriters by Tom Vickers of Almo-Irving music: "Bathe the listener's ears with pleasant sounds that people will want to hear over and over, don't scrub them with abrasive material."

You can learn these and a hundred other lessons from books, from history, from your own experiences and the experiences of your peers. But to understand the metaphysics of the matter you must look into your soul and into that mysterious place — is it in your own being? Is it in the culture? Is it in the stars? — where lucky accidents are born.

TWO WRITERS' PATHS

Let's examine the differing paths of two hypothetical short story writers. The first doesn't secure a career for himself. The second does, although not the one he would have predicted. Let's take it for granted that both writers are talented and creative. Talent and creativity are not the issue. The issue is the metaphysical one of the interrelationship among product, personality, and marketplace.

Joseph K.

As a young man our first writer, Joseph K., decides that he needs to write short stories. He loves the stories of Yevgeny Zamyatin, James Joyce, Jorge

Luis Borges, Grace Paley, Eudora Welty, and Franz Kafka, loves the compression and precision of the form, doesn't much revere poetry or the novel, and isn't interested in literary criticism or nonfiction writing. He calls himself a short story writer and determines to spend his life writing. From a business point of view, the path he has chosen is an unfortunate one. How much can a short story writer expect to earn? How much do even the highest-paid short story writers earn? But these are not questions Joseph K. puts to himself.

His own stories, as he begins to write them, bear a family resemblance to those of Kafka. We may guess that he is not a people-pleasing sort of person. We would not expect him to have a calculating way about him with respect to the marketplace. We would not expect him to agree with Truman Capote, who said, "I never write — indeed, am physically incapable of writing — anything I don't think I will be paid for." We would not expect him to agree with Samuel Johnson, who said, "Sir, no man but a blockhead ever wrote except for money."

Rather, we expect him to be a wounded, depressed, and lonely fellow with an excellent imagination and a fine way with words, who, like Kafka himself, is more than a little ambivalent about interacting in the marketplace. Our writer likely neither knows nor cares whether this is a good or a bad time to be writing Kafkaesque short stories. He is writing the stories that flow out of his imagination and soul, without calculation. His dreams of fame, recognition, and respect, which he does harbor, do not influence in the smallest measure what he writes or how he writes it.

Throughout college and afterward, Joseph K. spends a lot of time at his desk, in coffeehouses reading and writing, and on his sofa thinking. He works at odd jobs, goes to the movies, has a friendship or two, is shy with and estranged from women, has a stormy relationship with his overbearing father and polite mother, sleeps a good bit, is fonder of marijuana than of other drugs, writes letters, and continues to polish his stories.

When his car breaks down for the final time and his teeth hurt so much that he really must find a dentist, he sets about looking for a steady job. But because he considers himself no better at the game of academia than at the game of publishing, and because there are relatively few teaching jobs anyway, and because, a little arrogant and a little hurt, he despises teachers, he chooses not to pursue an advanced degree in English. Nor does it seem to him wise to seek a job that might violate his principles or get under his skin too much — say, a job in advertising. He decides, instead, to work in a bank.

A year or two later, with three complete and several incomplete stories sitting on his desk, he picks up his first copy of *Novel & Short Story Writer's Market*. Reared on the classics and with too many of them still to read, he knows little contemporary fiction and has no ready way of distinguishing one literary magazine from another. With some care but still with only half an eye, he selects several magazines and sends them his stories, which are rejected. A few of the rejections are personal and encouraging. A few are vitriolic. Most are form letters.

He writes more stories but sends none of them out. Several years pass. He now has a book-length collection of stories. A co-worker at the bank, one of the few who know that he's a writer, tells Joseph K. that her sister is an editor with a medium-sized literary press. He ignores this information since, based on those early rejections, he doubts the ability of editors to recognize the worth of his stories. Although not aware of it, he is also made extremely anxious by her offer.

Our writer's only good friend, a teacher named Max, provides him with much sound advice about how to market his book-length collection, and Joseph K. finally decides to listen. He tries certain publishers who seem likely, varying his query letters and altering the sequence of his stories. He gets only form-letter rejections.

After the manuscript is rejected ten times, he puts it away and begins to work on a novel, harboring the not-quite-conscious idea that novels, at least, can sell, and when his novel sells, then his short stories will be wanted. When his dark, brooding, and strange novel is finished he sends it out. It is rejected ten times. By now he is thirty-two years old.

Everyone in the trade knows that Joseph K. is to be pitied. Edwin McDowell, writing in the *New York Times*, commented on the forces working against him: "The odds against an unknown writer getting a manuscript published by simply sending it directly to a publishing house are astronomical." This sentiment is echoed in a *Time* magazine article: "It is virtually impossible to get published what is known in the trade as an 'over the transom' manuscript." Bookstore owner Walter Powell wrote: "Few of the major trade publishers will take a chance on a manuscript from someone whose name is not known."

Does Joseph K., hunkered down in his studio apartment, know this? Does he realize that blindly and hopefully sending out his collection of short stories or his first novel is a nearly futile gesture, the equivalent of buying a lottery ticket? In a way he does, for he has at least his own experience to guide him. But in an important way he doesn't, for first novels and collections of stories are regularly published. On balance he continues to think that his marketing strategies, as minimal as they are, are essentially sound — and that one day he will be discovered.

He does make one new decision. Some experts contend that with an advocate in the marketplace — a literary agent — the odds of Joseph K. getting published would change from one in a thousand to one in ten. One day Joseph K. realizes this and begins to send out his collection of short stories and his dark novel to literary agents rather than to publishers. He gets many personal and pleasant rejections, all of which boil down to the same message: his work would be hard to sell. Roger Straus, president of Farrar, Straus & Giroux, explained, "It's harder for a new writer to get an agent than a publisher," but Joseph K., unaware of these long odds and of the need to keep trying, chalks up his negative experience to the venality of agents and stops communicating with them.

Over the next few years, two or three of Joseph K.'s stories appear in literary magazines. One is anthologized in a collection of neo-Kafkaesque stories. But his own collection and his novel will not sell. He reads a newspaper poll asserting that Stephen King is considered America's greatest living author, followed in descending order of greatness by Danielle Steel, James Michener, Louis L'Amour, and Sidney Sheldon. One forty-seven-year-old female fan explains why she adores Danielle Steel's novels: "It's pure escapism. Her heroine is always beautiful, the men in the novels are always handsome, the people are rich and everything turns out fine, unlike life." None of this upsets or educates Joseph K. He simply doesn't take it in.

But our now not-quite-so-young writer is perplexed that two different universes seem to exist in the same time and space. He has a shelf full of books that inform him that if he puts his manuscript together neatly, researches the market, and sends out a solid query letter to the correct publisher, he has a good chance of being published. At the same time he understands that to operate in such a fashion feels like a pathetic waste of time and looks like lunacy.

He turns forty. His best writing goes into the letters he writes to a woman he has never met, a cousin of a co-worker at the bank, who lives on a dairy farm in eastern Iceland. He begins to tell her that he loves her.

Finally he stops writing stories altogether. He stops reading fiction. Instead he reads books about early Christianity, especially about early Christian martyrs. By the age of sixty he is an expert on the subject, and what began as a modest monograph on an obscure martyr has turned into a thousand-page manuscript. Once or twice he sends the manuscript out. But of course no one wants it.

Something in each of us wants to pity, ridicule, and laugh at Joseph K. — even if, as artists, we may not be so different from him. Something in each of us wants to call him blind, foolish, and weak. And yet, with respect to his writing career, all he has done is carefully and conscientiously write what he felt it important to write and then market his writing following textbook advice. To be sure, he ignored some opportunities and the basic demands of the marketplace and never opted to change his ways or to investigate the shadows in his personality, but nevertheless he operated rationally enough. Didn't he?

We can call him a failure, as he can't help calling himself, but we would be wise to understand that he did not fail as a writer of excellent fiction. He failed to negotiate the maze constructed by his own personality and the demands of the marketplace. He failed, that is, to understand how he was fated to travel along a certain path, unless and until he changed himself and rethought his role in the universe.

Robert F.

Our second short story writer, whom we'll call Robert F., is not that different in personality from Joseph K. He, too, loves the stories of Zamyatin, Joyce, Borges, Paley, Welty, and Kafka. He, too, is essentially a proud, arrogant, antisocial loner. In fact, our two writers look rather alike during their twenties. They work at odd jobs, write stories, frequent cafés, send out their stories, and have their stories rejected. Neither attends marketing workshops nor experiences much internal willingness to meet the marketplace.

But there are major differences between them. We could draw the differences in any number of ways. We could say that Robert F. is the less impaired one — less wounded by his childhood, more able to form relationships, more flexible, or less anxious. We could postulate that Robert F. has been better supported by his parents, has higher self-esteem or a better self-image, or is less romantic and shrewder than Joseph K. Maybe he is less uncompromising, more self-aware, or more willing and able to listen to the advice of others.

However we draw the differences, they are such that Robert F. is able to enter an intimate relationship with a woman, marry, and have children. In this new context Robert F. arrives at a crucial turning point, for it begins to seem like an act of bad faith to stoically identify himself as a short story writer and thereby contribute so little to the household income. At this existential extremity, Robert F. tackles the question of choice. How should he fashion his life? What will appropriately serve his wife and his children as well as himself? What can he do in addition to writing short stories — or even instead of writing short stories? How should he change? What should he do with his life?

The answers do not come overnight, but the questions remain alive within him. He thinks about them, makes plans, makes decisions. He goes out into the world more often, in strategic fashion, to see what's happening and what's wanted. He battles his own antisocial tendencies and works to keep his artist's necessary arrogance in check.

He discovers, over a year or two, that the themes he has been writing about in his stories resemble those being addressed by the burgeoning men's movement. It dawns on him that he could probably offer a men's workshop. He thinks about this, works on the idea, and eventually presents his first workshop, which draws only three men. But he does a better job of marketing the second workshop, and the third. His fifth workshop earns him more money that all his previous short story sales put together. Just as important, it strikes him that his new path is not a repudiation of his dreams or a violation of his principles but rather a hitherto unforeseen way to do good work and gain recognition.

Over the course of a year he writes a nonfiction book proposal based on his workshop materials and experiences. This book interests an agent and is quickly sold. It does quite well, and his nonfiction career is launched. By forty, Robert F. no longer considers himself a short story writer. He no longer *is* primarily a short story writer, although he returns to his first love whenever he can. He finds his identity hard to pin down. If asked, he sometimes calls himself a writer, sometimes a teacher, sometimes a group facilitator.

New business challenges continually arise for him. Some of the compromises he makes are harder for him to swallow than others. Some of his choices turn out to be misguided. But on balance he is pleased to have a career and proud that he has squarely faced the issue of how to acquire and keep an audience. If asked, he would refuse to call himself better than Joseph K. But neither would he accept, even for minute, the purist's charge that he had sold out by rethinking his career in this particular fashion.

THE CHALLENGES NAMED

The hard truth about art is that you must think about it as a business. What is wanted? What is not wanted? Who are the players in the game? How does the marketplace operate? You must spend real time thinking about the business end of art: how it operates, what you need to learn so that you can operate in it more effectively, what move you must make to transform yourself into a smarter businessperson.

On both a practical and a psychological level, you must deal with the high probability that your art will not earn you a living. As a young artist it may be impossible and even undesirable to acknowledge this probability. But the day will come when it begins to dawn on you that the odds are heavily stacked against you. Then you will have to reconsider the rightness of your choices: your choice, for instance, to work any sort of day job no matter how demeaning or debilitating. Might a second career be a better idea? A willingness to do more commercial art? A mutually thrilling relationship with a supportive wage-earning gentleman or lady?

At every stage of your career you must consciously do business, if you want a career. If you are an actor you must do business as a twenty-year-old actor and, thirty years later, as a fifty-year-old actor. If you're a novelist you must do business as a neophyte and as a mature artist with six novels behind you. At each stage of the game you must understand the marketplace and make decisions based on that understanding. You must handle the hundreds of small and large details that are an integral part of plying your trade — the mechanics of the business.

You're likewise challenged to examine your career path to see if, metaphysically speaking, there are crucial turnings to take. Above all, you're challenged to keep your spirits up as you go about your business. Especially if you produce potatoes rather than peaches, you can be certain that your business road will be rocky and that you will get bruised as you journey along it.

STRATEGIES

How can you better conduct your business and make sense of the business of art? The most important strategies to employ involve the creation and implementation of a personal business plan of action, one that takes into account both the mechanics of doing art business and the metaphysics of your life in art.

Your business action plan won't look like a recipe or an agenda. What concerns you is too complicated to allow for simple, linear solutions. Your approach is more like the juggler's, who launches five apples into the air and keeps them all flying. Even as the juggler grabs one apple in order to take a bite out of it, she is aware of all the other apples. Sometimes she needs to take a small, hurried bite because a distant apple is falling. Sometimes she can take a more leisurely bite. The items you are juggling in your business action plan are the following. None should slip entirely from your awareness even as you pay closer attention to one or another of them.

Artist's Business Action Plan

Perform ongoing self-assessment. Your first step is to engage in a general assessment of your present relationship to the business of art. Consider the following questions in conjunction with point 7 of the guided writing program described in chapter 13.

1. Do I intend to create peaches, potatoes, or a mix of the two?

2. How effective am I at doing the business of art?

3. How effective am I at mastering my resistance to doing the business of art?

4. How effective am I at meeting the fears and anxieties that well up in me when I contemplate business situations or attempt to negotiate business situations?

5. What have I learned from my past selling experiences, and how have I built on that knowledge?

6. How much time do I devote to the business of art? Is it enough?

7. How much mind space do I turn over to the business of art? Is it enough?

8. What are my business goals and aspirations?

9. How would I like my career to look? Modest but solid? Immodest and dramatic?

10. What tools will I use in assessing how I do the business of art? Will I read the trade magazines and learn to comprehend the realities of my business environment? Will I engage in quiet conversations with friends and ask them how they see me as a seller of art?

Engage in ongoing assessment of your personality as a seller. Consider the following in an effort to assess and improve your selling and marketing skills:

1. What part of your personality can you enlist to enhance your ability to sell? Your intelligence? Your intellectual playfulness? Your sense of curiosity? Your slyness or sense of whimsy?

2. What part of your personality must you better manage in order to enhance your ability to sell? Your stubborn, nonconforming side? Your aloof, distant side? Your sarcastic side? Your estranged, hurt, defensive side?

3. Learn to empathize with a potential buyer. Get into her shoes. What is she thinking? What demands do others place on her? What does she need? Why should she deal with you instead of someone else?

4. Insofar as your products make this possible, have a polished sales pitch. Present graspable ideas — that you are saving Celtic harp music from extinction, that your collection of stories are linked by their Arizona desert setting.

5. Be able to say why your work should be wanted. Self-advertise. Become the expert. Give workshops on what you do. Create the demand for your work.

6. Set aside time to do business. Schedule time for it.

7. Create a team. Collaborate. Encourage reporters to write about you and interviewers to interview you. Make and maintain significant professional connections.

8. Develop selling awareness. Look for opportunities to sell. Network. Exchange business cards with others. Bring your strengths and not your insecurities to the cocktail hour, the gallery opening, the network party.

9. Make yourself accessible and visible. Go out. Nurture your extroverted side. Be present. Make small talk. Watch to see if you self-sabotage. Are you drinking too much? Hiding in a corner? Can you manage your boredom, your arrogance, your shyness?

10. Acquire business savvy. Learn about contracts. Honor deadlines. Spot the trends early. Learn to read between the lines. What is really being said when people comment on your work? "Your paintings are very large" may mean "My gallery makes most of its money from graphics." "You lost me when your character went to Finland" may mean "You violated the genre formula." "This doesn't seem very focused" may mean "This is too painful to read." Try to intuit the real message and respond to it, or ask clarifying questions.

11. Practice your new skills. Practice exercising your personality in the selling arena. Practice pricing your art. Practice asking for what you

want. Videotape yourself asking and answering questions. Interview yourself. Practice being a businessperson and a professional. Rehearse business situations. Role-play them with friends. Arrive at ideas about what you want and what the other person might want before you set off for a meeting with a curator, a collector, or an art dealer. Step into the other person's shoes. Walk around the block in them. Be prepared for his agenda and his savoriness or unsavoriness.

Practice ongoing anxiety management. Doing business raises the anxiety level of most artists. You may feel anxious contemplating the business you have to do, anxious because you doubt yourself as a salesperson, anxious because you have no clear idea how to proceed with your business. To handle your anxiety you will need to assess it and to learn general anxiety-management techniques, as well as some specific techniques that apply to you as an artist. Answer the following questions, and others you'll need to frame for yourself, to help yourself really learn how anxiety operates in your business life:

- How do I presently manage anxiety? By using drugs and alcohol? By avoiding situations that make me anxious? By acting agreeable, self-deprecating, or nice? By acting out aggressively and sabotaging myself?

- Which business situations make me most anxious? Discussing my product? Negotiating contracts? Making decisions about whom to hire for my band or my play? Choosing between the options in front of me? Studying trade magazines to learn about trends? Talking on the phone with agents or curators? Meeting in person with directors, gallery owners, publishers? Auditioning?

When you have assessed how anxiety affects you, consider using the following general anxiety-management techniques:

1. Meditation and breathing techniques

2. Getting enough exercise and rest and eating a balanced diet

3. Biofeedback and autogenic training

4. Stress-reduction practices incorporating guided visualizations and affirmations

5. Behavioral and cognitive approaches: learning new thoughts, inoculating yourself against old thoughts, and systematically desensitizing to anxiety-producing situations

6. Rehearsal and role-playing in preparation for anxiety-producing situations

For more information on these and other anxiety-management techniques, please consult *Performance Anxiety*, in which I describe these techniques in detail.

Some specific anxiety-reduction techniques for artists include the following:

1. Have a marketable product. If you do highly personal art that has a questionable chance of reaching an audience, also diversify.

2. Don't identify with your product. You are not your painting, novel, or performance. When your agent asserts that your novel is not working for her, she is really talking about your novel — she is not calling you incompetent or a failure. Be able to step aside and hear what an agent, director, or curator is saying.

3. Demystify the process. Ask questions of friends. Read books. Learn what to expect and what not to expect. Listen to the players in the game. How are things done? When do you turn to your agent, and when do you consult your entertainment lawyer? How much must you socialize? How important are personal contacts and personal relationships? What does a good contract look like, and what does a bad one look like? Take a dose of reality.

4. Acquire advocates. A room is less intimidating with a friendly face in it. People who have already bought one of your paintings are on your side. An agent who has sold a book of yours is on your side. A playwright whose play you lit up with your performance is on your side. You can approach these people with confidence.

5. Prepare for business events. Rehearse. Ask yourself potential questions and answer them. Meet potential objections. Role-play with an art buddy, your intimate other, or your creativity coach.

Engage in ongoing market analysis. This strategy applies to both the practical and the metaphysical side of your art. Analyze what sells in your field. For example, is it regional art but only from a certain region? Mysteries but only British-style atmospheric mysteries, police procedurals, stories featuring an old-fashioned, hard-boiled private eye, or cozy narratives featuring a female amateur detective? New Age music but only on one or two labels? Students of a certain teacher? Clients of a certain agent? Artists represented in certain galleries?

If someone is selling in your field, what exactly is that artist doing? Is he adhering to a certain formula? How does he market himself? How does he keep himself in the public eye? Who represents him? With whom does he network? If his product is essentially uncommercial, how has he managed to obtain an audience? How has he managed to get his symphony performed or his quirky film financed, produced, and distributed?

Perform ongoing audience analysis. Who is your audience, in general and specifically? What are some of the characteristics of audience members you know personally? Do they come to all modern dance performances or only to see certain companies? Do they like all live theater or only feminist theater, drawing-room comedies, or plays by playwrights with name recognition?

What do they claim to like in general? Are surveys available? Questionnaire responses? Can you take your audience's pulse? What do they say they like about your work? Do they have favorites among your paintings, books, songs, collages, or repertoire pieces? Do they say that your fiction is difficult but that your nonfiction is useful? Do they say that your watercolors are charming but that your oil paintings are scary? Do they say they could listen to you playing Mozart sonatas all day but can't really tolerate any modern music? Do they like your ballads, angry message songs, or upbeat tunes the best?

Work to acquire a small respectful and knowledgeable audience, in addition to your larger audience, by searching out one or a few art buddies. Is there someone who really understands and appreciates your work? The person who holds Greek drama and Russian literature in the same high regard that you do may be your most valuable reader.

Accept that, insofar as you have an audience, you are a public figure. Have a public face. Realize that there will be misunderstandings — that your fans will not really know you, that they may not understand your message, that sometimes you and they will get caught up in the unreality of your status as a known artist.

Work to retain your audience. To the degree that it's in your heart to do so, play your hits, produce your trademark work, repeat yourself, be recognizably you. When you want to stretch or change, plan strategies to minimize the risks involved in offering your audience what they are not expecting. Help them understand.

Do ongoing product and portfolio analysis. Be able to talk about your products in detail. Prepare a written statement, for example: "I paint large-scale abstract Expressionist paintings in primary colors, with a recent emphasis on cobalt blue and cadmium red. I paint in two scales: roughly five feet by eight feet and three feet by five feet. In feeling, my paintings are like those of Hans Hofmann and Nicolas de Stael, but my inspiration is drawn from the look of contemporary Los Angeles."

If *you* are the product, learn to talk about yourself as a dancer, actor, or musician. Practice by preparing a written statement, for example: "I've worked in the theater for the past dozen years. During my time with the One Act Repertory Theater I performed in more than twenty contemporary plays and a dozen revivals. My performance in Simon Gray's *Butley* and Wendy Wasserstein's *Uncommon Women and Others* were singled out for praise, as was my performance in the revival of Bertolt Brecht's *Mother Courage*. My strengths are my voice (both speaking and singing), the conviction I bring to roles, my discipline, and my look, which reviewers have called 'exotic' and 'extraordinary.'"

Think about which of your products have been commercially successful. Why were they successful? How can you repeat those successes or make use of what you have learned from them? How might your present products be altered — without sacrificing or compromising too much — to better meet the demands of the marketplace? Might you paint in a smaller scale? Add more plot to your fiction? Tailor your songs to a certain market? Can you do private, idiosyncratic work *and* commercial work?

What other products might you attempt that would allow you to diversify? Nonfiction along with your fiction? Mysteries along with your poetry? Multiples along with your one-of-a-kinds? Solo performance pieces that you write and perform? Music of your own composition? Might you audition for unaccustomed roles? Would you do commissioned pieces? Send your band in a new direction? Create products in another medium?

Prepare answers to the following hard-to-answer questions:

- In what tradition do I work?

- Which work by a famous or popular artist does my work most resemble?

- What makes my work unique?

- Of what technique or style am I the master?

- Why do I paint or play the way I do?

- Why is my work important?

- Who has loved my work and will vouch for it?

- Who collects me? Who reads me?

Dream up other difficult questions and answer them, too.

Do ongoing financial-support analysis. There are essentially eight sources of income available to you as an artist. You may want to treat them as if they comprise a buffet meal from which you select items according to what's available and most palatable. These eight sources are:

1. Art products and performances

2. Commercial products (including commissions, genre work, commercials)

3. Grants, residencies, gallery stipends

4. Related careers (including tutoring, teaching, producing, agenting, editing, doing art therapy)

5. Unrelated careers (as lawyer, doctor, psychologist, etc.)

6. Unrelated day jobs

7. Income from a mate or spouse

8. Income from family and friends

Although you might prefer to live on income from the first category only, that's not generally the most plentiful source. Accept that perfect solutions are rare and that any financial-survival program you put together comes with its psychological fallout.

It is easy to picture a culture in which art and commerce are not connected and equally easy to picture a culture in which everyone has permission to create, does in fact create, and is supported in their creative efforts. Ours is not that culture. You can live an artful life and an art-filled life without worrying about the connection between art and commerce, but if you intend to live an art-committed life, then the challenges that we've discussed in this chapter are yours to face.

No question may be more difficult for you to answer than this deceptively simple one: What is your work as an artist?

This is not an academic or a trivial question but a core question, the answer to which an artist undertakes to live. Artists without a sufficient answer to this question, even if they never articulate their doubts and uncertainties, are likely to block and flounder. But even artists who do possess a rich, sustaining understanding of their work will sometimes face crises of doubt, developmental turning points, and other natural road markers on their journey. Therefore all artists can profit by taking some time to examine this question, which can be reframed as, "Why am I an artist?"

EXERCISE 1. STARTING OUT

Reflect on the following questions. What is your work as an artist?

- Is it the novel you're working on now, the play you're in, the preparations for your upcoming concert tour?

- Is it attending gallery openings, reading the latest psychological fiction from eastern Europe, learning audition monologues?

- Is it everything that you are and that you do, everything art related and life related, so that your work and your life are inseparable?

- Is it as much about negotiating the six months between shows as the two months that the show runs, as much about surviving the two years of trying to get your novel published as the two years of writing it?

- Is it only your personal work: your performance pieces but not your voice-over work, your experimental novels but not your genre fiction?

- Is it maintaining a certain stance as outsider, rebel, witness, trickster, wise woman?

- Is it networking, self-promoting, marketing, wheeling and dealing?

- Is it more your inner process or more your products or performances?

- Does it defy description or understanding? If so, what sort of problem or challenge does that raise?

EXERCISE 2. THE ARTIST'S PATH

Why are you walking the artist's path? Please expand on any of the following that seem true to you, with an eye on ending up with a robust, personalized sense of why you have committed yourself to a particular art discipline.

I am walking the artist's path:

- because I must.

- because art has tremendous value.

- because every other job pales by comparison.

- because it gets me — or may get me — things I want, such as sex, recognition, power, money, love, adulation, glory.

- because it allows me to communicate what's in my heart.

- because I'm talented.

- because other pursuits seem ordinary and run-of-the-mill.

Creativity for *Life*

- because doing art suits my personality.

- because it's a family tradition.

- because it helps me heal.

- because it's great work for a deranged person like me.

- because it was expected of me.

- because, as a child, I fell in love with my medium.

- because I'm not really suited to do anything else.

- because it is the very embodiment of freedom.

- because it has social utility.

- because the bug bit me.

- because it's as noble a calling as a saint's or a hero's.

- because it lets me get up late.

- because...

EXERCISE 3. VARIETIES OF WORK

You may have never attempted to define your work before or tried to think about it in exactly these ways. You may even believe that such exercises are wrongheaded. If so, you still may profit from learning why you feel this way. Try to spend some time looking at these issues with a fresh eye.

Can you define your work with a single adjective? Look at the following list, and select the word or phrase that resonates for you. Define each one you select, and give an example, either from your own work or from that of another artist.

I see my creative work as:

- dignified
- sacred
- courageous
- idiosyncratic

- willful
- socially relevant
- escapist
- existential

- commercial
- playful
- entertaining
- professional
- passionate
- career-oriented
- important
- culturally relevant
- useful
- innovative
- marketable
- personally relevant
- beautiful
- political
- true
- controversial
- simply mine

EXERCISE 4. WORK PARADOXES AND CONTRADICTIONS

Your definition of the work you do as an artist may include apparent or real paradoxes and contradictions. Comment on whether any of the following seem to you contradictory or paradoxical. For those you select, answer the following two questions: 1) Is the contradiction merely apparent, or is it real? 2) If it is real, should I embrace it or work to unravel it and effect some changes in my life?

1. I want to do highly personal art that nevertheless reaches a large audience.

2. I am both a truth teller and a trickster.

3. I want to do work that is socially relevant and that is also entertaining.

4. I want to work in solitude, but I also want to be part of a community.

5. I want to be on the road as much as possible, but I also want a home life.

6. Performing makes me very anxious, but I want to perform as much as possible.

7. I am not sure about the value of art, but I also think that there is nothing more valuable.

8. I want to do the art of my choosing, but I also want to make money.

9. I want to do classical art that nevertheless reaches a contemporary audience.

10. I see the following as a contradiction or a paradox...

EXERCISE 5. A MANTRA FOR YOUR WORK

A mantra is an incantation, imbued with meaning, that resonates powerfully for you. In traditional Hindu practice brief hymns or portions of Vedic text were chanted as mantras. Try out the following phrases, making each into an incantation, and see which of them have power and meaning for you. The goal is to hit on a mantra that points to an important source of your work and that serves to remind you of that source. If any of the following mantras have meaning for you, use them by memorizing them and regularly repeating them:

- "I have something to say."
- "We must never forget."
- "See me."
- "Come with me."
- "Beauty matters."
- "Truth matters."
- "I am a mystic."
- "I stand alone."
- "You are in me."
- "I am a hero."
- "Be happy."
- "I sustain life."
- "What I do is needed."
- "I serve in this fashion."
- "I will be no less than fully alive."
- "I am unafraid."
- "If not me, then who?"
- "I must."
- Your own mantra...

For a more in-depth look at how you can make use of mantras and incantations, I recommend *Ten Zen Seconds: Twelve Incantations for Purpose, Power and Calm*, in which I marry ideas from Eastern practice with strategies from cognitive and positive psychology.

EXERCISE 6. PERSONAL NEEDS

What inner qualities must you possess in order to do your work? It will pay you great dividends if you develop strategies to meet the needs that you select from the following list:

1. I need sufficient peace of mind in which to work.

2. I need fewer worries about how I'll survive financially.

3. I need a better idea of what art I want to create.

4. I need to be more consistently creative.

5. I need to be more deeply motivated.

6. I need to take more risks.

7. I need to take fewer risks.

8. I need to feel more connected to like-minded people.

9. I need a willingness to do commercial work.

10. I need a more competitive attitude.

11. I need to accept the flaws in my work.

12. I need a more appraising (but not self-critical) attitude.

13. I need to better balance my commitment to art and my commitment to life.

14. I need to learn to accept praise.

15. I need to learn to tolerate criticism.

16. I need to better manage my impulses.

17. I need a better understanding of the art marketplace.

18. I need to recover from my addictions.

19. I need a more assertive attitude.

20. I need a less cocksure attitude.

21. I need to find my voice.

22. I need a better understanding of my personality.

23. I need a better understanding of my place in the world.

24. I need limitless faith and courage.

25. I need...

EXERCISE 7. PRACTICAL NEEDS

All artists have practical needs that must be met. They need canvases and gallery representation, quiet time and a receptive publisher, appropriate head-shots and a well-connected agent, a singular violin and a recording contract, and so on. Can you name your practical needs? Can you say how you mean to meet each one? Select at least ten needs from the following list and indicate how you intend to meet each one:

NEED LIST

1. more business savvy
2. practical coping skills
3. an art buddy
4. new business opportunities
5. inexpensive suppliers
6. some inspirational reading
7. a college degree
8. an advanced degree
9. marketable products
10. advanced technology
11. better technical skills
12. agency representation
13. a plan and a schedule
14. more training
15. an assertiveness class
16. an advocate
17. ongoing financial support
18. good books on the business
19. career counseling
20. a work space
21. a better filing system
22. a better mailing list
23. an award or two
24. a break
25. a change of place
26. less clutter
27. a residency
28. a grant
29. a mentor
30. a new teacher
31. health insurance
32. a second career

33. a teaching job

34. new markets

35. more connections

36. a financial planner

37. a sponsor

38. a union

39. like-minded friends

40. more time

41. short-term goals

42. a new long-term plan

43. a golden opportunity

44. a creativity coach

EXERCISE 8. WHAT IS YOUR JOB DESCRIPTION?

Write a one- or two-page job description that takes into account the many aspects of your job as a writer, dancer, photographer, painter, actor, director, singer, and so on. What does it take to be effective in your art discipline, both as an artist and as a salesperson? Include all of the following:

- skills (including marketing skills)

- training

- experiences

- personal qualities

EXERCISE 9. WHO'S WHO IN YOUR MARKETPLACE?

Do you know who is who in your particular art marketplace? To ground this question, let's focus on the world of writers and the people with whom they must deal and interact.

For most writers, even those who publish occasionally, the publishing world remains opaque and mysterious. While you're sitting alone in your studio, staring at your computer screen, it feels as if the world is made up of you and others like you, anonymous and mostly unpublished, and a huge, amorphous, indistinguishable "them out there" made up of hotshot agents lunching with up-and-coming editors, celebrity authors and their fast-talking publicists, readers lining up to meet their favorite author, all these folks swirling together in a surrealistic, agonizing vision of good times and merry laughter.

Let's get a clearer picture than that! Who's who in the world of publishing? Here are twenty categories of people (in alphabetical order) involved in the publishing world, with a short description of each. If you are a writer, make it your business to understand what they contribute, how they affect you, and how they're related to you.

Consider the functions and responsibilities of the role they play and the sort of personality that is likely to go with those functions and responsibilities. Best of all, get to know some of these people firsthand: begin to transform your vision of the publishing world from surrealistic to photorealistic.

As you read, think of how you would answer the following question: "What do each of these people need from me?" An alternative way of framing this question is the following: "What do each of these people need me to bring to the table so that they will want to work with me?"

1. *Accountant.* "Accounting" is a state of mind having to do with maximizing profits, minimizing expenses and losses, keeping an eye on the bottom line, and acting "businesslike." Accounting plays a role in keeping your advance down but vanishes when a publishing house wants to hold its semiannual sales meeting in Maui or gets the itch to pay a $4,000,000 advance to a celebrity. Everybody at a publishing house acts like an accountant sometimes and refuses to act like an accountant at others.

2. *Acquisitions editor.* The person, whatever her title, at a publishing house who buys books, usually with the advice and consent of others at her house, including the publisher, editor in chief, marketing manager, and so on. Her other jobs often include improving the manuscripts she has purchased by editing them, stewarding manuscripts through the publication process, and sorting through the hundreds (if not thousands) of query letters, query emails, synopses, proposals, and manuscripts that come her way.

3. *Assistant editor.* This may be a junior editor who functions as an editor, buying and editing books, it may be an administrative assistant who handles secretarial tasks, fields phone calls, and so on, or it may be a person who does both. An assistant editor is likely to become a senior editor one day (if she doesn't become a literary

agent, book doctor, book packager, or writer first) and already, even in her junior position, can get a writer's work read by the right people at a publishing house.

4. *Associate publisher.* This sort of title and others like it refer to a person who has climbed up the ladder in a publishing house and functions as an administrator and manager, minding the bottom line, handling day-to-day crises, and sometimes finding the time to think about the company's future. He or she is typically also involved, at least peripherally, in the acquisition of new titles, may still read manuscripts and buy books, demonstrates and generates enthusiasm for individual titles, and usually has a real role in deciding what sorts of books and which individual titles the house will publish.

5. *Book doctor.* A book doctor is a freelance editor who tries to turn a book that is currently not strong or publishable into one that is. His role may also be to help sell the book; very often he works with well-known writers who are guaranteed the sale or who have already made the sale but who need help turning their current idea or manuscript into something decent.

6. *Book manufacturer.* Book manufacturers, many of whom are in the Midwest, in Europe, or in Asia, are the folks who literally make the books. They are employed by publishing houses and by authors who choose to self-publish, and they can print a few thousand books (or even a few hundred) or zillions. With new technologies like print-on-demand and e-books, book manufacturing is changing dramatically; but there will always be someone who fulfills the role of actually making the book.

7. *Book packager.* A book packager is a middleman or -woman who helps authors put together books, often dealing with the graphics, design, "high concept," and the like, and who presents busy editors with already strong and even already manufactured books to add to their lists. Book packagers often associate themselves with highly designed books like coffee table books, specialty books, books with lots of photos and design elements, ans so on, but may collaborate on any sort of book, being of service (ideally) both to author and editor.

8. *Bookstore manager.* Each independent bookstore, each chain bookstore, and even each cyberspace bookstore is managed by someone, and that someone has his or her own taste. Individual bookstore managers can help make a book successful by prominently featuring it, inviting the author to speak, suggesting it to local reading groups, and so forth. You will often find that a book that became a bestseller had the support of an author who micromanaged her book by visiting scores of bookstores and chatting with scores of bookstore managers.

9. *Bookstore events' coordinator.* Many bookstores now employ a person whose prime or even sole job is to book authors for book signings, lectures, and other events, sometimes sharing the expense of the event with the publishing house but more often than not absorbing the expense as a cost of doing business. A bookstore newsletter may go out to tens of thousands of customers and serves as an excellent way for potential readers to learn about books. Even if the event is not well attended, a little more name recognition has been garnered for the title.

10. *Chain store buyer.* Chain store buyers determine which books will be stocked systemwide and in what quantities, as well as which books will be featured and which pushed. The next best thing to having Oprah select your book for her book club is to have your book appear in the window of every Borders or Barnes & Noble nationwide. Since such an appearance is so important in the life of a book, chain store buyers are very influential players in the publishing game.

11. *Conference organizer* (and lecture booker, public events' coordinator, corporate events' coordinator, and anyone else who arranges for writers to give talks, lectures, and workshops). To generate sales and publicize their books, writers will often speak at conferences (their editors certainly hope that they will). The conference organizer is the person whom the writer contacts to garner an invitation or who invites the writer to speak because the writer's work has become known to members of the organization. These and other speaking engagements can supplement a writer's income in important ways

and turn books that otherwise might sell ten thousand copies into books that sell tens of thousands of copies.

12. *Copy editor.* Copy editors are employed by publishing houses. They look at a manuscript after the book's primary editor has done his or her work and the book is considered to be in (nearly) final form. The copy editor works on the book's grammar, but he or she also works on its voice and logic, often peppering the manuscript with scores of questions designed to make the book clearer and more logical. So, although an author may feel as if her book is finished once her primary editor signs off on it, she will still have a copy editor to interact with.

13. *Freelance editor.* Freelance copy editors and developmental editors are often employed by publishing houses as independent contractors on a book-by-book basis and sometimes in a particular area of expertise. In some cases they are employed by authors themselves to help get a manuscript in shape for publication. It is not that unusual for an author to hire a freelance editor to help hone his manuscript, then get assigned an in-house editor when the book is purchased, and then be assigned yet another editor, a freelancer selected and paid for by the publisher, who works on the book in conjunction with the in-house editor.

14. *Literary agent.* Literary agents are primarily salespeople. Of the manuscripts and proposals they read, only a small percentage of them, perhaps 1 or 2 percent, seem to them saleable (which is not the same as good, valuable, or interesting). They then represent these saleable ones. Their sales techniques are extremely simple: they write, email, or phone editors they know personally or know of and indicate that they have something the editor may be interested in. Editors, recognizing that agents play an important screening role, tend to respond to these notes and calls promptly. Often an agent is the most valuable person in a writer's professional network. To be sure, in some cases the writer could do what the agent does and save the 15 percent commission. But the short answer as to whether a writer wants and needs an agent is a fairly resounding yes.

15. *Literary lawyer.* Writers tend to let agents look over the contracts that publishers proffer. Agents advertise themselves as capable of construing and negotiating these publishing contracts, and in general this is true. But a writer who works as his or her own agent, who has a special copyright law or libel question to answer, who wants a special collaboration contract drawn up, or who otherwise feels in need of a specialist, can turn to literary lawyers. Their numbers are small, but they can be found in New York, Los Angeles, the San Francisco Bay Area, and elsewhere; even if they are geographically far from you, most affairs can be handled via phone or email.

16. *Publicist.* Publicists tout books and authors. Publishing houses have in-house publicists, and writers sometimes also hire freelance publicists on a book-by-book or retainer basis. Publicists attempt to get an author's book reviewed in the print and broadcast media, try to set up author interviews and book signings, and work to get their authors on radio and television. A freelance publicist may charge an author $15,000 to $40,000 for a single campaign, which is at its most intense during the six months before and the few months after the book comes out; or the publicist may be hired on a piecemeal basis and get paid for each interview, review, book signing, or media appearance garnered (often at thousands of dollars for a television appearance).

17. *Publisher.* According to an old saw, editors hire writers, and publishers hire editors. A publisher is an owner or, in a large publishing house with many imprints, a division manager. At a small house the publisher and the acquisitions editor (and the publicist, secretary, and so on) may be the same person, but even at a medium-sized house the publisher will be one person (often with his name on the line of books), and editors will come and go under him. The publisher balances the demands of the sales force against the desires of the editors, adds and drops titles from the list, and often still buys books himself, should they come to his attention and catch his fancy.

18. *Reader.* Every reader has something to tell an author, and the early readers of a manuscript — friends, writing buddies, agents — can

genuinely help a writer figure out how to improve her manuscript and increase its chances of being sold to a publisher. At its best, the relationship between writer and reader is so intimate and profound that it borders on a love relationship, making readers qualitatively different characters in this otherwise business-oriented cast.

19. *Sales manager/sales rep/marketing person.* The publisher's salespeople are concerned with pricing books competitively; choosing titles, subtitles, sizes, formats, and covers that will sell their books; servicing their accounts; keeping returns as low as possible; and in general winning the marketplace game. They tend to predict future performance from past performance, so the fact that a forthcoming book is actually better or worse than the author's last is hard for them to factor in. Similarly, they tend to write off authors who don't perform the first few times out of the gate. The sales force does not quite dictate to editors or demand that certain books be bought and others avoided, but their influence is enormous and must be reckoned with by editors and authors alike.

20. *Smart and savvy buddy/fellow writer.* One of the more important people in a writer's life is a friend with common sense, wisdom, and some understanding of marketing and sales. That friend may listen to the writer's initial ideas and give useful feedback, read the writer's proposals and manuscripts and offer suggestions, and keep on the lookout for publishers interested in what the writer is writing. A good agent also does these jobs, but a smart, savvy buddy can provide a level of intimacy and a continuity of interest that agents rarely can.

EXERCISE 10. CREATE A TENTATIVE DEFINITION OF YOUR WORK

Look back at your responses to the exercises in this section. Highlight the most important points. Incorporate your conclusions into a single tentative definition:

My work as an artist is...

The Challenges of Relationships

9

The Rewards and Perils of Isolation

I am glad I chanced on a place so lonely and so still
With no companion to drag me early home.
Now that I have tasted the joy of being alone
I will never again come with a friend at my side.

— LI PO

A rtists in all disciplines spend a great deal of time living and working in isolation. For some, like novelists or painters, isolation may constitute the very essence of their lives. In this chapter we'll examine the important benefits and serious dangers to the artist of prolonged isolation.

Without such isolation, creativity cannot exist. An artist can't pore over negatives, learn a sonata, or write a novel while chatting with friends. An inability to seek out solitude, to love it and make use of it, is a crushing impediment to the creative process. By the same token, there is no greater peril to the artist's mental health than the failure to realize how risky a business prolonged social isolation can become.

Most artists are well aware that prolonged solitude is both necessary and desirable, on the one hand, and perilous on the other. Because they sense how perilous it can be, they are often conflicted about seeking it out; or they manage a bit of solitude and, suddenly feeling too alone, leave it too quickly. Artists who leave their work too soon may claim to be blocked, but they may actually be fleeing not from their work but from some sudden sense of loneliness.

Since many of the artist's personality traits, especially his habits of mind, draw him to solitude, his need for social isolation flows directly from his personality. Consequently, when he avoids solitude because, for one reason or another, he is afraid of it, he does violence to his own soul. He may indeed manage to avoid the risks of prolonged isolation and fill his social calendar, but at the same time he will understand that he is not living authentically.

Then again, since prolonged isolation can be the breeding ground for mania, depression, and virulent acting-in, artists who do manage to stay with their work hour after hour and day after day risk growing disturbed as a result of their loss of human contact and their preoccupation with their own thoughts. One artist can't stand solitude and can't get her creative work done; another loves it too well and grows alienated, lonely, and strange.

It is in solitude, and only in solitude, that artists manage to create. But in too complete an isolation artists despair and sometimes go mad. How, then, is a balance to be struck?

THE VALUES AND BENEFITS OF SOLITUDE

Solitude is the ground of creativity. As psychiatrist Anthony Storr described it in *Solitude: A Return to the Self,* "The creative person is constantly seeking to discover himself, to remodel his own identity, and to find meaning in the universe by means of what he creates. These moments are chiefly, if not invariably, those in which he is alone."

The French philosopher Michel Montaigne wrote, "We must reserve a little back-shop, all our own, entirely free, wherein to establish our true liberty and principal retreat and solitude."

While the benefits of solitude are in one sense self-evident, we also need to specifically name them. There are two reasons for this: because we need to be reminded why artists must spend such a significant portion of their lives in isolation (and why they're unhappy when they don't spend enough time there) and because each specific benefit has its shadow side — carries its own warning label, so to speak — and points the way to an understanding of the hazards of prolonged isolation.

The benefits of solitude, then, are the following.

Personality Fit

The artist is often a loner, a solitary introvert. This is generally as true for the performing artist as it is for the creative artist. As actress Linda Hunt expressed it, "I think most of my life I have thought of myself as a solitary figure. Over and over again, I express that solitariness onstage and on film. . . . I want to see myself as solitary in the landscape. It's the story I tell."

The introversion of the actor as he works among other actors on stage or of the musician as she sits among twenty other violinists is at first glance less obvious than the introversion of the painter, the writer, or the theoretical physicist. But all creative people appear to be on the introverted side and as a rule prefer solitude to social interaction. They desire to be alone with their work; often they just prefer to be alone.

In his paper "The Capacity to Be Alone," psychoanalyst Donald Winnicott referred to the upside of solitude: "It is probably true to say that in psychoanalytical literature more has been written on the *fear* of being alone or the *wish* to be alone than on the ability to be alone. It would seem to me that a discussion of the *positive* aspects of the capacity to be alone is overdue."

Creative and performing artists generally possess this capacity. They may nevertheless fear isolation, because they find in it too keen an aloneness and not a delicious solitude. They may avoid their studios or practice rooms and avoid their art altogether. But such avoidance doesn't alter the fact that, as a matter of personality fit, they really prefer solitude to social interaction.

Contact with the Work

In the bubble of absorption that is the most precious aspect of solitude, artists can be together with their love — their medium, their art, their work. They can connect with melody, meter, or color. They wake up dreaming about the work they'll get done in the solitude that a new day brings. As the painter Alice Baber put it, "I wake up in the morning and feel the need of a color and I begin to work."

By becoming thoroughly absorbed, thoroughly lost in the moment, artists can do sublime work. This is as true for the performer as it is for the poet or sculptor. The musician practicing his instrument is no more engaged in a merely mechanical enterprise than is the painter with her brush or the writer at his computer screen. The musician's rehearsal activity is larger, more profound, and richer than that. As Pablo Casals put it, the musician is out to "make divine things human and human things divine," work she does as much in solitude as in public performance.

Free Play

In solitude, artists can experiment, make a mess, sustain notes for the joy of it, imagine themselves on any stage in any play. In the studio or practice room, they are not on public display and need not wear their public face. They can be their secret selves, their best selves, and their worst selves. If there is a certain lack of freedom on stage or in the gallery, there can be total freedom in the studio. As the visual artist Allan Kaprow put it, "Artists' studios do not look like galleries, and when an artist's studio does, everyone is suspicious." Galleries are for show; studios are where messes are made and where the real work happens.

Working Out Your Life

In solitude, artists are also organizing their experiences, making connections, traveling through time and space, wrestling with the abuse that was heaped on them in childhood, searching out the color of the sunlight that once warmed them, listening to the sounds that once thrilled them. French writer François Mauriac described what transpires in his moments of solitude: "During those times I don't observe and I don't describe: I rediscover. I rediscover the world of my devout, unhappy, and introverted childhood. It is as though when I was twenty a door within me had closed forever on that which was going to become the material of my work."

Artists are working out their lives in this silence that they are compelled to seek. While they fix a print in a chemical bath, play a passage a hundred times over, study to become Oedipus, or create the biography of their protagonist's father, they are reaching for answers to the questions that most interest or that most trouble them.

Contact with Others

Artists, when they are absorbed in their work, are also deeply connected to other human beings. The theologian Matthew Fox said, "The journey the artist makes in turning inward to listen and to trust his or her images is a communal journey." Psychologist Otto Rank argued that "the collective unconscious, not rugged individualism, gives birth to creativity."

To be sure, artists are not making real contact with living human beings as they work in the studio. Indeed, the absence of the kinds of pressures that other people tend to put on them allows them, in solitude, to love humankind. Whereas in their day jobs they may despise their bosses and at Thanksgiving they must deal with their alcoholic parents, in the studio they can contact their best impulses, their most noble sentiments, and their compassion for others.

Spiritual Journey

In many religious traditions contemplation in solitude is considered an important — sometimes the most important — path to spiritual growth and understanding. A dictum of Buddhist teaching has it that no one can teach another to become a buddha; all must learn for themselves. In this sense, the sincerely working artist is engaged in a spiritual activity very much like that of the religious contemplative — he is becoming a buddha. For many artists, this so-to-speak spiritual enlightenment is the goal of their solitude, while for others it is a happy by-product of their devoted creative efforts.

Safe Haven

In solitude, the artist can drop her social masks and necessary social pretenses and stop smiling politely. She can let down her hair, put up her feet, and do what she pleases. In her study no one can criticize or reject her, demand that she describe her work, or badger her with questions. Solitude is an island of safety in a dangerous world. T'ao Ch'ien, fourth-century Chinese Taoist poet, put it well:

In my empty rooms are time and space.
I return to be myself
Unfretted and unfettered
In this self-like place.

Integrity and the Existential Encounter

In solitude, artists confront life with all the integrity, passion, and intensity they can muster. These existential encounters are the very essence of authentic living. Some experience the encounter as pain and others as joy, but in either case the artist knows that something real has transpired and that he has used that time meaningfully.

He may feel as knotted as a Beethoven, building laboriously with musical scraps, or as weightless as a youthful Mozart or Mendelssohn pouring out music whole; in either case he is living. He may be able to say, as E. M. Forster did, that he always found writing pleasant and easy; or he may resemble the Cézanne described by Rousseau: "He spent many more hours looking and thinking than he did painting. People who watched him say that he sometimes waited as long as twenty minutes between two strokes of his brush. He himself said that there were days when he looked at his subject so long that he felt 'as if his eyes were bleeding.'"

In either case, whether he finds his work easy or hard, he knows that he is living with integrity. As long as he remains in contact with the work — whether his brow is clear or furrowed — he feels he is spending his time honorably. Stephen Spender elaborates on this: "In my own mind I make a sharp distinction between two types of concentration: one is immediate and complete, the other is plodding and only completed in stages. A poet may be divinely gifted with a lucid and purposive intellect; he may be clumsy and slow; that does not matter, what matters is integrity of purpose."

Aliveness

For a great many artists, the time spent in solitude is the time when they feel most real and alive. It is when they have their most intense experiences, when they can vicariously live out any adventure, any dream. Tennessee Williams said, "I'm only really alive when I'm writing." The painter Robert Motherwell explained, "I feel most real to myself in the studio." At the end of the last century the young Russian painter Marie Bashkirtseff exclaimed, "In the studio all distinctions disappear. One has neither name nor family; one is no longer the daughter of one's mother, one is oneself and individual, and one has before one art, and nothing else. One feels so happy, so free, so proud!"

We may think of this aliveness as the accumulation of the many benefits we just named: as the artist working out her life, manifesting her creativity, suiting her personality, playing, avoiding unwanted social interactions, working authentically and with integrity, and living intensely — and as a result feeling most at home with herself.

THE DANGERS OF PROLONGED ISOLATION

While the time artists spend in solitude is of incomparable value to them, as just noted, isolation carries with it tremendous dangers as well, including all the following ones.

Lack of Relationships and Social Savvy

It is difficult for the artist who remains too long in isolation to forge or adequately maintain real relationships with other human beings. Artists who spend too much time in isolation not only experience grave difficulty in forming friendships, intimate relationships, social contacts, and community, but they also remain insufficiently practiced in the ways of the world. They find themselves painfully ill-equipped to handle the interpersonal moments they do seek out. At such times they stand shyly off to the side, speak too bluntly or too little, and in a hundred other ways demonstrate their lack of interpersonal skills and social savvy.

Lack of Knowledge

If we think back to the stories of Joseph K. and Robert F. recounted in the last chapter and consider them in the present context, we see that Joseph K. gains little new knowledge of the world as he works on his stories in severe social isolation. Robert F., who also loves solitude and is quite capable of making use of it, purposefully ventures out into the world, learns about social movements, and makes use of that information to create a highly desirable product.

Artists, because they spend such prolonged periods in isolation, frequently fall behind the times. They may gain great self-knowledge, spiritual insight, and understanding of their mediums as they work in private, but the price they pay is a lack of vital knowledge about the world around them.

Minimal Personality Challenge and Real-World Challenge

Because solitude provides artists with a safe haven, because it fits their personality, and because it offers them a kind of communal contact with other human beings through their work, it can also bring on stagnation. Without ever quite realizing it, artists can grow flaccid in isolation and begin to experience their solitude as deadening. The studio can become too easy and unchallenging a place.

The world outside the studio offers unmatched opportunities for growth and for the expression of authentic and courageous behavior. Artists often miss these opportunities and, remaining relatively untested, handle themselves poorly when they do venture out.

Workaholism

Artists, because of the demands of their personality, their sense of mission, and their need to create or perform, tend to be driven. Mixed with the love of their work can be a terrible pressure to do the work. For many artists, especially for the most productive ones, the line between love and obsession and between effort and compulsion blurs or disappears entirely. Are such artists freely creating, or are they slaves to their work?

In *The Artist and Society*, psychiatrist Lawrence Hatterer describes such an artist: "His most recognizable trait is his recurring daily preoccupation with translating artistic activity into accomplishment. The consuming intensity of this artistic pursuit brooks no interference or obstacles. His absorption with the creative act is such that he experiences continually what the average artist feels only infrequently when he reaches unusual levels of creative energy with accompanying output. He appears to be incapable of willful nonproductivity."

This is Picasso working for seventy-two hours straight. This is Van Gogh turning out two hundred finished paintings during his 444 days in Arles. The artist who is "incapable of willful nonproductivity" is a workaholic for whom little in life, apart from his artistic productivity and accomplishment, may have much meaning.

Prolonged Unreality

Because artists feel alive when they encounter their work in solitude, and because that work is real and important to them, they can easily make the mistake of believing that they can successfully live without ever venturing out of the studio. But for such artists, life becomes unreal, and their cherished studio turns into a prison.

Prisoners in penal institutions have written eloquently about their slide, after years of isolation, into a dark world of distorted reality. One prisoner, who had served fourteen years at England's Durham Prison, wrote: "Can you imagine what it is like being a prisoner for life? Your dreams turn into nightmares and your castle into ashes, all you think about is fantasy, and in the end you turn your back on reality and live in a contorted world of make-believe."

This is the danger Freud singled out in his writings about the artist's life. In a characteristic passage, Freud explained: "The artist is an incipient introvert who is not far from being a neurotic. He is impelled by too powerful instinctive needs. He turns away from reality, and transfers all his interests, his libido, too, to the elaboration of his imaginary wishes, all of which might easily point the way to neurosis."

Freud went too far in calling the artist's time in the studio a substitute for life and in portraying the artist as an essentially dissatisfied and incompetent neurotic. What the artist does in isolation is serious and important real-world business and not mere sublimation. To call it a substitute for life is both to misunderstand what is in the artist's heart and to make an unjustified claim for the preeminent value of the world outside the studio. But Freud was right to note the very real danger that exists for those artists who so turn away from the world that their self-enforced isolation appears pathological. For such artists, solitude becomes a nightmare and life a prison sentence.

Mental and Emotional Disturbances

Prolonged isolation is the breeding ground for emotional disturbance. As the painter Jim Dine put it, "I do not think obsession is funny or that not being able to stop one's intensity is funny." Much that goes on for the artist in isolation is unpleasant and unfunny, for in isolation obsessions build; rejections, rivalries, and grievances are rehashed; and wounds fester. It's all too easy to brood if you live cut off from the world, your shades drawn tight, entirely alone with your preoccupations, and it is altogether harder to obsess while folk dancing or playing softball, while building a barn or baking bread with others.

Aloneness, Alienation, and Estrangement

Aloneness is the chief theme of existential literature and as important a psychological challenge as any confronting us as human beings. Its other names are alienation and estrangement; it is also sometimes called the "problem of the outsider."

Artists in particular are likely to experience this existential estrangement. They regularly ask the question, "Is life worth living?" They demand personal answers to that question, frequently finding no satisfactory answer. One moment the artist feels connected to others, to her god, to her ancestors. She contemplates human happiness and, like Beethoven, attempts to find fitting music to accompany Schiller's "Ode to Joy." Then, in virtually the next second, she feels utterly alone and utterly empty. In this sudden coldness she contemplates and, in some cases, commits suicide, as did Vincent van Gogh, Sylvia Plath, Ernest Hemingway, and countless other creators.

This existential aloneness should not be confused with loneliness. Loneliness can be ameliorated by human contact. Aloneness, however, is an attitude that roughly translates as "Life is meaningless," "I do not matter," or "Nothing matters." It inevitably cries out for an existential solution, that is, a solution in the realm of new meaning or of old meaning reinvigorated. The artist experiences aloneness as a terrible existential lack — a chilling lack of purpose, a frightening lack of direction, a sudden, despairing lack of interest in the work at hand. This terrible coldness can strike in the blink of an eye.

When it does strike, artists stop working. If they force themselves to continue, out of discipline or inner compulsion, their art is often inferior. Too much of their consciousness has been distracted by the coldness. Their world becomes a mess — not the happy mess that a child makes, but the unhappy mess of unrealized art. As Jackson Pollock put it, "It is only when I lose contact with the painting that the result is a mess. Otherwise there is a pure harmony, an easy give and take, and the painting comes out well." Despair, caused by the failure of meaning to hold, leads to a loss of contact with the work.

The easy give and take with the work is gone. The need to fill the void becomes insistent. A common solution — the one chosen by Pollock and countless other creative and performing artists — is to take to the bottle. They may seek out drugs or engage in other distracting mischief. If the artist is practiced at intellectualizing, she may invent fine arguments to wrap around the moment. Denying that she's bereft of meaning, she may talk herself into believing that what she really wants is a certain book, which she can only get on another continent. As a character laments ironically in one of Margaret Switzer's *Existential Folktales*, "What means we go to to fill the emptiness!" The coldness and emptiness are incontrovertible, and the artist must do something.

FINDING A PERSONAL BALANCE

The upside of solitude is magnificent, and the downside of prolonged isolation is terrible. Like every other artist, you are challenged to find and maintain a balance between necessary isolation and necessary human contact. In order to work, you must be alone. But you must also get out and meet what the writer Suzi Gablik called our human needs "for relatedness, for rootedness, for a frame of orientation and an object of devotion."

What will prove the right balance for you? Is it 20 percent of one and 80 percent of the other? Or maybe 50 percent of each? Certainly we know that opting for 100 percent of either — for the extreme of complete social isolation or for a complete lack of meaningful solitude — constitutes an unfortunate and dangerous choice.

Speculate, for instance, on the possible differences between the journeys of two people who from an early age loved art; one became an artist, and the other did not. It is quite conceivable that the latter experienced isolation more as aloneness than as solitude, dreaded isolation more, and chose a social path. If she never comes to grips with her inability to tolerate solitude, she is likely to feel that she has failed herself and may come to despise the fact that she's embarked on a life of doing other people's work and not her own. This is the danger for the person called to art who sees so much danger in that empty room that she swears off solitude altogether.

Likewise, the blocked artist, the artist who is unwilling or unable to confront his art, the tired or anxious artist, the artist driven by a desire for sex or drink, may find remaining alone in the studio impossible. When, however, he escapes to the café or picks up the phone to call a friend, he's likely to instantly regret his decision. He knows that his flight is a loss of nerve and an uncourageous act; and his subsequent time out in the world is tainted by a secret sense of failure. Too many of these flights into the world of company, and his creative life is lost.

At the other extreme is the artist who remains in self-imposed isolation around the clock. She may sometimes go out, but she still contrives to bring her solitude with her. She may go for long walks or to the movies alone and congratulate herself on having been out in the world. It is very clear, for instance, from the following diary passage, that although he is out of the studio, Paul Klee is nonetheless still completely alone and hard at work: "Yesterday afternoon I took a nice walk. The scene was drenched in a sulphur yellow, only the water was a turquoise blue — blue to the deepest ultramarine. The sap colored the meadows in yellow, carmine, and violet. I walked about in

Creativity for *Life*

the river bed, and since I was wearing boots, I was able to wade through the water in many places. I found the most beautifully polished stones."

All artists are caught on the horns of this dilemma. If they spend too little time in isolation, they do not get their work done and they feel guilty and ashamed. If they spend too much time in isolation, they feel lonely, unhappy, and estranged. How will you strike a balance? How will you reorder your life so that you get enough of each and not too much of either?

STRATEGIES

You are challenged to find time for your solitude and to make real use of it in order to reap its benefits. You are likewise challenged to minimize the dangers of prolonged isolation. By using the strategies presented below and by creating others of your own, you will do a better job of maintaining useful solitude, combating existential coldness when it strikes, and engaging the world.

Engage in guided writing, as described in chapter 13. Several interrelated issues have been brought up in this chapter that you might focus on in your guided writing practice. Below I've broken them down below into five groups of questions.

ON GAINING SOLITUDE:

1. Do I have a place to go that is all mine? Do I have a room of my own, a sacred space, a sanctuary?

2. How much do I love my solitude? Does solitude fit my personality? If I seem to love it insufficiently, or if it does not fit my personality, what strategies will I employ to gain the solitude I need? Will I contract with myself for so many hours of creative work a day?

3. Do I make enough time for my working solitude? Do I set such time aside at the end of the day, when I'm too tired to make use of it? Can I instead begin each day with a period of solitude?

4. Have I prepared myself to make use of solitude? Do I have work to do? Am I really engaged in and committed to my art?

ON MAINTAINING SOLITUDE:

1. How long do I generally remain in solitude working? Can I stretch out that time by taking brief, strategic time-outs and then returning to my work, rather than fleeing my solitude for the day after a brief stint of creating?

2. Will I work on the blocks that prevent me from maintaining my working solitude?

3. What distracts or derails me as I try to work in solitude? My thoughts? My sense of aloneness, loneliness, or estrangement? My doubts about the goodness or importance of the work I'm doing? What specifically derails me, and what plan can I devise to combat this problem?

4. How much solitude can I tolerate? How much aloneness? If I can tolerate a great deal of solitude but relatively little aloneness, what will I do when I flip from one mood to the other? To regain my sense of solitude what strategies will I employ?

ON ADDRESSING THE DANGERS OF PROLONGED ISOLATION:

1. By remaining in isolation too long and too often, am I failing to really challenge myself? Am I failing to gain new, needed knowledge that I can only gain out in the world? Am I failing at the business of art?

2. Am I estranged from the world? Do I consider myself an outsider? What am I willing to do to change my mind or my relationship to the world so that I can feel less estranged?

3. Am I a workaholic? What, for me, are the dangers of leading the life of a workaholic?

4. Is there a connection between the social isolation I seek out and the emotional disturbances I experience?

ON DETERMINING WHEN TO LEAVE:

1. What are good, legitimate, or sufficient reasons for me to leave my solitude? That I've gotten enough work done and met my daily goals?

That I've spent all the hours I set aside and now have other important things to do? That, by staying longer, I will grow disturbed?

2. What are bad, illegitimate, or insufficient reasons for me to leave my working solitude? Is it bad to leave if all that has happened is that I've grown distracted or still don't know how to proceed with the paragraph at hand?

3. Have I made any rules about leaving — for instance, that I mustn't leave if it feels like I'm running away? Should I create a few such rules and test them out?

4. Might I create a ritual or ceremony of leave-taking to slow the process down, to ensure that it's really time to go, and to celebrate the completion of a work period?

ON CALCULATING THE BALANCE:

1. Am I severely endangered by my social isolation? Must I dramatically reduce the time I spend alone?

2. Am I severely hampered by spending an insufficient amount of time in solitude? Must I dramatically increase the time I spend alone working on my art?

3. Am I bound to a myth about how solitary I should be? Can I dispute that myth? Can I picture myself more in the world and work to effect that change?

4. What is the right balance between social isolation and social interaction for me? Can I calculate a rough percentage or tentatively determine how many hours I should spend alone with my work and how many hours engaged with people and the affairs of the world?

Engage in parallel-life work. You can best avoid the dangers of prolonged isolation by leading a robust and meaningful life apart from art. This life outside the studio also helps prevent existential coldness because it reminds you, unconsciously but clearly, that you have something to look forward to after work.

Begin now to cultivate a life full of real meaning apart from your art-committed life. If you do not have such a parallel life presently, start by making small but real changes in the direction of new relationships, new community efforts, and a new belief system. Do not disavow your present life as an artist, but rather take steps to procure for yourself some meaningful out-of the-studio interest that involves living people: a volunteer activity, a second career, new friendships, a family life, an intimate relationship.

Naturally your parallel life produces its own tensions and carries its own risks. Won't a second career, even one lovingly entered into, bring disappointments and frustrations? Won't a mate and children provide more than a few distractions? Won't giving some energy to a needy cause bring with it burnout and depression? These risks are nevertheless worth taking. You will possess more energy, suffer fewer depressions, feel less concerned about the success of a rival, enjoy the art of other artists more, and despair and doubt less as you work in your studio if you have a life outside it.

In his short story "The Artist at Work," Albert Camus described a fictional painter named Jonas: "For human beings and the ordinary circumstances of life he merely reserved a kindly smile, which dispensed him from paying attention to them." But Jonas does not fare well in the loft he builds for himself; his perfect isolation finally paralyzes him. The artist whose investment in art is too great or who finds the world of human interaction too difficult to manage ultimately is likely to feel martyred and cheated.

Following are some tips on creating a successful parallel life:

1. If you are highly productive and rarely leave the studio, give yourself permission to produce fewer art products or to give fewer performances than you otherwise might. Rest for a day on your laurels in the company of other human beings. Set more modest daily, weekly, or monthly goals. Incorporate into your schedule both in-studio and out-of-studio time.

2. Redefine success so that accomplishments outside the art arena count. Call it a successful morning if you spent it writing a letter to your sister, having brunch with a friend, and chatting with your neighbor.

3. Redefine the concepts of productive time and wasted time. The afternoon you spend at a town meeting, in the waiting room of

your son's orthodontist, or on a crisis hotline should be considered time appropriately spent.

4. Pay better attention to other people. Do this not because they are fascinating creatures and make for good stories or good conquests but to enter into serious and sometimes loving relations with some of them and to feel your common humanity with all of them.

5. Expand your repertoire of activities. Will you graciously host Thanksgiving dinner? Play with a child? Protect a principle? Make barbequed chicken wings for a picnic? Enjoy some leisure time in great spirits?

The pursuit of a parallel life, the contours of which will be different in each artist's case, is the single most important self-help strategy available to the artist who spends too much time in isolation, working hard but missing out on human warmth.

Take strategic time-outs. Even having inoculated yourself against existential coldness by obtaining a parallel life, you will still experience icy moments. What will you do? You might take a strategic time-out from your work, your brooding, and your doubts and just do something pleasant. For instance, you could:

- make a bowl of popcorn
- take a hot shower
- play with your child
- recall a grand encounter
- shoot a rack of pool
- read a chapter of a mystery
- call a friend
- melt cheese on a tortilla
- sun yourself in your rock garden
- take a brisk walk
- meditate

- have a cup of coffee with your mate

- kick a soccer ball up and down the hallway

Prepare a whole array of fanciful strategies. Existential coldness may be better banished, and at less cost, by a hot shower or a brisk walk than by drugs or alcohol, a misadventure at the local tavern, or a bout of depression. If a brief time-out proves inadequate, step into the rich parallel life you've been cultivating and make contact with another human being.

10 *The Place of Culture*

An artist, like every other human being, is embedded in her culture and continually shaped, affected, and manipulated by it. She will like aspects of her culture and dislike other aspects of it, feel kinship with certain subgroups within the larger culture and animosity toward others, and stand in diverse relationship to the many elements that make up her society. She will form conscious cultural associations — that, for instance, she prefers tennis and PBS to bowling and cable, or vice versa — and also not be very aware of the ways that she is fully an American, or an African American, or an African American from Louisiana. All these conscious and unconscious cultural rules, roles, and effects mold her and constrain her, both as a person and as an artist.

Each of us is acculturated in ways that we would have a hard time analyzing or acknowledging. We simply do not know to what extent we have been formed by the television shows we watched growing up, the streets we walked as children, the churches and temples we entered, the values and norms our parents communicated, the songs we heard, or the books we read. Nor is all that formative pressure in the past: every evening newscast is a salvo of cultural messages that manipulate us and to which we are bound to viscerally react.

To what extent is our art even "ours," and to what extent is it born out of our cultural associations, out of the pressure our culture exerts on us, or out of a certain event in the culture that has caught our attention? Would we be doing a coffee table book on Gothic churches if we hadn't spent our formative years attending mass in a Gothic cathedral? Would we be penning protest songs if there weren't a war to protest? Would we be painting our particular abstractions if we hadn't grown up in the West Village opposite a modernist gallery? Is there any conceivable way to step outside our past and our present and gauge our motives for doing what we do? Is there some way we could guide ourselves to the work we would love to do if we weren't "trapped in culture"?

One proof of how deeply we are embedded in our culture is the fact, discussed earlier, that being dropped in a different culture has been known to produce psychotic episodes in previously mentally healthy individuals. The milder but still very real disorientation we feel when we enter a radically different culture goes by the name of "culture shock." We are shocked by the new culture in part because we are reminded how our life is bound up with the rules of our culture. In our culture, people come on time; in this other culture, they come today, or maybe tomorrow, or maybe the next day. Isn't the very way you breathe, move, sit, and think different depending on which culture formed you? And could the artistic choices of an artist growing up in one culture possibly be the same as the artistic choices of an artist growing up in another? In that moment of realization we recognize that culture is bondage.

Does this cultural bondage really matter all that much? It does, and for all the obvious reasons. We do not want to feel like slaves and, more important, we do not want to *be* slaves. We do not want our efforts rendered ridiculous by the fact that we are not acting out of own motives and in our own voice but rather only reacting to the forces of culture that are every-where around us and thoroughly within us. If we are art-committed, we want our art to reflect our best understanding of our true intentions and to possess a personal, rather than a cultural, logic. In short, we want to be our own person and to do our own work — and the ways in which culture influences and infiltrates us makes us wonder if such freedom is even remotely possible.

Take just one example. Say that in your culture the only people who pay for art are kings and priests, and that they only buy portraits of themselves. You grow up seeing paintings of kings and priests and begin to paint portraits in that genre, despite your worry that this can't be the only kind of painting worth doing. Still, everyone around you is painting this way; all the art you see is of this sort; and so you unconsciously conclude that this and only this is art and that everything else isn't. This inability to see beyond the borders of your culture has been dubbed the "cultural trance" and, to a lesser or greater degree, it affects everyone.

Some of those itches that you can't scratch, some of those depressions whose sources you can't identify, and some of the vague doubts you can't shake off may well have their roots in this particular dilemma, that each of us is more or less caught in the cultural trance. The effects of culture may play out in matters of class (you find yourself choosing classical music when you really want to play bluegrass music), matters of group identity (people from your group have permission to paint only realistic landscapes, and only on Sunday), or matters of ideology (causing you to try to write a "spiritual" book because that is the word people in your group use to describe a certain feeling). They may play out in any number of ways that, because they are artifacts of culture and not integral to you, produce in you a vague sense of unease.

The obvious irony and difficulty is that if you are deep in a cultural trance — and we all are — how can you know it and how can you break free of it? Still, the contemporary intelligent, sensitive person, having been made aware by her reading that culture is not only around us but within us, and having a rudimentary understanding of the problem, is liberated at least enough to know that she must continually examine her relationship to her culture, to see how it affects her and her art. By examining it, she gets free of it as best she can.

CULTURAL PRESSURE AND SELF-CENSORSHIP

Because we live embedded in culture, surrounded by neighbors, the watchful apparatus of government, and a million eyes, we almost invariably censor ourselves. We do this so as not to offend the culture and to remain safe within the culture. One of the main results of being social animals who share values, band together emotionally and psychologically around common traits (like skin color or political ideology), live in watchful proximity of one another, and get punished when we upset others, is that each of us practices self-censorship.

We go along to get along and try not to make waves. We do this because we do not want to be ostracized and because it can be dangerous to disagree with cultural norms. But if you are going along and not making waves, what do you do with your values, cherished principles, existential intelligence, and sense of right and wrong? To be sure, you certainly don't have the power to right every wrong. But what if your fear and unconscious self-censorship prevent you from even painting about it, writing about it, or singing about it?

Only a relatively few artists take their culture to task, and only a small percentage of what we see in the arts has arisen from a questioning of culture. While there are many possible reasons for this, including the reality that art arises from many sources, high on the list of reasons must be individual self-censorship. Indeed, Freud argued that writer's block is *always* a function of self-censorship, that the blocked writer censors himself to prevent himself from saying things that would disturb his psychological equanimity or his relationship to his community and as a result ends up saying nothing at all.

How many artists are unwittingly censoring their work and making "conventional" art — the very definition of culturally acceptable art — because they fear the reaction that edgier, radical, or provocative art would engender? And, if this happens regularly, what are the consequences of that self-censorship for the artist? Don't smart, sensitive, existential creatures like us get anxious, depressed and emotionally tuckered out if we spend all our time keeping ourselves from speaking?

Here is how one artist, Beth, came to grips with this issue:

My first response to the question of whether I regularly censor myself was to feel guilty. Suddenly, caught-with-my-pants-down guilty; bad-girl guilty. Not only do I not truly understand what I wish to communicate via my art, but I fear that it's not rage about the awful inequities in our world or the cultural conformity that robs countless people of joy and self-expression. Then I began to recall all the bad, sledgehammer-in-the-face political art that I've viewed on walls, as installations and performances. They were obvious, polemical, literal, boring, or garish; there was nothing persuasive about them. I never wanted to make art like that. So even if I do want to take a valiant stand against oppression and cultural entrapment, I still must figure out a way to do it with grace and lyricism and originality.

Suddenly I realized that I had been telling myself that there was a correct way to make art and a correct reason for making it. Talk about oppression and self-censorship! I oppress myself! We like to think that we are not subject to subtle cultural and political oppression and that we rage at external oppression, but we fail to watch the ways we control ourselves with it. Well, this week I didn't censor myself, I took myself seriously, and I felt anger about all those times that I have not taken myself seriously.

Self-censorship takes many forms. You might hold yourself back from attempting to write a certain screenplay because you are convinced that the "movie culture" would reject your script out of hand. You might hold yourself back from commenting on a cultural issue, like the place of religion in the state, because you have no stomach for the potential (and probable) backlash. You might hold yourself back from producing "ugly" art because of some not-quite-conscious internalized cultural injunction against producing anything that isn't pretty. Most likely of all, you might hold yourself back from expressing rage or outrage in your art because emotions that large feel dangerous and seem likely to provoke wrath and reprisals.

It isn't that you don't *feel* the outrage. It would be surprising if a smart, sensitive, principled person like you didn't experience regular outrage at some aspect of your cultural milieu: at some position taken by your local, state, or federal government or at some local, national, or global injustice. Almost certainly a lot outrages you. What, then, happens? If you are like most people, you "stuff it," vent it only at the dinner table or among like-minded friends, or engage in protests that protect your anonymity and safety. You do nothing more assertive for a host of reasons, first among them that personal protest is dangerous.

Leslie, an art student, put it this way:

Do I experience outrage? Yes, lately with respect to the "war on ter-ror." I see patriotism and nationalism as a type of global racism. I'm tired of reading accounts of terror overseas where many hundreds die but because two Americans perish, they are the only ones we are allowed to mourn. When will we ever be a global community?

For one of my drawing classes, we went to the New Britain Museum of Art in Connecticut. One painting there was of September 11, complete with the two towers, angels, and doves. The imagery made me ill because it seemed so clichéd. I'm reminded of the Dixie Chicks and how they publicly announced that they didn't agree with Bush's decision to go to war in Iraq. People immediately began destroying their CDs, and they received much negative press.

Our culture tells us to keep our minority opinions to our-selves. I think that if I actually drew pictures to represent what I feel about today's culture, I would produce more meaningful work, but out of fear of being shunned I sit quietly and draw "cute things." This year I'm working toward being more honest and authentic. Maybe if I can censor myself less, I will uncover more meaning in my work — and in my life.

There is nothing simple about our relationship to our culture or our relationship to our art. Deborah, a creativity coach, posed the issues described in this chapter to some of her clients and artist peers and got the following varied responses:

Some artists fully believe that they are making art that expresses their outrage. One is currently working on a series of narrative paintings depicting the plight of the homeless; another is creating a series of large paintings focusing on garbage and the overall disrespect of the environment. A client recently completed a solo show that dealt with the subject "Where do you draw the line?" She was focusing on urban sprawl, housing developments that destroy our natural habitat, and our dependency on cars and oil.

Some didn't feel that they were expressing their outrage through their art but rather that they had found other ways to do so, such as through financial contributions, volunteering, writing to their politicians, and so on. One stated that expressing outrage through her art didn't feel authentic to her. She describes herself as a person who appreciates beauty and genuinely looks for the good in life. She feels it is important to express this in her art rather than the "ambivalence and darkness that so often shows itself in our culture."

Some artists commented on how difficult it was to stay in the tension of creative work that continually expressed outrage. After months in such a project, they often felt drained, exhausted, and bordering on depressed. They felt that if they were to focus on the outrage with such intimacy, it would have the potential of becoming detrimental to their physical and mental well-being. They wondered if it was worth it and if there was any way to maintain their balance while dealing with such large emotions day after day.

You may opt not to fight a given cultural battle, and you may opt not to use your art to fight that battle. You may decide not to disclose something about yourself, because you don't want your neighbors to know, and you may decide not to disclose that information in your art for the same reason. Those choices are plausible and legitimate. What serves you less well is censoring yourself when you actually *want* to express yourself on some matter, either in your art or in another way.

The consequences of speaking may be exactly as grave as you fear them to be, and perhaps holding your tongue is the right course. Still, your fears may be largely unfounded, and quite possibly you owe it to yourself to speak up. As someone who is committed to lifelong creativity — that is, to a life of self-directed self-expression — you have a responsibility to notice when you are censoring yourself, why you are censoring yourself, and whether you intend to continue censoring yourself.

CULTURE AS RED HERRING AND EXCUSE

Say that you write a novel and then begin querying literary agents in the hopes of interesting one in representing you. If, after three or four form rejections, you get angry at the "culture of publishing," you are on the road to cutting off your nose to spite your face. Artists need to be careful not to turn a truth, that there are cultural norms and cultural realities, into a global defensiveness and a way of avoiding fighting the good fight.

If you stop sending out your novel after receiving those relatively few form rejections, then you need to grow a thicker hide. It may be that you don't much believe in your novel and presume that it really has no chance, that you have entirely misunderstood the level of competition involved, and that you have presumed, for no good reason, that the first agent you contacted would fall for you, and in other ways managed to mix up your fears about the work and your fantasies for yourself with cultural reality. In this scenario, the "culture" really isn't to blame for anything.

A host of issues, only a few of them cultural, are likely at play when a writer stops submitting his novel, and maybe stops writing, after three or four rejections. It would be smart of that writer to let go of his "us and them" mentality and to better understand what is going on in his mind, in his heart, and in the marketplace. Too-early withdrawals from the marketplace, rooted in something quite different from the artist's expressed antipathy toward and contempt for that marketplace, cause countless creative people to needlessly suffer. They end up closing doors that, if they could have dealt more effectively with their fears and their feelings, might have opened wide to them — after some considerable knocking.

Janice, a creativity coach, described one artist's struggle:

I know one wonderful picture book author/artist who has given up her work on books because she does not feel that the culture appreciates the work she does and that the market only wants the latest celebrity effort. I would love to see her produce more books but, as it has turned out, she is much happier now, focusing on producing new artwork rather than writing books.

It may be that her view of the culture was not completely accurate and that she had more of a chance than she thought. But she may have needed that belief as justification for redirecting her creative energies in a direction that she wanted to go anyway. Sometimes we unconsciously spin culture to our own purposes, using what is outside ourselves to bolster the tentative yet crucial personal directives we feel inside ourselves.

It is true that culture constrains us. But we need to be careful not to turn that truth into a self-fulfilling prophecy by announcing our unwillingness to interact with it, when in fact what we are feeling is hurt, anger, disappointment, or some other painful emotion. Better to get back on the horse and ride it into the breach than to use culture as a handy way to stop the pain.

EXPROPRIATING OTHER CULTURES

It is one thing to belong to a specific subculture and to comment on it as an artist: that is, to take your own group to task, to write a song about your people for your people, to sculpt in the idiom of abstract artists like yourself, saying something new to them by the work that you do, and so on. It is a different matter to speak about another culture, to comment on that culture, or to make use of that culture. When you do that, many interesting complications arise, among them the risk of romanticizing that culture, as anthropologists often do, unwittingly insulting it, or, most likely of all, simply misunderstanding it.

What is a non–Native American doing when she makes use of Native American imagery in her paintings? What is a screenwriter who knows nothing about the CIA doing when he portrays it in his suspense thriller? Are such appropriations and portrayals ever legitimate? This is not a question for the art police to answer; it is a question for the individual artist to answer as she finds herself investigating another culture and making use of it in one way or another. It is her job to evaluate her motives.

Here are the thoughts of one artist, Marcia, on this issue:

I have been mulling over the matter of appropriating culture in light of my current work, "Lead and Follow: The Connection." As a blond, blue-eyed American painter, I reflect my "outsider's" experience of Argentine tango onto my canvas. I am pulled toward all things Hispanic, from the lilt of the language to the pure color sensibility to the arts of the various indigenous peoples of Latin America. Despite this appreciation — indeed, passion — I will not transform myself into something I am not. I remind myself that I am a guest in the culture of my tango paintings, and remain sensitive to that fact.

The issue of culture *must* be a part of my process as I paint this tango series. To what extent do I leave my culture at the door of the studio and enter into the Argentine culture, in order to paint my *tangeros* from a point of heartfelt understanding? To what extent am I trapped in my own status as an outsider, separated from the culture of my subjects? How does my outsider point of view color what I see? In my current painting, the woman is blond, and shaped quite like I am, with her face obscured as she steps gracefully away from the viewer. That wasn't "intentional" — or was it? I have much more to think about.

An artist isn't obliged to be politically correct. But an artist is obliged, I think, to take seriously her portrayals of other cultures, just as she takes her work seriously in general. She is just as entitled to satirize a culture she believes is deserving of satirizing as she is to applaud a culture she believes is splendid. But whether she is satirizing or applauding, it is her duty to ensure that she is doing something that she can stand behind.

THE PARTICULARITIES OF CULTURE

One artist lives in China, another in Peru. One artist lives in a place with no art galleries or museums and no cultural connection to galleries and museums, another grows up being taken every Sunday to the Museum of Modern Art and the Met. One artist lives in a place where it will literally cost him his life to speak his truth, another lives in a culture where everyone gets to speak but no one is listening.

In the same small town there may be a dozen cultures, the small Hispanic community across the tracks, the small Chinese community, the ecumenical Protestant community and the evangelical Protestant community, the police community and the criminal community, the two Jewish families, the secular culture of the professional class and the business class, and many more. On top of all that is the mass culture, coming at us through television, radio, the advertising flyers that fill our mailboxes, and the books that we read.

These cultural groupings and divides are everywhere, and they really matter: socially, psychologically, and practically. To know yourself, you need to know how you are made by culture and how you fit into culture. You need to comprehend the dominant culture, including the mass media and the power elites; the many cultures around you, the forces that make up and divide your town, your city, and your state; and your own culture, the one into which you were born and that circulates in your blood.

This is too much to understand in any comprehensive way but not too much to think about, at least a little, for the sake of waking yourself up from the cultural trance. Then you will have a better understanding as to why you make the art you do and why it may be difficult (and even impossible) to be the artist you would like to be in the culture in which you find yourself embedded.

Here are the thoughts of Ingrid, an artist who was raised in Europe and lives in Asia, on her experience of culture:

> I have been living in cultures other than my own for the last ten years, in Canada, in Europe, and now in Asia. Living in Singapore and creating art in Singapore are particular transcultural experiences: this is a country that permits only limited personal expression and limited personal freedom and yet recognizes that it is important to develop people's creative minds in order to stay competitive as a country. So there is something like a budding freedom side by side with deep restrictions and a real antipathy toward speaking out in your own voice.
>
> People my age have had nearly no exposure to art during their school years and very little appreciation for all things "art." This means that they have not learned to see art or to accept it as a medium to challenge views, dispute the established culture, or express rage, disapproval, or negative feelings of any kind. These limitations on

the individual are likewise enforced as limitations on the size of canvasses: only small canvasses are allowed. One of the key discussions I had with local patrons of my exhibitions was their interest in how I dared to work in canvasses that were so large.

Set aside an afternoon and think about your culture and your place in it. This is an exotic exercise, since it requires that, like some contortionist, you see your culture clearly even though your culture made you. But this exotic investigation is cheaper, and rather more important, than traveling three thousand miles to "have a cultural experience." Have a cultural experience right in your own backyard by sitting down and fathoming the effects of your culture on your creativity and on your willingness — or lack thereof — to express yourself.

STRATEGIES

In conjunction with the guided writing program described in chapter 13, consider the following questions:

- How have you been formed by the culture in which you grew up?

- How do you continue to be shaped and manipulated by the culture in which you now find yourself?

- What differences do you notice between the rules — especially those related to creating and to personal expression — of your present culture versus some other culture in which you've spent time?

- Are there things you would say, avenues you would investigate, and/or art that you would make if you didn't fear cultural reprisals?

- Do you use "culture" as an excuse not to network or market your wares?

- Are you clear about what you are doing when you represent other cultures in your art?

- Does the concept of "cultural trance" make sense to you? If it does, try to identify areas in which you are its victim.

11 Social Interactions and Community

The artist brings his complex, contradictory nature with him whenever he ventures out into the world, and while his personality may serve him extremely well in the studio, it may just as easily fail him in social situations. Each of the artist's personality traits produces social effects, as do his moods. Even the artist's vitality and passion can prove an impediment in the social arena. He may fly wildly out of his studio full of manic energy, his vitality hardly spent by two hours of painting or writing, and into the company of others. The dancer John Prinz recalled, "I was like a volcano. In fact, everybody called me the 'Volcano.' I had all this incredible energy that kept exploding."

How do *you* approach interpersonal encounters? Does one aspect of your personality predominate? Are you consistently ironic, assertive, frightened, silent, or prideful? You may find it immensely profitable to determine what sides of yourself you present to the world — to determine, in effect, how others see you — so that you can decide whether you need to make any changes to your public persona.

In this chapter we'll examine artists' social interactions and relationships. Whether the relationship is with a parent, sibling, or spouse; with a teacher, mentor, or business associate; or with a colleague, fellow artist, or rival, there are five specific areas that are important to reflect on in determining how successful you'll be at establishing and maintaining relationships. We'll also examine the important topic of whether or not artists can find community among themselves.

OUTSIDER FEELINGS

The writer Colin Wilson wrote, "The atmosphere of the Existential Outsider is unpleasant to breathe. There is something nauseating, anti-life, about it: these men without motive who stay in their rooms because there seems to be no reason for doing anything else." Most artists are not quite as estranged from their fellow human beings, as bereft of reasons for existing, or as alienated from the common values and enthusiasms of the world as are the outsider characters created by existentialist writers like Kafka, Camus, and Sartre. But insofar as artists do regularly feel different from other people, a difference experienced both as a sense of oddness and a sense of uniqueness, they identify with the outsider's concerns and are often guarded or distant in the interpersonal realm.

In part, artists are outsiders because of the personal mythology they cultivate. This mythology is a blend of beliefs about the importance of the individual, the responsibility of the artist as a maker of culture and a witness to the truth, and the artist's ordained separateness. Artists often stand apart on principle, splendid Napoleonic figures perched on a hill overlooking the battle.

The artist may also find herself speechless in public. Around her people chat, but she has little to offer. Too much of what she knows and feels has gone directly into her art, and too much has been revealed to her in solitude

— infinitely more than she can share in casual conversation. In this regard she is not unlike the biblical figure Zacharias, described in the Gospel according to St. Luke: "And the people waited for Zacharias, and marveled that he tarried so long in the temple. And when he came out, he could not speak unto them: and they perceived that he had seen a vision in the temple: for he beckoned unto them, and remained speechless." How can an artist communicate or paraphrase what has transpired in the studio? And if she isn't to communicate that, what is she to speak about?

The artist is also aware that she was born into a ready-made society. She didn't choose it, and she can see clearly much that she doesn't like about it. By the same token, she can't lead the life of a Balinese composer, a Pueblo Indian potter, or a Greek dramatist; she must make do where she is, in an avid, heterogeneous, fragmented, disharmonious, mercantile society, a society she perhaps doesn't respect. This disrespect easily translates into a disdain for the people she encounters, for implied in every social gathering and interaction (with the exception of a protest event) is a shared acceptance of the status quo.

How much of an outsider do you feel yourself to be? How much outsider energy do you bring to your social interactions? Do you feel certain that other people see less clearly than you do and fall short of the mark? What sorts of relationships are possible for someone who interacts as a stranger in a strange land? It is well worth your effort to address these questions and perhaps even to cross-examine yourself about them, for outside in the cold is where outsiders find themselves.

ART OBSESSIONS

To put it simply, artists are often lost to the world because of their obsessions with their art. They may be equally lost as they incubate a new idea or in the feverish days when they make their final film cuts or race toward a publishing deadline. They may obsess about artistic questions day and night, alone or in the company of others, in the middle of a shift at their day job or on vacation in the Bahamas.

Lost in time and space and in love with the traditions that underpin her discipline, she may feel more connected to Pablo Picasso, Emily Dickinson, Ingmar Bergman, Gertrude Stein, George Handel, or Tennessee Williams than to the people in her immediate world. The living past holds extraordinary meaning for her, and she travels elsewhere, removing her spirit and attention from the present. She may reside, as she works on her novel, in the childhood of a character, walking the garden paths and living the household dramas there. She may come upon a Rembrandt drawing and find herself wrenched, not to any particular place or time, but just *elsewhere*, as she re-experiences the greatness of her traditions, measures herself anew, and dreams again of her future.

One musician explained to me that when he heard his first Beethoven symphony as an adolescent he experienced a tremendous disruption in his life that lasted two full days. He knew that his life had changed; he felt agitated, awestruck, in love. To the world, however, he seemed preoccupied, inaccessible, and self-involved. While connecting with a new, powerful, and hitherto unknown universe, he disconnected, in both subtle and obvious ways, from the world of everyday affairs. Artists often lose the present moment in exactly this way and live surreally.

Obsessed by their art, artists often find it difficult to make room in their lives and their psyches for flesh-and-blood human beings. Fyodor Dostoyevsky's wife, Anna, said of her husband, "I think that he is incapable of love; he is too much occupied with other thoughts and ideas to become strongly attached to anyone earthly." Lucy Audubon, wife of ornithological painter John James Audubon, complained, "I have a rival in every bird!"

The relationship between the artist and her art is a central, core relationship. The visual artist Eleanor Antin declared, "For art I could do anything." The dancer Starr Danias said of herself, "During layoffs, I miss dancing the way I would miss a person." The composer Georg Phillip Telemann claimed that "music requires a man to give himself entirely to it." The novelist William Faulkner advised, "The writer's only responsibility is to his art; he will be completely ruthless if he is a good one." The playwright George Bernard Shaw echoed this sentiment: "The true artist will let his wife starve, his children go barefoot, his mother drudge for his living at seventy, sooner than work at anything but his art."

Are you willing to care about other people more than this? Since all art and no love is an unbalanced equation, let us hope so! Are you willing to practice really letting go of your art some portion of the time? Can you make an effort to avoid snubbing those around you, even if that means losing an idea or an image? Can you interrupt your work when someone needs you? Can you let other human beings matter? Not every artist is able or willing to answer these questions in the affirmative.

DEPENDENCY, AUTHORITY, AND CONTROL ISSUES

Artists consider themselves independent and hope to remain more independent than the next person. At the same time their independent, rebellious, nonconforming nature, coupled with their introspective habits of mind, make them wary of social interactions. Whereas the firefighter, for example, has no reason to believe that keeping company with other firefighters will diminish his ability to fight fires, the artist, keenly aware that her journey is a personal and independent one, often fears that contact with her peers will slow her down, detour her, contain her, limit her, or unduly influence her.

An artist knows that other artists are opinionated and have their own agendas. Won't he be distracted, he wonders, by those opinions and agendas? If he wants to paint realistically, and the abstract painters he encounters announce that what he is doing is ridiculous and pathetic, won't that have some negative effect on him (or cause him to commit murder)? If, as an actor, he feels unwilling to audition for commercials and industrials but his peers tell him that he must if he is to eat, will that peer pressure cause him to "lower his standards" and sell cereal? Will the modern dancer, who has no desire to study ballet and, in her own mind, no need to study it, feel diminished — and psychologically prevented from competing — by her ballet-trained peers? In each case, the artist would just as soon avoid the interaction and not know the answer.

Because the artist must know for himself, do for himself, and believe in himself, he is unwilling to cavalierly agree with his peers or placate them when they disagree with him. If they say New York, where he lives, is the only place for an artist, but his journey is about to take him to Santa Fe,

Arles, or Nepal, he will buy his ticket anyway. If he's leaving his regional theater for Los Angeles, or leaving Los Angeles for a regional theater, he will leave. If he means to photograph in black and white, he will photograph in black and white. He will not let other artists define or deter him. Similarly, he will resist attempts to label him as a member of their particular school, for that, too, is a blow to his ego and a limitation of his freedom.

By the same token, it is also true that artists can't live as independently as they would like. At the simplest level, they are often financially dependent on parents, a mate, or a day job. They also depend on publishers, film distributors, curators, producers, and other industry professionals to put their work before the public. Because there is such a sizable discrepancy between the way artists view themselves and the realities of their situations, conflict almost inevitably arises. On the interpersonal level, these conflicts emerge as issues of dependency, authority, and control.

Not only don't these issues vanish with time, but they often become even more troubling. For example, in the first years of an artist's career, through school and in his first steps away from school, the question of financial independence may not strike him as being of paramount importance. He works and gets some help from his parents. Maybe he receives a partial scholarship or uses his savings. His art may bring in a little money. Perhaps he enters into a relationship in which he is dependent on his mate's income, but that dependency isn't much of an issue yet, because both partners believe that one day he will break through and make more money.

The contours of this life will prove different for each artist. The dancer will have a different experience from the painter; two dancers will themselves have different experiences. Each, though, is likely to share the artist's experience: that her art does not produce enough income to live on. Over time, she becomes less and less eager to think about her finances or to talk about how she's supporting herself. As the painter Susan Schwalb put it, "Most artists don't like to talk about money, and how they survive. Most artists don't like to admit how they make a living, or who helps them."

Even as she tries not to think or talk about money, she continues to worry. How will she be supported if she doesn't achieve stardom? Will the average person buy her oil painting for $4,000, when a plastic-framed

Monet or Warhol print can be purchased for $20? Craving entertainment and a good read, will the average person pick up her difficult novel? Committed only to a yearly visit to *The Nutcracker*, will the average person support her fledgling dance company? Expecting the production values of a $100,000,000 movie, will the average person rush out to see her grainy $100,000 epic?

As a rule, the average person will not. Nor will society's representative, the government, help the artist much. As Israeli artist Zvi Goldstein put it, "Western society never pays a cultural tax." The few pennies each citizen puts into the pot to support the creative and performing arts can't go far toward sustaining artists.

Eventually the artist gets tired of this lack of financial reward. He begins to realize that the odds are stacked against him. He may demand of himself that he do more commercial work, that he compromise to meet the demands of the marketplace. What was an appropriate and even charming life of poverty for the art student and young bohemian artist wears thin as the artist leaves his twenties. It is no longer charming that his car doesn't run, that he has no medical insurance, that he's still waiting tables, transcribing court trials, or driving a cab. As performance artist Eric Bogosian put it, "It's not fun to be poor. We used to romanticize the artist's life; we used to romanticize poverty. We spent years in art school studying the lives of artists, learning how to live like an artist. It was going to be cool to come to New York and live on the Lower East Side next to dope dealers. But we became frightened by the squalor and the poverty. I didn't want to live in a slum the rest of my life."

The composer Philip Glass, describing the early decades of his music career, underlines the point:

The first problem an artist has is how to survive. I began writing music when I was fifteen and was not self-supporting as an artist until I was forty-one. So for over twenty-five years I could not entirely support myself through the work that I wanted to do.

To begin as an artist means to take on a life of struggle, so that at forty-one you can finally make a living as an artist. My European artist friends say, "My gosh, it took you so long!" But in this country you'd say, "You mean, you did it so quickly?" It can just as easily never happen.

Sooner or later the artist's social interactions are affected by this lack of independence. He may find it hard to take from anyone...or hard not to take from everyone. He may maintain a feeling of independence by rebelling in any small way he can — by walking out of his acting class when the teacher criticizes him, by writing an angry letter to the small-press editor who has rejected his poems. His social interactions — with his mate, his business associates, with other artists in the café — may demonstrate a volatility that can be traced to his need to retain a feeling of independence. Some of his interactions, which may look self-sabotaging and may otherwise seem incomprehensible, can be roughly taken to mean "You can't do that to me!" or "I'll do what I damn well choose!"

Many of the rivalries and unpleasantnesses in the arts stem from the unhappy feelings associated with this lack of real or felt independence. The artist, his pride wounded, is hard-pressed not to consider anyone who appears successful or who occupies a position of authority an enemy. He may see every social interaction as a kind of threat and attempt to maintain control in even the most trifling matters.

Both subtle and flagrant battles over control may pepper his private and public life. The battles may be loud, ugly, and perverse; the artist, fighting for control, may connive, challenge, manipulate, attack. He may adopt a passive-aggressive stance and agree in principle to everything demanded of him by his agent or his mate but then make sure to arrive late, forget the milk, or "accidentally" break a vase — or his foot. He may take a heroic (or heroically foolish) stance in order not to feel pushed around by circumstances; he may become, as Whistler said of himself, the "Quixote in the battle fought by painters."

The artist, motivated by a sense that he's a caretaker of culture and certain that it's his right to be free, is at once unlikely to achieve independence and highly likely to mourn the fact that independence eludes him. Since no person can be as independent as romantic mythology and two centuries of idealization of the individual have led him to believe he can be, each artist is obliged to regularly reassess his ideas about independence and inter-dependence.

SELF-ESTEEM ISSUES

An artist with low self-esteem or one whose self-esteem has eroded over time enters into social interactions burdened by her feelings of inferiority. The fact that her art happens to be appreciated is no hedge against these feelings. As one celebrated rock musician put it, "I believe in what I do, but not in who I am."

Much can erode the artist's sense of self-worth. Even a successful career as a member of a good symphony orchestra may bring with it a sense of failure. The musician Carl Fischer explained: "The tragedy of the orchestra violinist's career is that his activity from the very first is equivalent to a renunciation, that it does not represent a beginning supported by joyous hopes, but in most cases forms the close of a period of painful disappoint-ments and hopes destroyed. Nearly every orchestra violinist, once upon a time, has dreamed of becoming a celebrated soloist."

When an actor, dancer, or musician is led into group activity, he may struggle, in the end unsuccessfully, to hold on to his artistic identity. He may blend into the group effort even while fighting to retain his individu-ality in the face of the conductor's efforts to maintain control and provide direction. This tension frustrates him and wears him down, and finally he may submit to the demands of the institution in which he finds himself — and lose self-esteem in the process. As the author Donald Henahan put it, "Without anyone's willing it, an orchestra bends to its common purpose (some would say flattens) all the diverse human types that enter it. There comes to be a recognizable symphony orchestra personality, an orchestra level of talent, an orchestra temperament. Like any walled city, the orches-tra demands of its inhabitants submission to authority and unquestioning response to a leader."

Pride may prevent the artist from sharing with others this central expe-rience — that he has fallen short of realizing his dreams. Because his self-esteem is being eroded, because every day he feels less whole and less adequate, he may experience great difficulty entering into relationship with anyone he supposes is healthier than he. Indeed, he may find himself drawn to the dregs of society, so as to feel superior to them or because he identifies with them, thus descending another notch and further eroding his already diminishing self-esteem.

ENVY AND COMPETITION ISSUES

Our discussion of the reasons creative and performing artists find it so difficult to interact in satisfactory ways would hardly be complete without an acknowledgment that artists typically compete fiercely with and envy one another. Alex Gross, founding editor of *Art Workers News*, expressed the problem: "It would seem that there is no sum of money so small, no crumb of reputation so paltry, no opportunity to show one's work so uninviting, that it will fail as the reason for one artist to stab another in the back."

Although many important dynamics operate between artists — including fellow feeling and mutual respect, a sense of shared purpose and joy during the run of a play, and so on — as often as not it is envy that most defines the relationship between two artists. The actress Danielle Brisebois agreed: "I was in *Annie* about three years. All of us kids were jealous of each other, even though we never let the others know it. No one wanted any of the other kids to have more than them."

It's not that the artist sits at home making lists of his rivals. When he's absorbed in enjoying a fellow artist's work or in his own art-making, he has no rivals. At such times his fellow artists are his spiritual companions. But at other times he can't stop comparing his lot to theirs. They are getting the parts he covets, they are having important shows, they are being rewarded for their dull acting, flat singing, amateurish painting, or sloppy writing. Their novels occupy the few spots on the bestseller lists. His own good friends withhold information about grants and group shows. His own good friends attend parties and rub elbows with people whose elbows they would invite him to rub if they were really his friends. All this eats away at him.

Artists are often aware of their envious feelings but not of how deep they run. An artist may claim, for instance, to hate realistic painting (or abstract painting, figurative painting, installation pieces, environmental art, miniatures, photographs, or murals), not realizing that this position may be a way of dismissing out of hand an army of potential rivals. Their successes become irrelevant to him because their work doesn't count. By taking a dismissive stance, the artist reduces the arena in which he competes.

An artist's envy may manifest itself in any number of ways. In the past she may have loved to read; now she avoids contemporary fiction completely. All living authors have become her rivals. Or she may avidly read contemporary fiction, but only to assure herself that it's bad. Or she may read only the works of an author she knows is an alcoholic or near death — a rival she can pity or feel superior to.

How is an artist to alter this unfortunate relationship with his peers? We live, after all, in a society and a cultural milieu that foster envy. Because there are relatively few jobs in art, the ones that do exist are precious. For an artist to unilaterally work on quieting his envy is tantamount to enacting unilateral nuclear disarmament — a noble idea with many risks attached. If he undertakes to love and respect his fellow artists, to support them, to attend their shows, to buy their books, and to judge them generously, will they return the favor? Will they notice and be transformed themselves? Or will they exploit his generosity?

Each artist is challenged to make sense of this dilemma. The artist has great gifts to offer her fellow artists — love, appreciation, and understanding among them. However, these gifts are bound to be withheld by an artist disabled by her envy.

IS COMMUNITY POSSIBLE AMONG ARTISTS?

The need for innovation in art exists as much as ever, but its challenge at this point surely lies in more comprehensive goals that link the personal with the global.

— SUZI GABLIK

The above discussion inevitably leads us to the observation that only rarely do artists establish or maintain meaningful communities. While they can and do join groups — orchestras, bands, repertory companies, writers' groups, and graphic artists' coalitions on the one hand, and unions, 12-step programs, religious institutions, and the PTA on the other — they retain a dream of community that reaches far beyond what they manage to experience.

Maybe the dream they cherish is romantic or utopian. Its undeniable power may be a product of the isolation and estrangement they feel — a powerful wish that can't possibly be fulfilled. They may need to believe that such community exists somewhere, maybe in Paris, Berlin, or some locale they've heard rumors about. They may need to dream about moving to Taos or Bali. If they do spend their obligatory year in Paris, however, they are likely to be disappointed, for the odds are great that reality will fall short of their expectations.

What, after all, are they seeking? What does this elusive community look like? What do we even mean by the word? A brochure for the Association of Humanistic Psychology begins with the following observation: "We know less about community than any other social form: is it an emotional state, a small group, a local place or a collection of widely shared values?" What is the artist actually looking for?

M. Scott Peck, in *The Different Drum*, his book on community building, provides one answer, describing community as a group where all are leaders, a place of inclusiveness, commitment, and safety. Artists would certainly want their definition of community to resemble Peck's, with the addition of the following conditions, which taken together make for a utopian picture. An artist's community would be a place where artists experience a sense of shared values and ideals, collaborate, experience a general enthusiasm for art and share a general prosperity, see the aims of art regularly furthered, feel support for the growth and maturation of each artist's work, and experience mutual respect and love.

If we try to envision a leaderless group of artists gathered to form community, we are struck by the fact that each artist will bring to the group his or her inability to relate. Each will bring a sense of estrangement, a need to maintain independence, a need not to be swayed by the opinions of the others, an artist's necessary arrogance, feelings of envy, art obsessions, and all the rest.

To take an extreme example, imagine for a moment spending two hours every Thursday night in a hypothetical 1880 men's group made up of Van Gogh, Wagner, Dostoyevsky, Gauguin, Tchaikovsky, Hardy, and Tolstoy. Can you imagine such a group working to support its members? Wouldn't such a group more likely provide two hours of utter mayhem and be more a miracle to survive than a joy to attend?

Van Gogh, isolated and longing for community during his years in Arles, wrote to his brother, Theo: "The problem is simply this: If I looked about for someone to chum with, would it be a good thing, or would it be to my brother's disadvantage and mine? Would the other lose by it or would he gain? My mind is running on these questions." As Van Gogh's infamous episode with Gauguin (in which he threatened Gauguin with a razor and then cut off his own ear) attests, the artist is right to wonder how his personality may mesh with another artist's. Several artists together multiply the effects. In short, any community formed by artists is likely to look more divisive and operatic than mutually supportive.

Many of the challenges discussed in this book contribute to the artist's inability to create and sustain community, but few artists will talk about their mood swings or about how they hunger for recognition or envy their fellow artists. Walls of strained silence and small talk stand between one artist and another. The artist remains a member of an orchestra, a ballet company, a writers' circle, an art school, but she still wears her public face. Around her she sees the public faces of her fellow artists. She feels the coldness, as they do, but concludes that her only course is to keep her distance.

Still, even if artists come to distrust the very idea of community effort and decide to measure their well-being in strictly personal terms, the desire for community remains strong. Even if they are discouraged from helping one another and don't believe that help is available to them, they still desire to give and receive help. Even if they grow tired of dreaming about fantastic community, their ears still prick up when they hear stories about the art colonies of Bolinas, California, or of Sedona, Arizona. Even if they remain in isolation, tending their own gardens, and even if they believe that modern artists are doomed to have their desire for community thwarted, the desire does not die easily.

In an attempt to have some measure of community, they may rally around causes, give benefit concerts and readings, march against censorship, meet to play softball, give and attend classes, attend self-help support groups, or spend one Saturday night a month at their local Mystery Writers' of America meeting. They may make an effort to connect with their fellow actors during the run of a play. In these and a hundred other ways, they assert that they are trying to come together, trying to share their common humanity. But, despite these efforts, artists remain largely disappointed at the lack of community in their lives.

This analysis may not ring true for you. You may experience a strong sense of community in your church, among your friends, in your writing group, as a member of your culture, or in your neighborhood. You may not hunger for any special community of artists, or you may already experience that community. You may, however, be among the many artists who do identify with the picture drawn here. If so, you're challenged to determine whether and in what ways to seek out the community of other artists. Do you want to exert yourself in this way and transform yourself and the world a little in the process?

STRATEGIES

To serve both yourself and others in your social interactions, you need a clear understanding of the issues addressed in this chapter. To have a fair chance at acquiring better relationships and a richer community, your first step is self-assessment, followed by personal transformation. The artist who is too envious, arrogant, estranged, or obsessed, who badly lacks self-esteem or who too quickly dismisses other people, must recognize the nature and extent of the problem, create a plan for personal transformation, and practice it in public. Make use of the following strategies to begin accomplishing these goals.

Engage in guided writing work, as described in chapter 13. I've raised many different issues in this chapter. To help you narrow your focus, I've divided the guided writing questions for this chapter into eight sections.

ON GENERAL PERSONALITY ISSUES:

1. What features of my personality most hamper me in social situations?

2. What features of my personality best serve me in social situations?

3. What social situations best fit my personality?

4. What social situations bring out the worst in me?

5. What are the qualities of a person who finds it easy to be in the world? Are any of those qualities attractive to me?

6. If I wanted to make over my personality so that I could function better in the world, where would I start? What would I change first?

ON OUTSIDER ISSUES:

1. How much do I feel like an alien from another planet?

2. Do I feel that people regularly misunderstand me?

3. Do I feel that people regularly fail to truly see or hear me?

4. Do I find it difficult to share in the general enthusiasm of the moment?

5. Do I disagree with or find reprehensible or shallow the values and concerns of most people?

6. If I do in fact experience life as an outsider, and if that issue greatly influences my interactions with others, how do I mean to address the issue? Do I mean to change? Will I try to come in from the cold?

ON ART OBSESSION ISSUES:

1. Am I always working? Do I seem incapable of letting go of my thoughts of and preoccupations with art?

2. Do I feel more obsessed at certain times, for example, when a book deadline or a major performance approaches? When I'm learning new material or puzzling over an especially riveting problem?

3. How do my art obsessions affect my relationships? Are they a full block to intimacy or a mere impediment?

4. How can I release the obsession, even if only for a few hours? What strategies have worked in the past? What new ones might I try?

5. Do I allow myself a real break between projects, a time when I can be present for others and free from thoughts about my art?

6. What do I obsess about with respect to my art? That I haven't done enough of it and should get back to it? Does everything I see make me want to paint; does every conversation I overhear make me want to write a story? Can I sometimes quiet these impulses and learn to relax in the world?

ON DEPENDENCY, AUTHORITY, AND CONTROL ISSUES:

1. On whom do I feel dependent? In what ways are my dependency feelings disempowering and destructive? Can I work to put any such relationship on a new footing — by, for instance, asserting myself more, disputing statements meant to diminish me, and demanding fair treatment?

2. How would I define a dependent relationship? A codependent relationship? An interdependent relationship? Can I generate some guidelines for myself so that I can distinguish one from another?

3. How do I handle being the one in authority?

4. How do I handle having someone exert authority over me? Do I act out? Do I regularly prefer to sabotage my chances rather than compromising or submitting?

5. Would it be in my best interest to dispute authority figures more? Am I too meek, submissive, and ineffectual? Do I hurt my chances by my lack of assertiveness?

6. Am I wise about knowing what I really can and cannot control? Do I understand how little other people's behavior is in my control? How little I can control their reactions to my work? How much or how little artistic control I can hope to retain in my particular art discipline?

ON SELF-ESTEEM ISSUES:

1. Do I come to social interactions feeling small, vulnerable, or unworthy?

2. Do I look confident but not feel confident?

3. Do I have trouble asking for what I want or need because I feel I have nothing to give in return?

4. What would most increase my self-esteem? A certain kind of success? A better acceptance of myself as I am?

5. Do I need to take certain risks so that, by proving to myself that I can handle them, my confidence will grow? Do I need to speak more directly, maintain greater visibility, or actively lobby for my interests with people who can help my career?

6. Do I know any self-confident people? What can I learn from the way they carry themselves in the world?

ON ENVY:

1. How often do I feel envious of other artists? Sometimes? Regularly? Almost all the time?

2. Is envy a significant problem in my life? Even a disabling problem?

3. How might I address the problem of envy? What options are available to me?

4. How much do my envious feelings prevent me from enjoying other artists' work?

5. How much does my envy prevent me from forming friendships with other artists?

6. Do I experience other artists as envious of me? How can I best handle their envy? Can it be addressed openly?

ON SPECIFIC RELATIONSHIPS:

1. How would I characterize my relationship with my parents? What about that relationship would I like to change? How might I effect such a change?

2. How would I characterize my relationship with my siblings? Do they understand my life as an artist? Is it important that they understand it?

3. Have I been troubled regularly by interactions with my teachers? Am I still troubled by such interactions?

4. Was I harmed by any one teacher? What are the present repercussions of that unfortunate relationship?

5. How do I generally react when I find myself in a student-teacher relationship? With wide-eyed enthusiasm? Uncritically? Submissively? Suspiciously? Combatively? Is there any aspect of the way I approach such relationships that I would like to change?

6. Am I able to speak my mind with my teachers? Do I ask for what I need? Do I protect myself from abuse?

7. Am I regularly successful or unsuccessful at maintaining an intimate relationship? If I'm unsuccessful, to what do I attribute the problem?

8. Am I interested in addressing the problems that arise in my intimate relationships?

9. Do I devote enough time, energy, and care to my intimate relationships? Or do I put them second to my art and generally treat them cavalierly?

10. How would I characterize the dynamics of my intimate relationships? Do I understand them? Is it important that I understand them?

11. Do I value my significant other? What about him or her do I value? Do I acknowledge and celebrate what my partner gives me? Does he or she value me and acknowledge my contributions to the relationship?

12. What do I believe are the best ways to cope in social situations? Relaxing more? Ventilating feelings on the spot? Speaking directly? Becoming a more practiced listener? Understanding my feelings better and making informed decisions based on this understanding?

ON COMMUNITY ISSUES:

1. How would I define community, both ideally and realistically?

2. Have I ever experienced a sense of community? When? In what circumstances?

3. Do I need to actively work on community building?

4. What about me do I need to change so that I'll have a better chance of joining meaningfully with others?

5. Is friendship, communal feeling, and/or a sense of shared purpose available to me:

   - with my immediate family?

   - with my extended family?

   - with one or a few close friends?

   - with other women? with other men?

   - in a fraternal organization or cultural club?

   - in my present religious institution? in the one I was born into? in a branch or offshoot of it (one, say, that affirms my worth as a woman or as a gay man)? in one that I have consciously selected?

   - in a 12-step or other self-help group?

   - in an activist organization?

   - in a political organization?

   - with people from my day job?

   - in a recreational group such as a skiing, hiking, bicycling, or gardening club?

Use the following strategies to become someone who, by remaining true to herself, is better equipped to enter into social relationships:

Affirm yourself. You'll experience less anxiety, act out less, and have less reason to repress or displace your feelings if you interact with others in ways that are respectful of your principles and desires and that affirm your right to exist.

Hold yourself in high esteem. Someone may be more talented, better connected, more powerful, or more authoritative than you, but that person is not worthier than you. Do not bow to others, and do not vanish.

Acquire new language habits that support your independence. To questions that have as their subtext a desire to master or control you, reply with "Let's talk about it" or "We'll see," rather than with a meek yes or a defensive no.

Free yourself from the disabling parts of your past. Engage in inner work or individual therapy to gain such freedom. Assert yourself, affirm yourself, and free yourself from the bondage of your character.

Practice habits of independence. Take an all-day vacation. Detach from everyone. Speak clearly, directly, and powerfully in conversation. Take a one-hour sabbatical from your obsessions. Practice walking meditation and cross the city. Act the equal of a powerful figure. Talk face-to-face with a rival. Take it for granted that you will be heard and seen.

Remember that you aren't the equivalent of your sources of income. Engage in inner work so that you won't feel diminished by the fact that you receive a check each month from your parents or that your day job is unsatisfactory. If possible, achieve a measure of financial independence through your art; construct a strong business action plan and implement it. At the same time, make peace with the psychological fallout of your real position in the world, as a laborer in an industry that rewards a few people well and most people not at all.

Manage your anxiety. The agoraphobic is one sort of unfree soul, hidden away at home, and the obsessive-compulsive is another, quelling anxiety through endless, repetitive rituals. The more anxiety rules your life, the more enslaved you'll feel. Begin an anxiety-reduction program that really addresses the sources of fear in your life.

Clean up your act. Begin the process of recovering from your chemical dependencies, addictions, and compulsions. Consider such recovery a crucial piece of your personal definition of independence.

Don't agree unless you mean to. Cultivate social skills, but don't be "nice." Attune yourself to your own needs before you volunteer. Think for yourself. Dispute arguments that rely on the logic of authority.

Watch out for your displays of independence. Check to see if they are angry outbursts, displaced aggression, a lack of impulse control, cover-ups for sadness or envy, or self-sabotaging behaviors of one kind or another.

Honor the independent parts of your personality. Remain skeptical, thoughtful, nonconforming, curious, and passionate. Honor the idea that you are on an important personal journey that no one can deny you.

Use the following strategies to become a more "interdependent" person:

Affirm others. The aloof artist, prideful and busy with his personal pursuits, gains "complete independence" at the expense of his humanity. Practice the art of contact. Collaborate. Make friends. Join the world.

Honor the interdependent parts of your personality. Your ability to empathize with others, your love of art, and your need for an audience are among the many important aspects of your personality that draw you to people and require you to interact socially. To deny the reality of your desire to be with others is self-delusion. Serve this part of your nature by entering into a single strong intimate relationship, by having a few close friends, or by joining with several others in a worthwhile project. Go out of your way to honor the part of you that is dissatisfied with a life of estrangement and isolation.

Learn interpersonal skills and practice them. Holed away writing, painting, or practicing your instrument, you have probably missed many opportunities to practice your interpersonal skills. It's also likely that you never much cared for small talk and the other conventions of social interaction. Improving these skills — learning to actively listen, to negotiate and compromise, to network — will serve you both in your business relationships and in your personal relationships.

Engage in conscious community building with other artists. Enlist other artists in a common cause — in painting a mural, for example. Evolve meaningful rituals and ceremonies for your time together. As feminist author Francine du Plessix Gray explained, rituals are "structured sequences of actions that bring us a heightened sense of our own identity and meaningfulness." The dimming of the lights before the play begins is part of the ritual that makes the stage a sacred-feeling space. In the same way, you can gather artists for a sacred event that you create together.

Don't idealize independence or interdependence. They must coexist. Affirm both your independence and your interdependence. Identify yourself both as an independent artist and as a community member. Bow to the orchestra's will in the afternoon, but play your own music in the evening. Write to make your mark and secure your reputation in the morning, but at lunchtime write letters in a campaign to free political prisoners. Master *and* serve.

12   *Artists* in *Love*

F̲ew people are spared relationship problems. For centuries the divorce
rate was kept artificially low by cultural injunctions against divorce, cultural norms that painted marriage as the only normal option, a vesting of
privilege and control in men, and laws limiting the grounds on which a
divorce could be sought. These artificial constraints forced unhappy couples
to remain together and kept closeted the relationship problems that were
indubitably present.

As individual liberty gained ground, religion lost its iron grip (in some
parts of the world), and women secured rights and power, a time came
when marriages had to stand on their own four feet if they were to survive.
In this country between half and two-thirds of them couldn't. It turns out

that if society doesn't step in to artificially shore them up, the majority of intimate relationships are likely to fail.

There is nothing surprising about this. It is a myth that it is easy for two people to live together in intimate relationship. It is a myth that someone or something is wrong if two people come together but can't remain together. Many relationships fail simply because the people involved do not possess sufficient reasons to share a bed, bodily fluids, and their dreams. This is true across cultures, in straight and gay relationships, and in couples consisting of two nonartists, an artist and a nonartist, or two artists. If an intimate relationship is to stand the test of time, the individuals involved must have not just some reasons for staying together but sufficient reasons. This sets the bar uncomfortably high but, in our age of freedom, exactly where it ought to be set.

For an artist, many special factors enter the equation and make her relationship options both more scant and more complicated. Like anyone, she would love her mate to be her friend, lover, partner, sympathetic ear, intimate other, and soul mate. But she also has some other requirements. She needs her mate to provide her with real freedom, the freedom to have her own ideas, to make artistic and human mistakes and messes, and to spend vast quantities of time in solitude.

She also needs her mate to appreciate her life project as an artist, that her commitment to the creative life is not "one of the things she is" but an imperative as real as breathing. Likewise, she needs her mate to put up with her inevitably rich and roiling inner life, which manifests itself as dreams, nightmares, a sudden need for Paris, a sudden desire to throw over painting for sculpture, and so on. To be sure, she may settle for a mate who does not meet these criteria — but if she does she will feel that she is settling.

She is also likely to have special survival needs because of the way our culture is constituted. If she could paint and pay her bills, she would not need a mate with a salary. Because so few artists in any of the disciplines can earn anything like a middle-class income, because typically there are only the extremes of poverty and celebrity, she is likely to be poor and to need to make calculations about how she might survive. One path, not necessarily held consciously but nevertheless held, is to look for someone who, rather than choosing to manifest his creative potential, has gone into accounting.

An artist knows that she is not entering a relationship of that sort with perfectly clean hands. By the same token, she may truly believe that there are enough good reasons in play to counterbalance her calculated decision (if she is aware of the calculation). The gal or fellow in question may be sweet, decent, charmed by the artist's life, happy to provide, genuinely encouraging, and so on. Still, an artist's choice to opt for this kind of security may well come back to haunt her.

Conversely, an artist may say to herself, "I will not choose a boring mate just because I could then get to paint" and instead choose her mate based on sympathetic resonances, resonances that will likely be found in the being and body of a similarly impoverished artist. Then the endless dramas and negotiations can't help but begin: who will work the day job, who has the better prospects and is more entitled to a full shot at an art career, who will sacrifice for the other, who will bite the bullet and go into the world when times are hard (which will be often), and so on.

The upshot of these difficult realities is that many artists find themselves spending long periods of time alone, since their needs are not that easily met by those they encounter. Many end up cycling through brief relationships, since their needs for intimacy collide with the fact that insufficient reasons exist for remaining with this or that partner. Others find themselves in distant relationships whose distance is a function of the basic incompatibility of the partners. Still others wind up in dramatic relationships, in which each partner feels unjustly treated and makes that dissatisfaction known. And a great many sink into depressed relationships, in which both partners feel emotionally and existentially under the weather.

THE MORE SUITABLE MATCH?

Is an artist more likely to make a good match with an artist or with a nonartist? I think it is fair to say that there is no way to answer this question in the abstract. It depends on the two people involved. Some artist couples are torn apart and ultimately defeated by rivalry and competition. Others aren't. Some artist/nonartist couples are defeated by the artist's sense that her mate doesn't understand her. In other artist/nonartist couples, no such problem exists. So we must let go of the idea that we can choose between one or the other and conclude, "It depends."

Nevertheless, when two artists are in intimate relationship certain difficulties frequently arise. For example, Jennifer, a painter, and Mark, a musician, came in to see me for couples' counseling (in the days before I began creativity coaching). Each felt blocked and daunted and blamed the other for not providing enough financial and emotional support. They were running through their savings and were fighting about who should go to work. Mark argued that the university administrative job Jennifer could easily land would hardly tax her. Jennifer countered that Mark's computer skills make him much more marketable and that he would bring in considerably more money. So they fought.

They fought continually. They argued about who should do the shopping, who should do the cooking, who should do the cleaning. They argued about everything with a time cost. When they came to see me, their main grievance was that neither of them was willing to make time to fix the broken window in their apartment. Jennifer wasn't painting (which he rather liked to rub in), so she should do it. Mark wasn't composing (which she rather liked to rub in), so he should do it. The matter of who should repair the broken window, standing in for their many elephant-sized underlying issues, looked about to do them in.

At about the same time I counseled two married actors. Both were reasonably successful in San Francisco theater, which meant that they both had to work day jobs to supplement their meager acting incomes. They framed their current problem as "loyalty issues." Jeremy felt that Alicia did not respect him as an actor. His proof was that whenever a role came up for a leading man, an actor/singer, or required a dialect, she would remind him of his hawk nose, his propensity to sing flat, and the difficulties he once experienced trying to play an Irishman. She, in turn, complained that he never came to see her perform, got on her about her weight, and dismissed the idea of moving to Los Angeles or New York.

Like Jennifer and Mark, Jeremy and Alicia lived in a state of constant tension that was in part caused by the demands of the art life they had chosen, in part by the constant bruising of their egos at the hands of the world and of each other, and in part by their feelings of envy, competitiveness, and rivalry. Had one half of either of these two couples become successful, you could lay odds that the couple's problems would only worsen; individual success was not going to be the answer. And had one of them made the decision to "sacrifice everything" for the other and, with gritted teeth and clenched jaw, worked full-time to support the other's art career, you could lay equal odds that the relationship would ultimately founder on that frustrated partner's misery.

Ronda's situation was different. She hadn't married an artist, she'd married a former artist (or, more accurately, a failed artist). Harry had once been quite a good amateur musician. But he had put his guitar away and opened a shoe repair shop in San Francisco. Ronda worked in the shop with Harry, dealing with customers and keeping the books. Their situation struck her as absurd and humiliating, but it did allow her to afford a painting studio and to get to the studio several days a week.

Ronda's main complaint was that Harry was always sabotaging her. He would fall over himself to seem helpful, pledging to pick her up from the airport when she got back from New York or run her slides over to the post office so they'd get to a certain juried show on time. Then he would fail to show up at the airport or to get her slides to the post office. His excuses were always perfect. He hadn't shown at the airport because he'd had a headache, which had caused him to take some medicine, which had made him drowsy, so he'd fallen into such a heavy, drug-induced sleep that even the alarm, which he'd remembered to set, hadn't awakened him. As to the slides, well, their cat had gotten sick, so he'd had to rush it to the vet, and in his anxiety he'd picked up the wrong package.

Harry's passive-aggressive behavior was no doubt connected to his failure as an artist; possibly the worst choice an artist can make in a life partner is a failed artist who refuses to acknowledge his or her anger and disappointment. Be that as it may, it is certainly true that an artist is inclined to mate with someone who has at least a little artistic sensibility, existential intelligence, and understanding of the artist's world. Complications instantly arise because that person will be hungry, driven, and complicated in his own right.

Meredith, a young painter, nicely captures something of this dynamic:

I'm afraid of commitment because I know myself and know that I have a powerful need for change. Luckily my current partner, who lives across the globe, feels exactly the same way. He is an artist who very much needs and loves his own space and independence. He, too, wants to know who he is and what his life would be like without a partner's influence. We love being together when we're together, and I feel lucky to have someone who is so like me and who understands my needs.

I've noticed, though, that we never seem to be creative at the same time. He seems to be less inspired to do his work when he is with me. I feel like he is losing out on more when he is with me, no matter how much I encourage and support him.

Still, I have this recurring daydream where we create heaps of artwork together and help each other to promote our work. I just wonder if that's a realistic scenario for us. I know my boyfriend loves to feel independent, as do I, but I would love one day to feel more like part of a team rather than on my own with everything.

Different challenges arise in artist/nonartist relationships. The artist, who may not bring in much money, is likely to feel dependent on the nonartist, disempowered because of that financial dependence, and guilty about her inability (and perhaps unwillingness) to contribute to the communal pool. She may have a hard time being taken seriously by the nonartist because, for example, her work requires that she stare into space and her mate, seeing her staring, presumes that she isn't busy. And she may consider her partner dull and his values too materialistic and conventional. Here is how one writer, Marilyn, described her experience of dating nonartists:

I met John through business. He'd been attracted to me for years; he used to say that I was the most fascinating woman he'd ever met. Now that we're involved, he no longer says that I'm fascinating. For the time and effort I put into my writing I have little to show, which he cannot help but see. I have a tendency to assign my own negative self-talk to him, and then I resent it when he doesn't say or do anything to reassure me that he doesn't feel that way.

I resent his lumpish inability to intuit when I need that just-perfect two-word touch that I can deliver when he needs it. I feel that I bring all the emotional intensity to our relationship. It seems like he just shows up and feeds at the trough. He doesn't have any big life questions he's studying. He's not attempting to raise his consciousness; he thinks he's okay just the way he is. That's the basic issue. Artists are striving for something; nonartists buy things.

Sarah, a painter, presents a contrasting view:

> It seems to me that relationships often work well when the partners have very different personalities — each ends up carrying the load in the areas of her or his strengths. I have always had relationships with women who have artistic sensibilities but have not chosen to pursue art to any degree. The pluses for me have been that my partners have always appreciated and admired my work, and that's a real ego boost and often a stimulus to keep going.
>
> I have gotten some excellent and helpful criticism from my current partner, too, and I am very open to that. I imagine that some artists would find that a distinct minus, but it works for me because my partner is not my competitor or my rival. If the nonartist partner is confident of her own gifts, skills, and talents, and if the artist appreciates and values them, things can be worked out. Always, communication is the key to making it work.

Every artist's intimate relationship, whether with another artist or with a nonartist, is a unique coming together of two distinct people. The relationship will succeed not because one of them is or isn't a self-identified artist but because the two of them are friends, mature enough to relate, genuinely on each other's side, and sympathetic and lively. It doesn't matter if your mate paints, and it doesn't matter if he doesn't paint; it only matters that the two of you have good reasons for sharing a bed and a life.

TWENTY BUILDING BLOCKS

The prevailing cultural myth about relationships, a myth only about a thousand years old but ubiquitous and rarely challenged, is that each of us should meet someone to settle down with permanently and monogamously. Together we are to raise a family and live in a prescribed way, ideally on a piece of land and in a house we own, earning a living through the sanctioned work that we do, maintaining ties with and being supported by family and a religious institution, and retaining a modest-sized individuality but in most matters obeying and conforming for the sake of social harmony.

This prevailing myth has it that the family is the basic unit of social currency and that permanent dyadic relationships are not only the best and most natural life arrangements but the only ones that are not suspect. Even feminism, our skyrocketing divorce rate, and other countermyth realities like single-parent families and intentionally childless couples have done little to deconstruct the myth of marriage and family that has settled in since the troubadours began touting romantic love in the eleventh century.

Artists, however, male and female alike, have always balked a little (or a lot) at this mythology. Concerned about their individual destinies, wanting to chart a course for themselves based on insistent internal demands and the felt need to make meaning, wanting to speak and be heard, feeling different from (and alienated from) those around them, and knowing that truth telling, solitude, and nonconformity possess real value, they have put a priority on actualizing their potential and plotting a personal course rather than on playing out a predetermined role in the social game. For these reasons artists have typically made less-than-stellar marriage and family material (with, of course, many exceptions); and they have suffered for this and made others suffer in turn.

Since artists tend to see through the pretty picture of romantic love and perfect relating as drawn by their culture and since they know that a great many relationships are long-lasting only because both partners have lowered their expectations or lost the wherewithal to leave, they need to come up with their own reasons for relating. Given that an artist's goal is not to make a good marriage and settle down but rather to be an artist, given that she may well hold the idea of marriage-and-family as compromising, and given that she sees herself as a loner navigating an unknown personal journey — given, in short, that she starts out with many potent reasons for not valuing relating — it is only if and when potent reasons to relate present themselves that relating begins to make sense.

What, in fact, is required of two people, when one or both of them is an artist, if the relationship is to succeed? Such a relationship needs to be built on the following twenty building blocks:

1. *Care of each other's solitude.* It must be all right and more than all right for each partner to spend significant time pursuing his or her own activities and inner life.

2. *Maintenance of emotional security.* Each partner is not only aware of the other's feelings but takes them into account and actively works to help his or her partner feel good.

3. *Maintenance of meaning.* Partners understand that meaning crises will arise and that, to be met, they may sometimes necessitate profound changes, such as in career, in art discipline, in subject matter, in geographic location, and so on.

4. *Maintenance of passion.* Partners will not let themselves become too busy for love, too tired for love, or too disinterested in love, unless they want to participate in an ice-cold relationship.

5. *Creation of at least occasional happiness.* Partners will actually ask questions of each other like, "What would make us happy?" and "What would make you happy?" and make requests, saying, "This would make me happy."

6. *A gentle demanding of discipline from oneself and one's partner.* Each partner will strive to work in a productive, undramatic, regular way, with few creative tantrums and few excuses about not being inspired or in the mood.

7. *A gentle exchanging of truths.* When something must be said, it will get said carefully, thoughtfully, and compassionately — and also clearly and directly.

8. *Acceptance of the limits of human beings and the facts of existence.* Each partner will expect a lot from himself and his partner while at the same time recognizing and accepting that floods, failures of nerve, and pratfalls do happen.

9. *A minimizing of one's own unwanted qualities.* Each partner will bravely look in the mirror, take a fearless personal inventory, and

identify and then change those aspects of personality that harm the relationship.

10. *Support of each other's careers.* Each person in the partnership is likely to have a career and hence will have career demands that need to be respected and negotiated.

11. *Maintenance of friendship.* Nothing is more crucial to the viability of an intimate relationship than that the partners be friends — and friendly.

12. *A monitoring of moods in oneself and one's partner.* Both partners will sometimes feel blue, and depression will likely prove an uninvited but persistent houseguest, one that must be regularly acknowledged and just as regularly banished.

13. *An acceptance of difficulties.* Both partners will understand that difficulties arise and that action must be taken to deal with them.

14. *Shared principles and values.* Both partners strive to build on their shared principles and deal calmly, intelligently, and compassionately with their differences.

15. *Management of one's own journey.* Each partner has the job of taking responsibility for his or her life, for setting goals, for making choices and taking action, and for proceeding as a responsible adult.

16. *Careful communicating.* Both partners will want to speak carefully and clearly about the large and small relationship matters that endlessly arise.

17. *A bringing of artfulness to the partnership.* A creative person can bless her relationship by bringing the same qualities to it that she brings to her art, qualities as diverse as whimsy, imagination, resilience, and meticulousness.

18. *Maintenance of a present orientation.* Each partner lets go of past grievances, even in the face of repeat offenses, not to engage in wishful thinking or denial but to deal with issues in their specific and current reality.

19. *Fair treatment.* Fairness in everything — the honoring of agreements, the equitable distribution of resources, the respect shown in word and deed — is the glue that holds together a healthy relationship.

20. *The creation of a supportive relationship.* Even if two people find it easy to relate, even if both are "low maintenance," they will still have to invest real time in and attention to what they have created together, an edifice that is certain to need the occasional repainting and new roof.

This is not to say that an artist can't live alone and thrive. Of course he can. Rather, it is to say that when an artist does decide to be in an intimate relationship, there will be work for each partner to do if they are to build a relationship that serves them. Imagine training to compete as an ice skating pair. Each partner has individual work to do in order to become fit, to learn moves, and so on. But the pair must also function beautifully together. Each artist has his own work to do to make him fit for relationships; but ultimately it takes two serious partners to make a partnership work.

PARTNERS AND PARTISANS

What does a relationship erected on these building blocks look like? Following are two reports, the first from Nancy, a painter:

> I have been a "starving" artist for forty years and have been supported by my advertising-writer husband. Nine months ago he was laid off, and we are now both "starving creatives." We are scrambling to figure out who will be paying the bills, and how. For the last two and half years I have been doing portraits and as a result have gotten a lot of publicity. My portrait business is increasing, but I am nowhere near being able to support anyone.
>
> It is hard to actively pursue something really artistic and still meet the demands for food. It is a constant balancing act between what we need to survive and what we need to grow and be happy. I can't imagine my life without art; and my husband and I made many sacrifices in order for me to be at home to raise our family

and to still have the time to pursue art. It takes a lot of work, but it is well worth it and I am sure that we will figure out this time in our lives as well.

Diane, also a painter, explained her situation:

Most of us know that we want to live the lifestyle of an artist, but finding the right person to share that way of life can be a problem. Speaking for myself, I met and married a fellow artist twenty-five years ago. What has worked for us is our focus on the creative process and the respect we both have for one another. We have balanced our life by working full-time nonart jobs, painting, selling, traveling yearly to Spain, and sharing the same studio space.

Times have been rough recently. John lost his job of twenty-five years and was out of work for two years. There were times he did not want to paint because his days were spent looking for work, and he had to deal with interviews, rejections, and anxiety. After his unemployment benefits ran out, I was the sole source of income keeping us afloat. Through it all we continued to support one another with faith, the realization that nothing stays the same in life, and the belief that things do work out. We are each other's best friends and lovers, and that's the way it's been for twenty-five years. Our focus has always been on our art and on making sure that nothing comes between what we have together.

That's the secret: that nothing is allowed to come between the two of you. Many things will try: your moods, his moods, money problems, differences of opinion, failures of nerve, small betrayals, bad habits. Real partners can weather these trials because they have made the decision to go it together.

This "being in it together" is different from love, different from respect, different from empathy, different from caring, different from compassion, different from commitment. It is a distinct quality, that of honoring an agreement to take the other person's side. You side with that one person above all others. The lovemaking, the conversations, the like-mindedness, the mutual love of art are frosting on a cake that will go stale unless each partner puts the other ahead of the rest of humanity.

You don't go out with your buddies if your wife needs you. You don't go out shopping if your husband needs you. You don't go back to the studio if your wife asks you to hold her hand. You don't visit your sister for the weekend if your husband needs cheering up. Each day you reckon what, if anything, your partner needs. Maybe it is the freedom to create. Maybe it is a bit of truth telling. Maybe it is dinner out. In turn, you tell him what you need, secure in the knowledge that he will listen and do his best to respond.

Are you willing to be your partner's real partner? Are you willing to be loyal and faithful? When you hear of an opportunity for your wife to show her art, do you make careful note of it and report it to her at dinner? When your friends take a few sarcastic potshots at your husband's latest enthusiasm, do you refuse to laugh along? Do you think of her first? Do you think of him first? If you don't, you haven't obeyed a good relationship's first commandment.

There is only one marriage vow: you are now the most important person in my life. When that changes, when the person you sleep with is not the most important person in your life, when he matters but not really that much more than the fellow with whom you share studio space, an intimate partnership has become just two individuals sharing a bathroom. No legal document can create such a partnership; no amount of love can guarantee such a partnership. It happens in a simple but altogether rare way: when two people shake hands and agree to become loyal partisans.

The ultimate goal for an artist and his or her partner is the creation by two ever-evolving people of a bastion of safety and sanity in a dangerous world, the creation of a close-knit unit in which each partner protects, supports, and enlivens the other, in which each respects the other's efforts and has his or her efforts respected in turn. This fine relating eludes most artists — indeed, most human beings — but it remains the prize on which we want to keep our eye.

STRATEGIES

Spend some time thinking about each of the twenty building blocks described above, and begin to understand what each one means and what each one requires, both of you and of your partner.

The Artist's World

No matter how hard you try to keep the world at a distance, you remain always in the world — there is just no escaping it. The world is your ground and your context, if for no other reason than because out in the world is where you find your audience. What, then, is your place as an artist in the world? The following exercises offer you the chance to wrestle with this question.

EXERCISE 1. AUDIENCE

Virginia Woolf wrote, "No audience. No echo. That's part of one's death." How will you bridge the gap that exists between you and your potential audience?

Insofar as art-making is a meditation or a process of self-actualization, an artist needs no audience. She can practice her instrument and love the music she makes in the practice room, she can learn about the character she is playing as she studies the text, she can meditate as she throws a pot on the wheel. All this she does happily in the absence of an audience.

But art-making is more than a meditation or an act of self-realization. It is also one of the most important ways we have of communicating what's on our minds and what's in our hearts. It is as much a potent means of making contact with others as it is a personal meditation. You therefore want and need an audience. As the pianist Eugene Istomin put it, "In order to function, I need a public. We all need it. And there is none of us who is free of that anxiety." Given that reality, how will you find your way to that audience? To begin with, tease out the meaning and implications of the following statements:

1. There are too many artists.

2. Most people are not really interested in art.

3. The main requirement of the marketplace is that you pander and compromise.

4. What I have to offer is not easily understood.

5. I have high standards.

6. I am not properly connected and doubt that I can get connected.

7. I have trouble communicating why someone should be interested in my work.

8. I don't play games.

9. I haven't the personality of a seller.

10. Nothing much in my genre is currently wanted.

11. The audience for the work I do is historically very small.

12. I put people off.

13. Something in my personality balks at making connections.

14. Nobody hears or sees me.

EXERCISE 2. DYNAMICS WITH AUDIENCE

The dynamics between artist and audience are often exceedingly complex. Some of these dynamics may encourage you to seek an audience, and some may encourage you to avoid one. You may, for instance, find it strange and unsettling that your audience knows you, while you know nothing about them. Or you may doubt that your audience really understands you, which causes you to sneer at their applause. Does something in the artist-audience dynamic prevent you from seeking an audience?

Comment on any of the following that apply to you, and outline how you might meet these challenges.

I may be avoiding acquiring an audience because:

1. I suffer from performance anxiety.

2. I'm shy.

3. I refuse to be criticized or judged.

4. I am waiting to perfect my work.

5. I doubt that I'll be understood.

6. I doubt my talent.

7. I don't know what to say to people when they congratulate me or want to talk about my work.

8. I don't much like people.

9. I hate to appear as if I'm hawking my work.

10. I'm uncomfortable in the spotlight.

EXERCISE 3. ART BUDDY

A popular concept among groundbreaking visual artists at the turn of the twentieth century was the idea of acquiring an "audience of one." By this they meant that, insofar as their art was too new, different, and disturbing to be liked by the masses, and insofar as they could not hope to obtain a mass audience, they would at least try to find one person — literally a single person, and often another working artist — who understood their work and would mirror them. You might also think of this person as your "art buddy." What qualities would you want your ideal "audience of one" or "art buddy" to manifest?

My art buddy should:

1. Respect my work.

2. Speak truthfully, but in a context of respect and love.

3. Have an eye for both the commercial and the artistic.

4. Share my worldview.

5. Extol my virtues to others.

6. Genuinely believe that I will succeed.

7. Offer me detailed analysis and concrete suggestions.

8. Call me great.

9. Respect me, even when my work fizzles.

10. Ask for something in return, so that I can express my gratitude by helping him or her.

EXERCISE 4. THIS TIME, THIS PLACE

Artists are often romantic daydreamers and ardent lovers of the art of other times and places. But the potential dangers of this orientation — or disorientation — are many. Artists so oriented may grow unnecessarily alienated from their own time and place. They may miss connecting with their own families, with their intimate others, and with their children. They may fail to understand their own milieu, losing the chance to contribute to or receive from it anything worthwhile.

Comment on any of the following statements that resonate for you either because they don't hold true for you or because they do:

1. I understand what it means to be an artist today.

2. The times are changing so rapidly that it's impossible to keep up.

3. It is better to be rooted in tradition than to be wedded to the present moment.

4. I am less interested in the here and now than in perennial matters.

5. These are desperate times, and I prefer to ignore them.

6. I understand what is required of today's avant-garde artist.

7. I prefer to live in my mind, where I am independent of this time and place.

8. I am unaffected by the goings-on of the world.

9. I would like to comment on or connect with the world I find myself in, if only I understood it.

10. Something in my past or in my personality prevents me from fully living in the present.

11. Neither my art nor my art business requires that I understand my time and place.

12. Great work was done in the past, but great work is not permitted in today's cultural climate.

13. People who are fully informed about current matters are faddish and superficial.

14. I respect no one working in my art discipline today.

15. I do not really identify myself as a contemporary American.

16. My artistic and cultural roots run deep into distant times and other places.

17. I am alienated from this time and place.

18. I am well oriented to this time and place.

19. It is to my advantage to become better oriented to this time and place.

20. If I wanted to feel better oriented to this time and place, I would know how to go about doing that.

EXERCISE 5. ESCAPING *INTO* THE WORLD

Carve out some time from your schedule, and run away to art. A creative escape is like getting away for a romantic weekend with your lover — except in this case your lover is your creative nature. Fall back in love with the visual world, with the art of others, with music, with poetry, with silence. If you can manage it, try to pencil in one day every few weeks and escape into the world to reignite your passion.

Here are a few creative escape ideas:

- Put aside your current project and start on an alternate one by working on it for a weekend in the country. Choose something that's a stretch, a new direction, or that's been percolating, or wait until you get into the country and let the landscape inspire you.

- Sign up for a one-day workshop on a subject that fascinates you — monoprinting, beading, mask making — that you haven't managed to make time for yet. Or, better yet, create your own workshop and learn a new technique through trial-and-error experimentation.

- Go to a bookstore, pull out all the books on an artist you love or an artist you would like to get to know, take them to a table in the bookstore café, and visit with that artist for three hours over coffee and some almond biscotti.

- Mark, a creativity coach and painter, explained, "I plan a play weekend with a friend once or twice a year. We do a sleepover, get out our art materials, and just play for the sheer joy of creating." Instead of going on a budget-busting retreat five thousand miles away, why not create your own retreat by inviting a few friends to spend a weekend falling back in love with art? Get out your day planner right now and pencil in your next creative escape.

EXERCISE 6. PAYING ATTENTION TO RELATING

Think through what sorts of issues are likely to arise when you relate. Let's say, for example, that you are a classical musician. What sorts of issues might arise in the following situations? (I'll put a few hints in parentheses.)

1. If the relationship is with someone who plays the same instrument that you play. (Issues that can arise include envious feelings, competitive feelings, and issues of pseudo-intimacy, that is, the two of you feeling close just because you both happen to be violinists.)

2. If the relationship is with someone who plays a different instrument from the one you play. (Issues that can arise include feelings of superiority, if you play the "sexier" instrument, or feelings of inferiority, if he or she plays the "sexier" instrument.)

3. If the relationship is with your violin teacher. (Issues that can arise include the pressure to please, boundary issues when your teacher gets too close, and depression resulting from criticism or disapproval.)

4. If the relationship is with your conservatory teacher. (Issues that can arise include issues of boredom and alienation if the teacher is treating the students inappropriately as beginners, feelings of frustration if the teacher isn't being clear, and feelings of fear and diminished self-esteem if the teacher is harsh, critical, and demanding.)

5. If the relationship is with the conductor. (Issues that can arise include a loss of self-esteem if criticized, as well as authority issues that can play out as fearful — and therefore mechanical — playing or as acting-out behaviors like making mistakes on purposes.)

6. If the relationship is with a virtuoso in the field. (Issues that can arise include envy and rivalry and an exaggerated shyness or heightened arrogance in the star's presence.)

7. If the relationship is with your parents. (Issues that can arise include their mistrust of your career path should your playing not afford you a decent living, and ongoing dependency, autonomy, and separation issues should you still be turning to them for a helping hand.)

8. If the relationship is with a nonmusician. (Issues that can arise include feeling that the other person doesn't appreciate the sheer amount of work involved in mastering an instrument or the intense challenge of performing at a high — or even just an acceptable — level.)

9. If the relationship is with a fan. (Issues that can arise include the unconscious desire to exploit adulation and the sense of alienation that arises when someone acts like he knows you — and feels like he owns you — simply because he has heard you play.)

10. If the relationship is with a marketplace player such as a booking agent. (Issues that can arise include the kind of anxiety that often

surfaces when we deal with people who hold our future in their hands, as well as authority and dependency issues that play out as a prideful stubbornness or a fearful squeamishness.)

EXERCISE 7. THE ARTIST'S TEN COMMANDMENTS

Reflect on these commandments as a way to integrate your thoughts about your personality, the creative work that you do, and your environment:

1. Look in the Mirror
2. Look out the Window
3. Do the Work
4. See the Synergies
5. Explore Your Anxieties
6. Become a Master Juggler
7. Practice Existential Magic
8. Relate
9. Get a Life
10. Artfully Adapt

Let's take a closer look at these.

Look in the Mirror. That is, reflect on the question, "Who am I?" The only person who can put the puzzling pieces of your personality together is you. The unexamined life may as a rule not be worth living, but for an artist not to examine her life is both foolhardy and dangerous. You are the one full of contradictory impulses and on a roller-coaster ride in the arts, and you are the one who must fathom your own being.

Look out the Window. You may be leading an isolated, introverted life, and this way of living may be a personality fit for you and your preferred mode of being. But there are obvious negative consequences of this insularity. Therefore it is your job to look out the window: to see the world, to learn as much about it as you can, and ultimately to connect with it in meaningful ways.

Do the Work. It is your job as an artist to wrestle with issues of blockage and procrastination, to manifest your creativity and your talent, to maintain the necessary motivation to look for and to do the work, to accomplish the work professionally when you obtain it, and to work both at your art and at the business of art. These are challenges that will confront you every day for as long as you remain an artist.

See the Synergies. The first three commandments involve your personality, the world you live in, and your work. These three aspects of your life are dynamically interconnected. When you audition, for instance, you bring your personality, your strengths and weaknesses, and your understanding (or lack of understanding) of the situation with you just as certainly as you bring your voice and your repertoire. Such moments, then, are your very best learning experiences, and it is your job to make use of them.

Explore Your Anxieties. Anxieties plague artists, and it is vital that you explore the role anxiety plays in your life. Anxiety may be preventing you from learning difficult new repertoire, from trying your hand at painting in a new idiom, from entering competitions, from talking to agents, from doing your artwork or taking care of your art business. Assess your anxieties, become friendly and familiar with them, and begin to manage them.

Become a Master Juggler. It's the rare person in the arts who doesn't pursue many paths of employment simultaneously, who isn't pushed and pulled in a dozen different directions every day of the week. You may dream of quiet and simplicity, but you're more likely to find yourself confronted by noise and complexity. The ability to juggle — to manage time, to manage commitments, to be organized, to move fluidly from task to task — is vital for an artist to master.

Practice Existential Magic. Practice the art of creating new meaning in your life, of investing meaning in new ideas and projects and of divesting meaning from ideas and projects that are no longer workable. Perhaps you've changed in the past decade or year. Have you really looked at your beliefs, your principles, your career, your circumstances lately? Remember that meanings change over time, and it's crucial to assess current situations based on your most current thinking.

Relate. Busy mastering your craft and pursuing a career in art, working a day job, determined not to be sidetracked by the agenda of others, criticized and rejected in the marketplace, you may grow wary of people and put relationships on the back burner. But as difficult as it can be for an artist to form and maintain relationships, relating with your fellow human beings — with a single intimate other, with friends, with an art buddy, with other people in the arts — remains a vitally important component of your life.

Get a Life. While you need to work hard in order to have a career, and while it's true you may obsess about your art or your career so much that you allow little else any mind space, it's still crucially important that you maintain a rich life unrelated to art. This rich life might include relationships, a meaningful second career, social activism, or a spiritual practice, and it should also include the ability to take time-outs, to relax, to enjoy, to visit with friends, to breathe. Whatever its specific ingredients, such a parallel life is necessary for mental health.

Artfully Adapt. The workable decisions and adaptive lifestyle of one artist may not be workable or adaptive for you. You will be faced with the bewildering complexities of the world, your own personality, and the difficulty of the work you undertake. No simple recipe is available to you. You must artfully adapt.

PART

4

Strategies and *Tactics*

13 Self-Awareness through Guided Writing

Only rarely do any of us determine to actively and consciously assess our current situation and guide ourselves down new pathways. Even if it dawns on us that it might be possible to systematically consult ourselves, we have little idea how to begin. How, after all, does a person consult herself? Isn't the idea something of a paradox? If we know what changes to make, why not simply make them? If we don't know what changes to make, how can we guide ourselves in the right direction?

A young man, a blocked writer, came to me for an initial coaching session. He wore a wry smile, which grew more rueful as the session progressed. Finally I commented on the smile. The writer replied, "Well, I feel like I'm getting exactly what I expected to get. I'm getting good advice. But I'm convinced that coming here was a mistake. I don't know what I need to start writing, but I know that I have to figure it out. The answer is figuring it out *for myself.*"

Still, even though he knew that he was his only true guide, he remained baffled. How was he to proceed? One way might have been by using focused, intentional writing. By using self-guided writing, writing that engages and demands more of the self than journaling does, you will be able to pinpoint the challenges that confront you — in your personality, with your art, and in the world — and to head yourself down new paths of your choosing. At the same time, the maintenance of a regular and systematic writing practice encourages you to be more disciplined, creative, and energetic, qualities that serve you as an artist even if your art is other than writing.

What is self-guided writing? It is writing that makes use of what Alan Watts describes in *The Way of Zen*, the "very genius of the human mind that it can, as it were, stand aside from life and reflect upon it, that it can be aware of its own existence, that it can criticize its own processes." Engaged in a long-term process of discovery, you ask yourself about your past, present, and future. You ask questions of yourself, and you endeavor to answer them. You make use of writing exercises of your own device that probe your experiences. You create new exercises to probe further. You examine pertinent aspects of your personality, relationships, and life circumstances.

As writer R. V. Cassill explained, "Writing is a way of coming to terms with the world and with oneself." The regular practice of guided writing helps you shape your journey. First, of course, the practice must be learned, just as the principles of meditation must be. But once learned, it becomes your own.

Use the following fifteen-point program on a regular basis — even a daily basis — as your primary self-help tool for maintaining lifelong creativity.

A FIFTEEN-POINT
GUIDED WRITING PLAN OF ACTION

1. Create a writing environment.
2. Begin to silence negative self-talk.

3. Use guided imagery.

4. Create a writing bubble.

5. Raise your level of tolerance for frustration.

6. Uncover problems and challenges by writing.

7. Narrow your focus.

8. Ask creative questions.

9. Write responses.

10. Read creatively.

11. Uncover tactics and solutions

12. Make a plan.

13. Add contingencies to the plan.

14. Evaluate the results.

15. Create new plans of action.

Let's examine each of these points in turn.

Create a Writing Environment

The best environment in which to begin your daily guided writing practice is one in which you can actually write. It need not be a quiet place, unless you require a quiet place to write. It need not be an organized space, unless you require an organized space to write. It should, however, be a place where you can channel energy and direct it from your deepest self to the paper or computer screen. You should be able to experience the sensation of being utterly lost in the present, absorbed, connected to your thoughts and feelings. That is the test. If you happen to choose an unlikely spot — an airport lounge, a hospital cafeteria, the corner of your yard next to the prickly pear cactus — and find you can write there, then that is a sacred spot, one of your writing haunts.

Still, in the beginning, such odd spots may fail to serve you. One will be too windy, another too noisy, another too public. In each, something will distract you. Of course, the problem will be only partly environmental.

It may involve your newness at writing and your desire to avoid writing. In a way, you can't know yet what your ideal writing environment will look like. So, in lieu of knowing, it's sensible to construct an environment that gives you the best chance of succeeding. Such an environment should provide sufficient quiet and privacy. You will have to bring the time and the courage.

Begin to Silence Negative Self-Talk

Even before you begin your guided writing program, thoughts may occur to you that drain meaning from the enterprise of looking carefully at your life. Why, you wonder, are you trying out this writing program anyway? Where will you find the time for it? Can it possibly amount to anything? Our negative self-talk tends to severely limit us and derail our efforts. These self-denigrating or merely distracting thoughts are terribly familiar swimmers in our stream of consciousness, doubly hard to combat because we rarely take real notice of them.

As it is said in the Bhagavad Gita, "You are your own friend, and you are your own enemy." You can be a better friend to yourself if you deal with the part of you that is functionally your enemy, the part that generates negative self-talk. These negative, self-deprecating statements may arise from anxiety, guilt, self-rejection, or a hundred other sources. Each such statement is distracting and demoralizing and needs to be silenced. Your first job is to notice what self-limiting, self-rejecting thoughts are present in your consciousness. Here are ten of the most common ones:

1. I'm so far behind, I can't catch up.

2. I write too poorly. My sentences stink.

3. I have so little time, I might as well not start.

4. I've always censored myself, and I need to censor myself now.

5. If I put down the truth, it will be an indictment of myself.

6. Criticism hurts, and I don't want to criticize myself.

7. Even though I'm the subject, I still don't know what to write, and that's humiliating.

8. I feel defeated.

9. My writing never satisfies me.

10. Why write? Nobody gives a damn about my struggles, myself included.

Some of these demon self-statements may be true. It may be true, for instance, that you censor yourself or that your grammar is shoddy. It may be true that self-criticism will hurt. Still, you must find ways of defusing these negative thoughts and self-indicting labels. Practice dismissing these negative self-statements using the following techniques:

- Learn not to overgeneralize. Don't translate ten minutes of weak writing into "I'll never be able to write."

- Learn not to catastrophize. Don't magnify your discomfort as you sit with pen poised by saying, "I've never felt this bad in my whole life."

- Don't predict your failure. Don't say, "That sausage sandwich I ate for lunch is bound to prevent me from writing this afternoon."

Use Guided Imagery

Guided imagery (also called guided visualization) is a technique using verbal cues to encourage you to create a particular imagined, interior landscape. For example, you might imagine yourself in the office of an esteemed director or in the waiting room of your dentist. Guided imagery helps you practice new assertive behaviors with the director or new stress-reduction techniques while awaiting a root canal. Or you might lead yourself back into childhood to re-experience some painful or joyful moment — in the first case to grieve or to rage, in the second to bring to the present moment a talisman of that past happiness.

A cancer patient might use guided imagery to picture an interior battle being waged between healthy cells and cancerous cells, leading to defeat of the cancer. You might picture yourself in a tranquil spot, select an object from that spot, and practice returning to that state of tranquility by retrieving that object from memory. There are many uses for guided visualizations;

the following one is designed to help you commit to beginning a guided writing practice.

VISUALIZATION: *Committing to Guided Writing*

Relax by seating yourself comfortably in a quiet environment. Close your eyes, and go deep inside yourself. Breathe easily and deeply — in and out, in and out. Maintain the sort of awareness you might keep on a journey. When you feel ready, go back, far back, thousands of years back, to the dawn of humankind.

Notice that every generation had to rear children in order for you to be here today. See those generations, those parents and children, in all parts of the world, speaking their different languages. Feel life in the caves, in the deserts, on the plains. See all that human spirit, that human activity, in all its richness and all its poverty — the pettiness along with the splendor; the hatreds, the fear, the superstitions; and the love, which has always been luminous and profound.

Now move toward the present, into this century, into your own family, your own times. Begin to feel your own history, visions of your childhood. Come closer to the present. Put no labels on who you are. You are not man, woman, wife, husband, actor, painter, but a human being on a journey. Connect your journey to the journeys of all men and women, and approach the present moment.

Imagine the journey continuing in ways that excite and exhilarate you — in ways as rich as your grandest dreams, in ways that make use of your being, that support your sense of aliveness, that challenge and invigorate you. Feel the journey continuing. Commit to it continuing. Commit to your mission. Commit to supporting yourself on your mission by examining the challenges in your life through writing.

When you feel the reality of this commitment in your body — in your heart, in your stomach — open your eyes and proceed with your guided writing work.

Create a Writing Bubble

The next visualization is designed to help you create a writing bubble, where you can remain with the thoughts and feelings that the practice of guided writing stirs up in you. A writing bubble is a self-created private space. Translucent and semipermeable, this bubble encircles you and isolates you from distractions. Because it is translucent and semipermeable, you can see the pot boiling over on the stove, but only indistinctly; you can hear your baby crying, but only in a muffled way.

In the bubble, your sense of time is altered. Time passes without your noticing. You are utterly lost in the present. When your writing bubble is in place you are more distanced than usual. Rather than being at the world's beck and call, jumping at every outer command, and rather than being a slave to inner turmoil, jumping at every inner command, you — and your writing — are armored.

You can will your writing bubble into existence at any time. It takes only a few seconds to construct it. In bidding it to return you are making manifest your resolve: you are saying to yourself, "I am working." The following visualization will help you create your writing bubble. Record it and play it for yourself as needed at the beginning of a writing session.

VISUALIZATION: *Developing a Writing Bubble*

Relax now. Seat yourself comfortably, close your eyes, and go inside yourself. Breathe easily, deeply — in and out, in and out. Feel your feet firmly planted beneath you, feel the regularity of your breathing. Attune yourself to your breathing. Let go of all that has no relevance at this moment. Let go of your worries, your doubts.

Begin to feel the presence of your own writing. Feel the words. See the words. Feel their presence within your sphere of being. You and your words are together. Build a bubble around you and them. Create a rich, protective sphere, a private universe. Let in what you want, keep out what you want. You and your words are together.

Feel the sensation of being inside your writing bubble. Make it spacious and comfortable. Here you can write. The world will keep its distance. The bubble allows in light, allows in whatever you need. Inside it you and your words are together.

When you are ready, open your eyes. Continue to hold the feeling that you are present in your own writing world, protected and engaged. You and your words are together.

Raise Your Level of Tolerance for Frustration

For most people the knot of resolve and the sense of missionary zeal needed to engage in hard self-examination come regularly enough but last only fleetingly. After an involving workshop or a charismatic lecture you feel ready to tackle the tasks you've set for yourself, but by the time you reach home that resolve has dissipated.

The ability to tolerate an uncomfortable state for minutes, hours, and days on end, to tolerate that discomfort again and again, week in and week out, is the key to maintaining resolve. An inability to tolerate uncomfortable feelings will bring the enterprise of guided writing — or anything else — to a grinding halt.

If you stop writing out of frustration, acknowledge that you feel frustrated. Walk around your chair and ask yourself, "Even though I'm frustrated, can I go on?" If the answer is a resounding no, shake off the feelings of guilt or failure that may begin to well up in you and go about the business of your life with an easy heart. But in a corner of your mind make a deal with yourself that you will return to your important work of self-examination as soon as you can.

Each time the feelings of frustration and discomfort return, acknowledge them. Say to yourself, "I am not going on with this investigation of my father's many failures because it makes me feel uncomfortable to think about them, and I don't like feeling uncomfortable!" Wait a moment to see if, by acknowledging your discomfort and by giving yourself a few seconds to breathe, you find your willingness to continue your investigations returning.

Slowly you may learn to better tolerate frustration. You may begin to feel more comfortable, or at least easier with discomfort. You may leave your work far less often or return to it more quickly. One day you may complete a rich, eye-opening piece of self-examination without once moving from your chair and exclaim, "That was easy!" Such ease is the fruit of a practiced ability to tolerate frustration.

Uncover Problems and Challenges by Writing

You are ready and willing to write. How do you begin? The first (enormous) question you want answered is: "What is really going on in my life?" If the issues that prompted you to begin this writing practice are very disturbing, you may want to push them away rather than look at them closely. This is therefore a time for courage and deep breathing.

Write at length, over as many sessions as it takes, addressing your most important questions until you begin to uncover the problem areas that are presently troubling you. Ask big questions, such as, How do I see myself? How do others see me? What in my personality is preventing me from feeling happy? What relationship has wounded me most? About what am I most self-critical?

There is no one perfect question to ask, and there are few wrong questions to ask. Your goal is to invite in your best understanding of how to meet the challenges in your life, and whatever question has the power to help you start knowing yourself is a good one. It might be, "Do I dare take a frank look at why I'm not published?" or "Since I know that I'm feeling a lot of rage these days, why am I not painting more angrily?" You can ask any question under the sun, as long as it flows out of your desire to understand yourself and to meet your current challenges.

Narrow Your Focus

The problem areas you uncover may be large. They may be hard to grab on to or badly out of focus. They may involve important aspects of your personality or the way the world is constructed. The next challenge is to find methods for dissecting such large problems into a series of workable subproblems.

One way to begin narrowing your focus is to ask yourself questions based on the challenges I've been describing. Sample questions that you might use as the basis for your investigations are offered throughout the book.

As each new area of concern or interest comes into focus, you will be adding a new ball to the ones you are already juggling. Be prepared to become a master juggler. There is an endless series of questions and an endless series of answers. Accept that life is the sort of project that demands ongoing self-awareness and self-investigation.

Ask Creative Questions

The issues that begin to come into focus require creative, rather than rote, exploration. Sometimes our thoughts are so stale on these matters, since we may have been brooding about them for a long time, that only fresh, innovative questioning will allow us a new perspective on them.

For example, if the issue is self-esteem, you might make a list of questions, such as the one below, and choose to ask yourself the question on the list that sounds least familiar or most intriguing:

1. What would it take for me to feel really proud of myself?

2. How would it feel to step into a powerful person's shoes?

3. What do I most fear hearing about myself?

4. When do I give away my power?

5. Why do I feel so ashamed of myself?

If the issue is your "work identity" or "artist identity," you might generate the following sort of list:

1. What impact does my work identity have on the rest of my life?

2. Am I the equivalent of my art products or my performances?

3. How many work identities do I have, and how do they coexist?

4. How would I define what an artist does?

5. What is my job description?

Write Responses

Once you've chosen the questions you mean to address, write responses that do the questions justice. Spend time at it. Lose yourself in the writing. Many fears, blocks, and distractions may prevent you from engaging yourself. You are, after all, asking yourself the hardest questions imaginable. You may fear that such poking and probing will do some unalterable damage to your life. But have faith that you will survive your revelations. Remember the three maxims of Zen Buddhism: great faith, great question, and great courage. Continue faithfully and courageously with your great questioning of yourself.

Try not to censor the writing. When you feel the urge to stop, continue. Write for forty minutes, sixty minutes, ninety minutes. Fill up pages. Shake away your writer's cramp. Feel drained if the experience is draining, frightened if the experience is frightening, but will yourself to continue. Then, when you feel you have finished, congratulate yourself: you have been working in a way that few people dare to.

Read Creatively

Read your responses as creatively and courageously as you wrote them. Look to gain understanding and insight. Try to avoid the following pitfalls: feeling self-conscious about your writing mechanics or style; feeling unduly disappointed or impressed by your own words; or wondering whether the writing ought to be turned into a story or poem. (We are always looking to make creative products out of our experiences!)

Take care of yourself as you read. You may be opening up old wounds. You may be looking into dark corners that you've avoided looking into all your life. Your realizations may depress or enrage you. Remind yourself that your painful realizations are part of a process meant to serve you, not defeat you. Search out support if you need it.

Uncover Tactics and Solutions

By engaging in this practice, you have begun to understand which challenges are presently the most troublesome in your life. You may have a clearer idea of the ways in which several different challenges interconnect. Have tactics for meeting these challenges also suggested themselves to you?

Possible solutions to the problems you've pinpointed, or directions to head in to get to those solutions, are embedded in the writing you just completed. If, for example, in the course of writing about the issue of self-doubt, you say in many different ways that you don't know whether you can complete the art project you're currently embarked on, it will seem natural to ask yourself next if you need to learn some new skill, enlist the aid of a collaborator, or muster the courage to persevere in the face of fear. Think about each possibility, and choose the one that seems best to you.

Make a Plan

Once you've made your choice, you will want to construct a plan to implement that choice. Constructing a plan of action is a crucial part of the process. Create as specific and detailed a plan as you can. What will you do, and when will you do it?

Let's say that you've determined that you're not happy with specific parts of your life as a dancer. First, you understand that something goes profoundly wrong in your intimate relationships, although you can't articulate what it is. Second, you sense that dancing is much less fun for you now than it once was, even though you have just been accepted into a prestigious dance company as a soloist. To have gotten this much clarity about your present situation is a real triumph.

Now you must tackle these issues. Each concern is a serious challenge and requires a specific (and different) plan of action. Certain strategies may have already suggested themselves to you in your writing; but in any case, whether you have a clear sense of what you need to do or must sit down and figure it out on the spot, producing two different action plans is your next step.

A plan of action designed to meet your first challenge (your putative failure at maintaining intimate relationships) might begin with a thorough self-examination of your personality. Are you unable to trust because of certain childhood or adult experiences? Is dance your first love, and do human beings run a poor second? Are you so critical of yourself and others that no one, yourself included, can stand up to the scrutiny?

A second element of the plan to meet this challenge might be to ask certain friends for their insights into your relational difficulties. The plan would also include your willingness to listen to their comments. Does a theme emerge? Do they see you as too intense, too overbearing, or too critical to maintain intimate relationships?

A third element of the plan to meet this challenge might involve researching the subject of dancers in intimate relationships. What have other dancers said about their ability or inability to maintain intimate relationships? For instance, John Gruen's interviews with Alexandra Danilova, Rudolf Nureyev, Rosella Hightower, Alvin Ailey, and seventy other dancers in his book *The Private World of Ballet* might prove informative and revealing.

A plan designed to help you meet the second challenge (to discover why dancing feels less rewarding to you these days) might include some or all of the following elements: an analysis of whether dancing with an injury has sapped your strength and enthusiasm; an analysis of the developmental rhythms of dancers' careers to see if you are in one of the predictable valleys in a dancer's life; an existential analysis focusing on whether your values have shifted in such a way that dancing is less meaningful to you now; and an analysis of your definition of success to see if, now that you have achieved solo status, you perhaps need a new goal and a new dream.

Add Contingencies to the Plan

Your plan, which has the goal of effecting real change in your life, is likely to be hard to implement. You may balk somewhere along the line. You may backslide into habits you had hoped to eliminate. You may fail the first, second, or tenth time at doing your business more assertively or relating with your fellow actors more positively. Such setbacks are natural.

What will you do if you have trouble following your own plan of action? One possibility is to make use of a behavioral contract, one of the tools of behavioral psychotherapy. Such a contract should contain, according to psychologist Philip Zimbardo, the following seven elements:

1. Explicit benefits and privileges, such as reading a magazine in the bath tub, gained through a specific performance.

2. Specified consequences for failure to meet the terms of the contract, which could be a promise to flush $20 down the toilet for each day missed.

3. Bonuses for compliance with contract terms.

4. Monitoring of contracted activities, which simply means keeping track of your promise and noting your compliance.

5. Record keeping of benefits earned.

6. Voluntary participation.

7. The right to outside arbitration in instances of alleged contract violation, a task that should fall to a close friend.

Evaluate the Results

Periodically evaluate the results of your self-shaping work. How far have you come? What benefits have you reaped? What remains to be done? What sorts of things do you need more practice in? What feelings remain troublesome? Are there new steps to add to your plan? Have new tactics occurred to you? Do you need to set new goals for yourself?

This process of self-examination, planning for change, implementing the plan, and analyzing the results of your work is a subtle feedback loop, in which you continually feed yourself new information and make changes based on the data you have uncovered about yourself. Though I am presenting it in linear fashion, it is nothing like a straight line. It is much more like life — only a fully examined one.

Create New Plans of Action

You will be led down many tributaries as you make changes. One tributary will lead to another. The plan you made in May to handle a certain challenge may not be an appropriate plan of action in December. By then the challenge may be to find effective ways of handling your extraordinary success!

You will benefit in many ways if you maintain this program. You'll become more disciplined and will overcome some of your natural resistance to self-exploration. You'll begin to identify problem areas in your life and to plan more effectively for change, to bring about real change, and to monitor the changes you make. Give this guided writing program a shot — it is well worth your time and attention.

doesn't want to; that he watches his diet and passes on the hot fudge sundaes, even though he craves them; that he visualizes success and in other ways talks himself into the right frame of mind. We picture him taking charge of his mind and his body and engaging in a goal-oriented process that naturally includes pushing himself in ways that, on many days, he hates.

Martial artists provide us with another model. We picture their formality: the way they bow when they enter the studio and when they face an opponent before a match. We picture their intensity: the way they shout, the way they drive themselves, the way they focus on a given move and a given routine. We picture the value system by which they live, which revolves around the honorable use of force and sanctifies self-control, including the self-control to walk away rather than to fight.

Then there's the path of the dedicated thinker, someone who lives for intellectual problems to solve and whose main meaning investments have to do with unraveling the laws of the universe, finding cures for diseases, or inventing ever-better mousetraps. We picture a self-directed person who takes it upon himself to pick his path, even if it runs counter to the path his peers are following, to bite into his problem as a starving man bites into a juicy sandwich, and to demonstrate a resolve and tenacity that are sometimes punctuated by joyous shrieks of "Eureka!"

And what if someone tells us that she has spent a lifetime battling for the rights — and the release — of political prisoners? In our mind's eye we see her engaged in a dedicated, daily way, in the face of setbacks and indifference, with an enterprise that she is convinced is important and righteous. We don't picture her smiling much; we don't picture her life punctuated by that many prisoner releases; but we understand why she is bringing every ounce of fortitude she can muster to this enterprise.

Last but not least, what if we meet a woman at a cocktail party and learn that she has written and published twenty novels and thirty nonfiction books? Certain thoughts about how she must live immediately come to mind. We picture her chatting easily and regularly — maybe even every day — with marketplace players such as agents, editors, and publicists. We see her attending book signings, giving interviews, and going on book tours. If she has somehow managed to avoid all that, we have the sure feeling that she did so for the sake of her writing.

THE ELEMENTS OF YOUR PRACTICE

You can construct a creativity practice that incorporates core elements of all these models. Rather than create in a hit-or-miss way, without sufficient motivation, energy, or regularity, you can construct a routine that minimizes your disinclination to create as well as your personality shortfalls and that maximizes your natural abilities and your love of your art discipline. The following twelve elements comprise that practice.

Simplicity

Our creative work may be complex, but our practice is simple. It is as simple as showing up. It is as simple as saying "I will write every day" and then doing it. It is as simple as learning to sculpt by actually sculpting. It is so simple that it can be said in very few words. For instance, you hold the thought "I will write every day," and you write every day. You hold the thought "I will write my first novel," and you embark on writing your first novel, with everything that entails, from false starts to mushy middles to multiple revisions. You hold a simple goal and take daily action in support of it.

What this quality sounds like:

"My work doesn't exist separately from my life." — Richard Ford

"I just say to myself, 'Just give it another hour. Just plod along, one foot in front of the other.' And then six months later I see it's a beautiful piece." — Virginia Cartwright

"I think that people who are not artists often feel that artists are inspired. But if you work at your art you don't have time to be inspired. Out of the work comes the work." — John Cage

Regularity

Our creativity practice requires that we create, every day, or on as many days as is humanly possible. We do not skip our practice because it is gloomy out or because we are gloomy inside. We pledge to show up every day at our creative work, and then we honor that pledge. Every day means every day: that is the essence of regularity. We hold the thought "time to paint," and we move ourselves, joyfully or unwillingly, to our studio. If we are blocked, we take it upon ourselves to remove the block. If we are resistant, we crack an egg and proceed. If we are in the middle of a crisis, if we are very busy, if we are really tired — if we are anything — we remind ourselves of our commitment to turn to the work every day.

What this quality sounds like:

"Writing every day is wonderful." — Maria Irene Fornes

"If I don't paint for one day, I don't feel well physically or mentally." — Raphael Soyer

"If I don't practice for one day, I know it; if I don't practice for two days, the critics know it; if I don't practice for three days, the audience knows it." — Ignacy Paderewski

Solemnity

We engage in our creativity practice because it matters to us. It is meaningful; it is respectful of the vision we hold for ourselves; it is a primary way in which we show our heroism, our humanity, and our love of life. Because we hold it in this high esteem, we treat it seriously and solemnly, even if the art we are producing is comic. We hold the thought "my research matters to me," and we seriously research. If your research doesn't in fact matter to you, you solemnly stop everything and recommit to your research, inaugurate new research, or find a different meaning container. You solemnly do your work and, just as solemnly, you make sure that you have work to do.

What this quality sounds like:

"[Life] feels like a real fight — as if there were something really wild in the universe which we, with all our idealities and faithfulnesses, are needed to redeem." — William James

*"My lifelong ambition has been to unite the utmost seriousness of question
with the utmost lightness of form."* — Milan Kundera

"A symphony is no joke." — Johannes Brahms

Honesty

Our practice amounts to nothing if we are not honest. If we play a passage
that isn't strong yet, we are honest and say, "This isn't strong yet." If we
write a sonnet and can't say for sure what we think about it, we say, "I will
look at this tomorrow and see what I honestly think." We acknowledge that
it may take all our resources to create honestly, to appraise our creations
honestly, and to reckon with the marketplace honestly. We are not honest
for the sake of taking some perverse joy in our flaws and blemishes — this
isn't some kind of self-flagellating honesty. We are honest so that our creative work can rise to the level of our aspirations.

What this quality sounds like:

*"If you start with something that's false,
you're always covering your tracks."* — Paul Simon

*"It may be that the deep necessity of art
is the examination of self-deception."* — Robert Motherwell

"I care about truth, not for truth's sake but for my own." — Samuel Butler

Self-Direction

You and you alone guide your creativity practice and your life in art. You
may learn from others, but you make your own decisions. You decide
which novel to write; you guide yourself through the process; you make and
learn from your mistakes. You listen carefully to your agent, your editor,
your readers, and even to the wind, but you decide whether to write this or
to write that, whether to stop for the day or whether to continue on for
another two hours. Your thought is "I decide." Your thought is "I plot my
course." Only rarely do you look for teachers, since you are committed to

learning by doing. Only rarely do you look for models. When you do not know what to do with the painting in front of you, you take a deep breath and say to yourself, "Don't bother looking for relief or a way out. It's all on my shoulders."

What this quality sounds like:

"If the universe does not belong to me, to whom does it belong? If I am not master of it, why am I not?" — Eugene Ionesco

"It was important that I learn that what I wanted was no different from what other artists wanted: confidence that I could be my own censor, audience, and competition." — Beverly Pepper

"I have no master and shall never have any." — Winslow Homer

Intensity

You can exercise lackadaisically, or you can exercise intensely. You can write your screenplay absently or with real commitment. You can care only a little about your efforts, or you can care a lot about them. You can bring your full wattage to the creative encounter, or you can bring a fraction of your passion and energy. Your practice demands all your intensity: every muscle fiber, every moral conviction, every brain cell, every ounce of passion. For those several hours of your daily practice, as you strive to bring your symphony, sculpture, or theory into existence, you spend, if need be, your entire capital of energy. Do not worry about tiring yourself out. Do not fear plumbing your depths. Work with intensity; and only afterward relax.

What this quality sounds like:

"I have never seen such a great musician as that soloist. He looked very ordinary, but there was some inner fire in him that felt like a volcano." — Ravi Shankar

"To say yes, you have to sweat and roll up your sleeves and plunge both hands into life up to the elbows." — Jean Anouilh

"I am not a human being, I am dynamite." — Friedrich Nietzsche

Presence

When you come into the studio, you mean to be present. You intend to be right there, in front of the canvas, and not elsewhere. You aren't half-thinking about the bills that need paying, half-thinking about your child's grade-point average, half-thinking about your husband's complaints. You are here and nowhere else, not in the past, not in the future, not preparing your grocery list, not doubting your talents. You are either thinking about your painting, or you are thinking about nothing, that not-thinking that means your brain is readying itself. You are full of your painting, or you are empty and primed. You have shaken off distractions, quieted your nerves, and geared up for the encounter. You are in contact with this canvas, settled and committed to the work directly in front of you.

What this quality sounds like:

"The discipline of the writer is to learn to be still and listen to what his subject has to tell him." — Rachel Carson

"There are wonderful moments, those rare moments when there is silence, a tangible silence out there, a silence deeper than silence." — Derek Jacobi

"In beginning to throw pots, I worked for a long time to get the clay centered. I soon discovered that if I were not centered myself, the clay would not become centered." — William Galbreath

Ceremony

There is ceremony in digging the earth for the clay, ceremony in kneading the clay, ceremony in making the pot, ceremony in lighting the kiln, ceremony in contemplating what has been wrought. There is ceremony to every aspect of the process, if we treat it ceremonially and give it that added measure of respect and poignancy. You can take your violin out of its case in a certain ritualistic way that communicates your willingness to pay attention, or you can remove it absently, tune it absently, and play it absently. We add a ceremonial feel to what we do by translating our good intentions into small, studied gestures that we repeat. We may add this ceremonial feel to the way we apply our makeup before a performance, or to the way we ready ourselves as our computer boots up: we add that sense of ceremony.

What this quality sounds like:

"Over the door of the sacred tepee, they painted the flaming rainbow. It took them all day to do this, and it was beautiful." — Black Elk

"Art class was like a religious ceremony for me. I would wash my hands carefully before touching paper or pencils. The instruments of work were sacred objects to me." — Joan Miró

"I never practice; I always play." — Wanda Landowska

Joy

Our practice brings us joy. It does not bring us joy every day, and on any given day it can bring us at least as much pain as joy. But when, one day, we find a cure for a disease, secure the release of a political prisoner, see our book published — or just feel good about our own heroic effort to make meaning — a kind of joy wells up in us that, even if gone in an instant, is proof that we are living authentically. Joy accompanies our practice, even if it manifests itself as rarely as a sunny day in a period of bad weather. We want to invite in that joy, remember that it is nearby, and call on it as we would call on a friend. Let quiet joy be the background feeling of your creativity practice.

What this quality sounds like:

"I so love carving. It seems to me to be the most rhythmic and marvelous way to work on living, sensuous material." — Barbara Hepworth

"I've learned what 'classical' means. It means something that sings and dances through sheer joy of existence." — Gustav Holst

*"A strong endeavor that brings you joy is
the greatest thing in life."* — Sono Osato

Discipline

Our practice hinges on our willingness to be disciplined, at least with respect to our creating. Every act of the right sort, even the smallest — an extra hour of instrument practice, an extra thirty minutes of learning new repertoire, an extra fifteen minutes of songwriting — is the measure of our discipline and the way we build our muscles for further disciplined action. Be disciplined in your approach and in your efforts, doing whatever your current work requires and whatever your career requires. Have you come to a hard part in your novel, a dry spell in your career, or a disinclination to continue? Say, "I am disciplined, and I will do what is required of me." Make the effort to crack through your resistance and then, face-to-face with the work, rise to the occasion.

What this quality sounds like:

*"I prepare myself very intensely. I am at the theater four hours
before the performance. That allows for complete concentration
and preparation."* — Natalia Makarova

*"In order to be a good writer, you need to be a bad boss. Self-discipline and
stamina are the two major arms in a writer's arsenal."* — Leon Uris

*"Dedication to your work is the only possible
sanctification."* — Cynthia Ozick

Self-Trust

Our practice rises on self-trust and crumbles if we do not trust our decision to work in our chosen medium, if we continually second-guess ourselves, if we doubt that we have what it takes. You can paint even if you have doubts about your current painting; but what if you don't trust that painting is the right creative outlet for you? That is a deal breaker. Bring to your practice a new or renewed belief in your choices and your abilities, even if some serious doubts remain. Every day say to yourself, "I trust myself implicitly and completely." Say this for the sake of your practice, so that, by honorably working, you can earn your self-trust.

What this quality sounds like:

"Never, even as a child, would I bend to a rule." — Claude Monet

"An artist, under pain of oblivion, must have confidence in himself." — Pierre-Auguste Renoir

"Learn to trust your own judgment, learn inner independence, learn to trust that time will sort the good from the bad — including your own bad." — Doris Lessing

Primacy

Many things in life are important. But few require the attention and work that our art does. Our child may be more important than our recitals, but our child is three thousand miles away and living on her own and doesn't need our active attention throughout the day. Our mate may be more important than our novel, but our mate is off at work and our novel is happening, or not happening, right here. Much that is important in our life does not require our constant or immediate attention. But our art does, which means that we must accord it a certain moment-by-moment primacy in our lives. In every moment we can choose to attend to it or to do something that is likely much less important.

What this quality sounds like:

"I must take responsibility for my work. That word may be grandiose, but there's an ethic involved in creation." — Cecilia Davis Cunningham

"Some rainy winter Sunday when there's a little boredom, you should carry a gun. Not to shoot yourself, but to know exactly that you are always making a choice." — Lina Wertmüller

"The artist himself may not think that he is religious, but if he is sincere his sincerity in itself is religion." — Emily Carr

YOUR CREATIVITY PRACTICE

At the simplest level, what does your creativity practice look like? The bare-bones outline of your writing practice might look like the following:

- You pledge to write every day.

- You intend to write every day.

- You write every day.

- You think about your writing.

- You care for your writing.

- You affirm the importance of your writing.

- You stay put when you are writing.

- You do what the writing requires.

- You send the writing into the world.

- You steadily create a body of work.

The bare-bones outline of your musical practice might look like the following:

- You learn your instrument.

- You affirm your love of music.

- You open up to the music you love.

- You practice every day.

- You make music.

- You strive for performance opportunities.

- You accept the realities of performing.

- You create new music.

- You create performance possibilities.

- You show up each day as a musician.

The bare-bones outline of your research practice might look like the following:

- You fall deeply in love with a subject.

- You think about it, read about it, and dream about it.

- You do not posit a hypothesis for any reason except that you believe it to be a way to the truth.

- You learn material that you don't really want to learn if that material helps you understand your subject.

- You get up off the mat, simply and gracefully, if your research leads to a dead end.

- You do all the mundane things required of you to gain funding for your research and to situate yourself so that you can pursue that research.

- You stare into space, if staring into space is what is required of you, and you pore through journals, if poring through journals is what is required of you.

- You show up each day as a researcher.

Creativity practices naturally differ according to personal differences and according to what your particular art demands. A writer's primary practice is writing, while an actor's primary practice is made up of preparation, job hunting, and producing in a group setting. A theoretical mathematician's practice may be largely staring into space, coupled with mastering mathematical material and elaborating ideas as they arise. An inventor's practice is endless fiddling and noodling at all hours of the day and night on his gadgets and latest ideas. A soloist's practice is maintaining her instrument, maintaining her repertoire, and maintaining her physical and emotional health throughout an arduous performance schedule. What each practice shares with the other is its seriousness, its felt sense of purpose, and its commitment to daily attention.

What distinguishes, say, an actor with a thriving creativity practice from one without such a practice? The actor with the practice takes his roles more seriously; takes looking for roles more seriously; takes the production he is in more seriously; and takes his preparations more seriously, whether those preparations involve new headshots, creating a personal website, or mastering accents.

He doesn't make a fuss about auditions; he simply auditions. He doesn't make a few phone calls in support of his career; he makes many. He solemnly swears to find good roles, even if they are few and far between, and he honestly appraises his efforts, redoubling them when he finds that he hasn't been active and persistent enough. In these and similar ways he can be said to be living his creativity practice.

It will pay real dividends if you take some time and describe the creativity practice you want for yourself. Explain to yourself how you will keep your practice simple, how you will keep yourself honest, how you will foster real presence, and so on. Think about each of the twelve elements, and picture yourself living your practice. Picture yourself trusting yourself; picture yourself imbuing your creative life with ceremony; picture yourself putting your creative life first. Do an honorable job of articulating and visualizing your creativity practice: then begin it, today or tomorrow at the latest.

15   *Transitions* and *Choices*

One enormous, life-altering transition that some artists decide they must make is the shift from one art commitment to another. They decide to stop dancing professionally and devote themselves instead to painting. They discover that their true love is weaving and not sculpting. They decide to let go of novel writing, which hasn't produced any sales, in favor of writing nonfiction, where sales have been abundant. Most creative people face transitions of this sort throughout their lifetimes.

For some artists, like dancers, the matter is thrust inexorably upon them with age. For others, for reasons of finances or personal fulfillment, leaving one art discipline for another feels like the appropriate and even the lifesaving thing to do. An artist who believes that he or she must make the transition out of a particular art commitment and into a different one can profitably employ the following nine-step program. It is also a good model for understanding the transition process in general.

NINE-STEP TRANSITION PROGRAM

1. Reflect on the question.

2. Change your internal language.

3. Make your parallel life rich and valuable.

4. Plan to be recognized in new ways.

5. Take vacations.

6. Begin a process of inner career counseling.

7. Say it out loud.

8. Pay attention to your emotions.

9. Live your new life.

Reflect on the Question

Carefully let the question in: "Should I make the transition out of my current art love?" A wall of denial may prevent you from asking this question directly, even though you've whispered it to yourself many times. When you first ask yourself this question out loud, a wave of terror may engulf you. You may feel as if you're drowning. But take comfort in the knowledge that your severe reaction to this particular question is absolutely natural. Expect to be buffeted by a host of contradictory and difficult thoughts and feelings. Begin, as best you can, to tolerate those thoughts and feelings.

Change Your Internal Language

Say you've decided to switch from writing novels to writing nonfiction (even though you suspect you might return to writing novels one day). Begin to let go of the charge attached to phrases like "The only thing I want to do in life is be a novelist." Doubt the truth of the threat "I'll die if I give up novel writing." Inaugurate the following crucial cognitive change: instead of saying "I am a novelist," say, "I am a creative person who makes meaning as I see fit."

A person is much more than a particular sort of artist, even if that art has been a great love and of great value. Once you viscerally understand that you will be able to make important meaning in your new discipline, you will likewise begin to recognize that your life holds more opportunities than you previously realized.

Make Your Parallel Life Rich and Valuable

Let more of the world in as you move between art loves. Meet your relational needs in new ways, too, not according to whether you are admired as a singer, dancer, or actor but according to the rightness and soundness of the relationships into which you enter. Parallel-life work, after all, requires that you learn new things, acquire new friends, and practice new actions; it requires, in short, that you live creatively in brand-new ways.

If you are making the transition from writing nonfiction to fiction, say, and you know that the move will feel scary and is likely to cause subterranean doubts and fears to surface, plan to do things in your parallel life in which you feel confident and competent. The goal is to have those well-earned feelings of confidence and competence help counteract any anxiety that wants to bubble up.

Plan to Be Recognized in New Ways

Begin to dream up new ways of satisfying the recognition-seeking part of your ego. Might published articles about your life in dance satisfy some of your need to remain known as a dancer, even as you begin your life as a painter? Would leading a workshop for actors, in which you teach the preaudition centering technique that has worked for you, gratify your ego and serve you as you begin your life as a screenwriter?

It would be nice to imagine that, as part of this transition, we might leave behind us, as a snake sheds its skin, what the writer William Thompson called the "trappings of the Wagnerian ego." Perhaps that is even part of the goal, to enter into our next commitment with a new definition of what recognition and success will look like. Still, it may be wise to chart a course that allows for at least some recognition during this transition period, just in case your ego needs to remain aggressively alive.

Take Vacations

As you make the transition from one art commitment to another and try to release any pent-up disappointment and fatigue that may have accumulated, take some real vacations from striving, worrying, practicing, auditioning, brooding, creating, selling, performing, priming, rewriting, and all the rest. Say out loud, "I don't need to strive today," "I refuse to worry about the goodness or badness of my writing today," or "I will not brood about being too old for all the good parts." Announce, "I am on vacation!" Go on vacation: take the afternoon off.

After your vacation, you may discover that you do not want to let go of your former commitment altogether but rather that you want to commit to both, enthusiastically beginning your new screenwriting life while still auditioning for acting parts, or beginning your life as a novelist while still entertaining nonfiction assignments. If you opt for this path, this is itself a major transition as you commit to two disciplines instead of one. Go back through all the steps of this transition program to help you deal with the added difficulties — and, of course, potential joys — to which this new double commitment will give rise.

Begin a Process of Inner Career Counseling

Allow all that you are — your full identity, your different interests, your complicated personality — to be part of this process. As you do, engage in what career counselors call *identification of transferable skills*. For example, Alan Pickman, a career counselor, names the following transferable skills that dancers typically manifest: attention to detail, perseverance, intense concentration, determination, self-evaluative skills, and the ability to take direction and to improve performance. If you are a dancer, how might you apply these skills to your new painting career?

Think through the contours of your new career. You may have pursued your first love without giving much thought to what was required to turn that love into a career. Now you have the opportunity to use all that you learned from your first journey to make this new journey a success. Will you network and market yourself more aggressively this time? Will you start earlier to learn what the marketplace requires? If one of your goals is to turn your new commitment into a healthy career, act as your own career counselor right from the beginning.

Say It Out Loud

A recovering alcoholic introduces himself at Alcoholics Anonymous meetings by saying, "Hi, I'm Bill, and I'm an alcoholic." Why this particular ritual? It turns out that there is no more powerful way to combat lingering denial or to step into a new identity than by saying something *out loud*. Begin to say to friends: "I'm starting my life as a painter and pretty much giving up dance" or "I'm not writing novels for the foreseeable future; I'm going to give nonfiction a shot."

Maybe you'll have to whisper this news at first. Maybe you'll have to practice it in front of a mirror. Maybe you'll have to spend a day recovering from the shock of saying it. Maybe you'll doubt your decision, change your mind, and suddenly want to audition or start a novel. These are all pieces of the transition puzzle. You add a healthy dose of reality and dynamism to the process when you announce your new intention out loud. Whatever you provoke in yourself by saying it out loud, you were going to provoke that same reaction sooner or later: you might as well face those repercussions right now.

Pay Attention to Your Emotions

As you make this transition from one art commitment to another, you may have real losses to grieve. You may experience a loss of identity, the shattering of your oldest, fondest dreams, the loss of a world you knew, the loss of friends and fellow artists, the loss of excitement, and the loss of a vessel that held so much meaning for you.

You may find yourself wrestling with anger, sadness, frustration, and despair. Depression may even set in. These are natural human reactions to profound, drastic change. The healing process may take a long time and, on some days, you will have to deal with powerful emotions and full-blown crises. Be alert to the powerful role your emotions will play in this transition process.

Live Your New Life

Accept the changes you initiate, try to make peace with the past, and find renewal and real joy in your new apprenticeship. Even if you're left with something of a hurt heart, and even if you struggle with thoughts about the past and about what might have been, you can still find great satisfaction in your new life, as you learn its ropes and as you begin to experience some successes in it.

MAKING CHOICES

Making the transition from one art commitment to another is a special case of the more general task that confronts creative people all the time: making choices. The choice might be whether to write this book or that book, whether to write a particular book one way or another way, whether to aim for personal, idiosyncratic work or more commercial and market-driven work, and so on. While it is obvious that you will face countless choices of this sort, it is not very well understood how anxious all this choosing makes you. How likely are you to flee from your work, your commitment, or your career because you don't feel equal to making a given choice?

Following are some of the choices that might arise in a writer's life, presented in lighthearted quiz form. The goal of this exercise is not to come up with the "right answer" for each scenario but to gain a better appreciation of how choices affect you emotionally, metaphysically, and practically. You decide to write your novel in the present tense: that choice affects you every day for the next two years. You decide not to contact an editor who has expressed an interest in your work: by making that choice you disappoint yourself and hurt your career. Life might even be defined as the activity of making one choice after another, each with its happy and unhappy consequences.

Scenario One

No agent has been willing to give your screenplay a reading. All you get are form rejection letters. Then, one day, you get a letter from an agent who has actually looked at the screenplay you sent him. However, his words aren't exactly heartening: he says that he could tell at first glance that the screenplay was strictly amateurish, since it went on for well over the maximum allowed 120 pages, the main character took several pages to appear, and the characters sometimes went on speaking for more than two sentences (who do you think you are, Shakespeare?). What do you do at this point? 1) Bring to his attention all the famous screenplays that have violated his so-called rules? 2) Hire a hit man and get even? 3) Cry hard, then leave the screenwriting business? 4) Laugh, shake your head, and send out your screenplay to six other agents? 5) Consider whether you must rewrite your screenplay, taking the agent's comments (demands) into account?

Scenario Two

You have come back from the world of mystery and silence with a poem. But one word is missing. You let the poem rest overnight, fully expecting the word to be there in the morning. But it isn't. Nor does it arrive in the afternoon. You have a poem you love, but it has one word missing and you can't show it to anyone or send it anywhere as long as there remains this gaping hole. A week passes — still the missing word hasn't materialized. What do you do at this point? 1) Wait for the word to come, even if it takes sixteen years? 2) Put in a word as near to the right word as you can muster and call the poem done for now? 3) Engage in some "word-finding" exercise, for instance, by searching cyberspace synonym sites? 4) Send the poem to some selected friends with the word missing and ask them to fill in the blank? 5) Rewrite the poem so that the need for the missing word vanishes?

Scenario Three

The initial royalty statement for your first published novel arrives, and you discover that no subsidiary rights earnings appear, even though your book was a book club selection and was serialized in a major magazine. This absence makes no sense to you, and a variety of strong emotions instantly surface, among them confusion, anger, disappointment, and the overall bad feeling that your publisher is using its might — and your smallness — to take advantage of you. What do you do at this point? 1) Call your agent and fume? 2) Call your editor and fume? 3) Do nothing and presume that the earnings will show up on the next royalty statement? 4) Do nothing, out of a sense of powerlessness? 5) Use this event as an excuse to stop working on your current novel, which you happen to hate?

Scenario Four

You and your mate are having dinner at a nice little French bistro, a place that is a tad expensive but very atmospheric. The wine is fruity and the music seductive. Your mate has come directly from work and, after a morning of fitful writing, you have just completed three good hours of afternoon television watching. You are already feeling a little furtive and defensive when your mate says, "Dear, we really need a car that runs." What do you do at this point? 1) Say, "You're right, honey! Why don't you work some overtime?"? 2) Say, "Just hold on, love! — I know that in a few years my psychological fiction will be all the rage and then we can have two cars *and* a dishwasher!"? 3) Say, "When did you become such a materialist?"? 4) Say, "What are you implying? — that I should stop writing?"? 5) Say, "All right — I'll look into that teaching job!"?

You can do nothing when the agent's letter arrives. That is one sort of choice. You can do nothing when the word for your poem fails to arrive. That is one sort of choice. You can do nothing when the royalty statement arrives. That is one sort of choice. You can say nothing when your wife remarks on the sad state of your car. That is one sort of choice. But these "not doing" and "not saying" choices are exactly as real, and come with exactly as many consequences, as any action you might take or anything you might say. By doing nothing and saying nothing, you can avoid some of the anxiety that comes with actively choosing — and, as likely as not, you will pay a high price for that avoidance.

LIFELONG CHOOSING

You can debate your possible choices endlessly and even make endless debating your choice. You can choose casually, thoughtfully, impulsively, decisively, furtively, pragmatically, intuitively: you can choose in any manner you like. What you can't do is eliminate choosing from your repertoire of human activities. Grow as easy as you can with that reality, and agree that you won't flinch from choosing.

You have chosen to live an art-committed life, and living that commitment amounts to negotiating an endless series of choices. Some are as "small" as choosing what to do when your poem is a word short of being finished, some are as large as dealing with your mate's unhappiness that what you compose isn't profitable. Some are as "simple" as choosing how you intend to deal with each rejection letter, some are as complicated as making the transition from painting to sculpting or vice versa. Whether small or large, simple or complicated, these choices stand before you, this afternoon, this evening, tomorrow morning...as far as you and the calendar can reach.

16   *Creativity* for *Life*

Imagine writing or painting for seventy-five years, from age twenty until you retire at ninety-five. Just for a second, consider the variety of products you might produce over those seventy-five years, the fascinating tributaries you would explore, the discoveries you would make, the moments of satisfaction you would experience. Yes, on many of those twenty-seven thousand days you might hit a wall, hate your work, or doubt your path. Maybe you would have more bad days than good ones. Certainly you would have to hike back out of the occasional blind alley and bury projects that never came alive. But just consider how much personal meaning you might make if, for most of those twenty-seven thousand days, you created.

Lifelong creativity isn't given to you. You must earn it and attend to it every day. You have so many methods of getting in your own way and of stopping yourself from achieving your goals and realizing your dreams, and life has so many curveballs to throw at you, that you will have to dig deep to find the requisite honesty, courage, and resilience to live an artful, art-filled, art-committed life. You must really want it and really commit to it in order to have it. Only if you treat an art-committed life as — depending on the language you use — sacred, meaningful, or simply the way you live, will you be able to crack through everyday resistance and create for a lifetime.

TEN CORE IDEAS

How can you help yourself maintain your creative life year-in and year-out? Here are ten core ideas:

1. *Reflect.* You need to get under the radar of your own defenses and reflect on your life. Worry and self-reflection are different things: we already worry too much. But we reflect too little, because self-reflection provokes anxiety. To have a chance at the creative life you desire, you need to reflect on your personality, your culture, your relationships, your subject matter, the marketplace, and more. What this means is that you must face the fear of knowing about yourself and your actual circumstances and continually ask yourself, "If I am not doing the creative work I intended to do, why am I not doing it?"

2. *Matter.* You have to make a pact with yourself to act "as if" you matter, even if you can come up with abundant evidence suggesting that you do not. Unless you can convince yourself in a heartfelt way that painting a portrait or writing a sonnet matters, you will have no motivational juice for creating. The question to ask yourself is, "Am I willing to believe that my efforts matter, at least to me?" If you can't get a "yes" to that question, you need to stop everything and have a heart-to-heart chat with yourself until that "yes" resurfaces.

3. *Forgive.* You need to forgive yourself and others so as to release stored-up pain and disappointment. You cannot make meaning in

the present if you are consumed by resentment about the past and if you are upset with yourself for your (all-too-human) failings and failures. The question to ask yourself is, "Can I forgive myself and others and let go of my stored-up emotional blocks?"

4. *Surrender.* Surrendering to the facts of existence is another vital component of your plan to maintain meaning, reduce depression, and create. Your anger, sadness, and anxiety about the facts of existence cause blocks, and the desire to have reality be something different from (and better than) what it is prevents change. The question to ask yourself is, "Given the facts of existence, what efforts must I make in order to have the creative life that I want?"

5. *Dispute.* You want to dispute your very human tendencies to deal with your meaning crises and your creative blocks in unhealthy ways (by working hard at projects other than your creative work, by creating life dramas, by giving in to the happy bondage of a drug or alcohol addiction, by engaging in obsessive sexual activity). The question to ask yourself is, "Am I in control of myself? If not, what sort of battle must I wage with myself in order to gain control?"

6. *Create.* You need to create work that you deem interesting, worthy, and meaningful. If you only do other people's work — as a graphic designer, writer-for-hire, and so on — you will find it hard to sustain personal meaning, unless you are producing a full complement of your own creative work at the same time. The question to ask yourself is, "Am I doing my own creating often enough?"

7. *Relate.* You need to relate. You need love relationships and marketplace relationships and friendly relationships. It turns out that a life of isolation and alienation, even a highly creative one, breeds depression, since human meaning and human intimacy are intertwined. A lack of intimacy is a severe meaning drain. The question to ask yourself is, "Do I have love in my life and the relationships I need?"

8. *Act.* Creative blocks and meaning crises breed inaction, and inaction exacerbates meaning crises and creative blocks. This common cycle can paralyze you. You may not recognize that the best antidote

is to take some action — any action — in the service of your creative life, no matter how apparently small. The second you get yourself in motion, resistance becomes less of an issue. The question to ask yourself is, "What action will I engage in today in support of my creative life?"

9. *Succeed.* You need to experience some success if you are to experience life as meaningful. It is not possible to maintain meaning if you find yourself defeated at every turn. However, it is crucial that you define success in ways that account for the facts of existence. If you define success as writing a bestseller, and if the odds against having a bestseller are thousands-to-one, then you will find yourself in the throes of a meaning crisis while you wait for that success, growing gloomier with each passing year, even as you write books and sell them. The question to ask yourself is, "Am I willing to define success in such a way that my successes feel like successes?"

10. *Hope.* Psychotherapists tend to define the goals of therapy as insight coupled with change. But a more primary goal is renewed hope. Each time a little hope returns, each time the flicker of a smile plays across your lips, each time you desire again and dream again, you arrive at a refreshed acceptance of the facts of existence and, for however long that acceptance lasts, of restored meaning. The question to ask yourself is, "Can I feel hopeful today? Can I give myself that gift?"

Take a few moments and think through these ten core ideas. If you feel in the mood, write out your thoughts about them. Here is how Vivian, a painter, responded to them:

It is good for me to think about these ideas, because I am fighting hard to maintain my creative life since the rest of my life is in such turmoil.

Reflect. My art/journaling enables me to reflect on my creative life and my "other" life on an ongoing basis. I force myself to continue to do this journal work as needed. It centers me, it gives me an outlet to be creative in a very nonjudgmental place, and it allows me to reflect on questions like, Where am I? How did I get here? Where am I going?

Matter. The most important thing I can do for myself at this time is to remember that I matter. I'm fighting hard to maintain this thought every day. You don't start out knowing that you are going to have to keep meaning afloat every single day through force of will, until finally one day you get it that meaning is fragile and your own responsibility.

Forgive. Facing the deterioration, probably the end, of a long-term marriage leaves a lot of room for forgiveness. I don't know whom I have to forgive more — there are many candidates for forgiveness in this disaster, including meddling parents on both sides.

Surrender. I have no choice but to face the facts that I have not wanted to face for many years, surrender to them, and figure out whom I am willing to forgive — and how completely.

Dispute. I spend my days trying to stay in control of myself, and my situation, a situation in which I have very little control. I must continue disputing, in the sense of asserting myself, rather than running or hiding. I want to exert as much positive influence as I can on myself and on my situation and dispute my entrenched, self-sabotaging habits of being.

Create. I have been creating for others, running classes, facilitating workshops. This is good work, important work, but others reap more of the profits and more of the benefits than I do. I need to be doing these things for myself. I owe it to myself to gain more from these workshops by offering them myself and by positioning myself right in the center of a personally creative life, not on the periphery of other people's creative lives.

Relate. I relate well to people, to most of the people around me, to the people I love, to the people with whom I work. But I have been faced with a lack of intimacy for far longer than I care to admit, and I am faced with making major "disruptive" life changes in order to give myself the chance to live and grow again. I always thought that I was a natural at relating, but I understand that I am going to have rethink all that.

Act. I force myself to act. I call a friend for an "art date." I take a workshop when I find one that appeals to me. I try to do things — and I try to create. But the hardest acts remain the ones directly related to my own creating, the acts where I am required to get really quiet and go off into the unknown, the truly creative acts. I know that if I don't do more of those, I don't actually have a creative life.

Succeed. I have had many successes, and I've done things I never could have imagined I'd do. I feel good about that, but it's hard to make those past successes count for anything when I'm not currently succeeding. In a way, those past successes are burdens — they remind me of what I don't have now. It makes me sad that my life has "gotten in the way" of my enjoying past successes and building on them to create present successes.

Hope. I could use more of that these days. But I know maintaining hope is something I need to do, not something that comes from outside. I have to be hopeful — and I choose to be hopeful. It isn't that I intend to put on rose-colored glasses, but I do want to continue dreaming about possibilities and believing in the future. I don't expect life to be easy, and I don't need life to be easy, but I do need it to be filled with creative energy and with creative products.

AN ISSUE-ORIENTED APPROACH

One sensible way to practice self-awareness with respect to these ten core ideas or any issue confronting you is to use the following tactic regularly. First, you name the issue confronting you. Next, you name the fears that arise with respect to that issue, the fears that are likely preventing you from meeting the challenge in an active, forthright way. Third, you remind yourself why you don't want to give in to those fears. Fourth, you name some concrete strategies to deal with the issue. Last, you announce what steps you mean to take "in the world" to handle the issue. Here is an example:

Issue: Finding the Courage to Be an Artist

UNDERLYING FEARS

1. I won't make it.

2. I'll starve.

3. I have no talent.

4. Creating is a dead end.

REMINDERS WHY NOT TO GIVE IN TO THESE FEARS

1. Creating allows me to feel whole.

2. I love it when I create well.

3. I only feel human when I create.

4. I only get to use my talents and resources when I create.

STRATEGIES FOR DEALING WITH THIS ISSUE

1. I will acknowledge the fear and create anyway.

2. I will learn one or two anxiety-management tools.

3. I will practice taking risks.

4. I will reduce my fear-based self-talk.

TO DO IN THE WORLD

1. I will take one important risk this week.

2. I will do one thing I am afraid of doing.

3. I will tackle my creative work, even if I'm anxious.

4. I will help my career along, even if I'm anxious.

Following is a (long) list of issues that regularly arise in the lives of creative people. If you would like to practice the strategy I just described, pick one of these issues and handle it using this method. Name the issue, the fears associated with that issue, the reminders to yourself of why you don't want to give in to those fears, the strategies for handling the issue, and the real-world actions you mean to take in dealing with the issue.

ARTISTS' ISSUES

Personality and Psychological Issues

1. Primary self-relationship issues (e.g., an inability to frame your "self" as central meaning-maker, a fleeing from yourself and the responsibilities of freedom, etc.).

2. Psychodynamic issues (e.g., devaluation at the hands of critical parents, anxiety syndromes resulting from disturbed family dynamics, enduring conflicts with regard to self-worth).

3. Personality trait issues (e.g., the excessive or insufficient manifestation of particular personality traits, such as passion and self-direction, a too-tame or too-wild personality arising from the combining of personality traits in a certain way).

4. Fears and anxieties (e.g., fear of negative responses and evaluations, fear of loss of self-esteem, fear of self-exposure, fear of the unexpected and the unknown, fear of failure, and fear of success).

5. Issues of individuation and separation (e.g., an inability to handle the stresses of independent living and decision making, an emotional dependency on others, which prevents a flowering of self-trust).

6. Ego defenses (e.g., the use of ego defenses to protect yourself from unwanted information and experiences that feel unsafe, so that you intellectualize about art rather than encounter the blank canvas, or you daydream and fantasize but not in the service of your creative work).

7. Depression (e.g., depression arising for existential reasons, because you have "seen through" the culture's commonly held values; this crisis causes a meaning loss, saps motivational energy, and leaves you without reasons to create).

8. Addictions (e.g., the long-term consequences of alcohol or other drug use, which quells anxiety, including artistic anxiety, in the beginning, but ultimately blocks and ruins you).

9. Personality disturbances (e.g., any number of severe disturbances, including psychotic and near-psychotic episodes, clinical mania, and profound anxiety disorders).

Culture and Climate Issues

1. Repressive and authoritarian childhood (e.g., an anti-intellectual, antiexpressive, antiart childhood, coupled with parental criticism, rejection, dogmatic rules and assertions, and punishing responses).

2. Repressive and authoritarian childhood culture (e.g., religious injunctions regarding sin, a tyrannical social environment in which governing metaphors and authority figures could not be questioned or taken to task).

3. Repressive and authoritarian adult culture (e.g., currently finding yourself in a group, culture, or social system in which creativity is despised or forbidden).

4. Group identifications (e.g., identifying with an inhibiting group stereotype having to do with a lack of intelligence, will power, skills, sensitivity, courage).

5. Lack of entitlement (e.g., a sense, arising from group or class identifications or as a result of family myths, that you are not entitled to be creative or successful).

Creative Process and Work Issues

1. Inability to enter or maintain a proper awareness state (e.g., the presence of an anxious, chaotic, or "noisy" inner environment or the presence of negative self-talk, doubts, worries, and fears, which prevents you from maintaining or achieving the awareness needed for creative effort).

2. Myths and idealizations (e.g., a naive or calculated misunderstanding about the place of intuition in the creative process, so that you "wait to be inspired" before beginning, and mythic idealizations about how talented, productive, effective, special, or different well-known creative individuals are; these idealizations serve to keep you in your place and spare you the pain of trying and possibly failing).

3. Lack of a clear, integrated sense of the creative process (e.g., not understanding or not accepting how comfortable you have to become with "not knowing" beforehand what something will look like; not understanding how to embrace, rather than battle, the anxiety that naturally attaches to the creative process; not understanding how to "hold the intention" to return to your work when you're on a break from your work).

4. Skill deficits (e.g., insufficient practice and attention paid to drawing, if drawing is central to your painting, so that you are never really satisfied with your paintings; this dissatisfaction leads to meaning drains and blockage).

5. Material blocks (e.g., becoming blocked by the difficulty inherent in the work you are currently doing. That work may suddenly require some research, without which progress can't be made; or the sculpture you've been chiseling may have been ruined by your last gouge, a fact you would rather deny).

6. Pressure paralysis (e.g., blockage arising because you've committed to too many projects or have too many deadlines approaching, or because an upcoming gallery show or concert is unusually important or you perceive it as unusually important).

World Issues

1. Alienation (e.g., a mistrust of, distaste for, or felt separation from the prevailing culture and the pursuits and ideas of others. This alienation provokes a meaning crisis. Why create, if you don't respect or like your potential audience? The presence of other outsider feelings — that the door is locked, preventing entry into

the marketplace, that you are too eccentric or iconoclastic to be accepted).

2. Pessimism and defeat (e.g., a repeated battering in the marketplace, failure to make products or give performances that feel worthy, rejection by critics, and other failures that lead to a pessimistic outlook and a pervasive sense of defeat).

3. Marketplace issues (e.g., a lack of opportunities, repeated rejections, an inability to break in, an inability to be heard by marketplace players, a lack of understanding about how best to approach the marketplace and "play its games," an inability to craft a career and maintain momentum).

4. Issues of showing and selling (e.g., blockage resulting from the conscious or half-conscious fear that, were the work to be completed, you would have to show it and try to sell it; this attempt might result in criticism, rejection, failure, and defeat. Blockage resulting from the accumulation of unsold products).

5. Role uncertainty (e.g., uncertainty about what you are attempting to "do" with your creative nature and capabilities. Are you supposed to enlighten or to entertain? Be congenial or abrasive? Tell hard truths or gain some popularity?).

6. Postmodern vacuum (e.g., feeling that all motives and all versions of reality can be questioned, leading to repeated intellectual, motivational, and existential crises).

Existential Issues

1. Meaning crises (e.g., suddenly feeling that dance, which once seemed so meaningful, no longer is, or that the writing of academic poetry, which made use of your ingenuity and cleverness, now only seems sterile and heartless).

2. Meaning drains (e.g., having your work repeatedly rejected, doing a string of work that you consider unrealized or inferior, sensing that your genre is no longer respected by the culture, concluding that your grand dreams will never be realized).

3. Meaning shifts (e.g., understanding in a corner of conscious awareness that "x" has become more meaningful to you than "y" — that writing is now more meaningful than painting, that biology is now more meaningful than poetry — but fearing that knowledge because of the great investment you've made in loving and mastering "y" and how far you would need to travel to master "x").

4. Fear of meaninglessness (e.g., an inability to confront creative work out of the fear that in the encounter you will experience the void or in some other way get too clear a whiff of meaninglessness).

5. Motivational malaise and existential doubt (e.g., being plagued by doubts about the importance of any work, creative or otherwise, arising from a profound, even more central doubt about the importance of your existence or the importance of the existence of the species).

Issues of Circumstance

1. Poverty (e.g., an inability to afford necessary materials or the latest technology; multiple crises including hunger, disease, dangerous neighborhoods).

2. Day job and second career issues (e.g., fatigue from a taxing day job, an abiding need to pay attention to your second career, increasing investments in your second career and decreasing investments in your art).

3. Relationship demands (e.g., spouse upset with your time spent in solitude or spent auditioning, the necessary demands of parenting or single parenting, the multiple demands of children and aging parents).

4. Particular wounds and traumas (e.g., receiving particularly harsh criticism from a teacher or editor, producing a kind of work that was wanted previously but that is not wanted today, becoming expert in a technology that has been replaced by a newer technology).

5. Real-world crises (e.g., floods, fires, economic upheavals, wars, personal crises, health emergencies).

6. Chores (e.g., endless small and large chores — shopping, cooking, cleaning, doing the laundry, paying bills, answering emails — as well as anxiety about all the chores you aren't getting done, how you aren't shopping around for the best auto insurance, keeping the roses pruned, saving for retirement).

Here is how three painters completed this exercise.

RON

Issue: Working to Succeed Despite Low Self-Confidence

UNDERLYING FEARS

1. Even if and when I succeed, the endless struggle with low self-confidence will create a background state of unhappiness.

2. When I succeed, I'll have to be responsible for it.

3. I'll find subtle ways to sabotage my own success.

4. I won't have the ability to persist in the face of market failures.

REMINDERS WHY NOT TO GIVE IN TO THESE FEARS

1. The most important goal is a sense of contentment and equanimity. Success can help create that.

2. My work has already enjoyed success in the marketplace. The hardest work (developing the skills) has been accomplished. My beliefs about myself are the only remaining obstacle.

3. My work deserves to be out in the world.

4. There's a strong possibility that, with success, the struggle with issues of low self-confidence will substantially lessen and perhaps disappear entirely.

5. I have this one life, this one opportunity, to develop my talents to their fullest. What do I have to lose?

STRATEGIES FOR DEALING WITH THIS ISSUE

1. When the voices of doubt arise, acknowledge them without criticism or anger. Relax. Counter the thoughts by thinking "I can do this."

2. Prepare. Do the market research. Create goals, plans, and strategies for success. Make the foundation of my plans so solid that my voice of doom has little on which to base its comments. Make success as likely as possible.

3. I will take one step each day, no matter how small, toward my goals.

4. I will research the topic of self-esteem.

5. I will nurture the habit of success and completion.

TO DO IN THE WORLD

1. This week, I will finish my marketing goals and assign daily tasks.

2. I will order one book on the issue of self-esteem.

3. At the end of each day, I will look back and find one task that I have successfully completed and celebrate that fact.

4. Every Friday afternoon I will look back on the week and enjoy and celebrate the progress that I've made.

JOANNE

Issue: Inability to Act "As If" I Matter

UNDERLYING FEARS

1. I'm not really creative.

2. If I take time for my creative work, I am neglecting my responsibilities.

3. I'm wasting time.

4. I don't have anything to say.

5. I do have something to say, but I'm reluctant to put it on display.

REMINDERS WHY NOT TO GIVE IN TO THESE FEARS

1. I can use my talents to create what I want — no one else can dictate what I do or how I do it.

2. It gives me a feeling of satisfaction to create something.

3. I have fun when I work on my creative projects.

4. My creative time and creative work matter to me because they are just for me.

STRATEGIES FOR DEALING WITH THIS ISSUE

1. I will acknowledge my fear and create anyway.

2. I will quiet my negative self-talk.

3. I will say "I matter, my creative work matters, and getting to my creative work regularly matters."

4. I will relax and consider my creative work as vital as eating and sleeping.

5. I will believe in my creative work, and I will believe in myself.

TO DO IN THE WORLD

1. I will tackle my creative work, even if I'm anxious.

2. I will schedule creative time at least four times a week and hold that time sacred (I know that it would be better if I created every day, but from where I am, this is a huge improvement).

3. I will work through the frustration of not knowing exactly what to do.

4. I will work just for me.

CONSUELO

Issue: Not Giving My Art the Time and Effort It Deserves

UNDERLYING FEARS

1. I have no meaningful things to say, and so spending more time on my art is a waste of time.

2. I lost my opportunity in life and now it is too late; now I have no talent to develop.

3. I would be regarded as a self-absorbed, egotistical person.

4. I won't be a good enough mother, since I will be taking the time from my son to be working at something that will get me no-where.

REMINDERS WHY NOT TO GIVE IN TO THESE FEARS

1. Going deep and staying centered are the ways to have meaningful things to express.

2. I will get older whether or not I work on my art, so I might as well keep doing it.

3. Others don't really consider me self-centered and egotistical; that is only a feeling coming from a deep unknown place.

4. My son will be happier growing up with a happy mother than with a blocked artist.

STRATEGIES FOR DEALING WITH THIS ISSUE

1. I will recognize the fear and anxiety that produce these kinds of thoughts and work anyway.

2. I will work on my self-esteem and keep working at becoming a better artist and person.

3. I will keep working on producing meaning in my life through art-making.

1. I will respect the amount of time I have already assigned to art-making in my week and try to increase it little by little.

2. I will practice doing a series of works that I think have meaning for me and when I feel they are ready, I will show them to people.

3. I will have a show!

4. I will counterattack my negative self-talk with affirmations.

5. I will honor my art by showing up at my studio regularly and working deep.

CREATIVITY FOR LIFE

This book is done. What will my next book be about? That is a complete mystery to me. How could it be otherwise? Who would want it to be otherwise? My next book will arise of its own accord, for its own idiosyncratic reasons, perhaps because a stray thought catches my attention, perhaps because an idea has been percolating for thirty years, perhaps because, walking from the post office to the café, I make a certain decision about what I want to tackle next. I am not in control of the creative process, nor do I have any doubts about the creative process. I am completely certain that there will be a next book, though I have no idea what it will be.

I will do what I do every day, which is stand ready (in an everyday creative way) and show up at the computer first thing each morning (in an art-committed way). This is the essence of my "creativity practice." It is like a snowflake — simple and anything but simple. I hope your way is like that too. I hope this book will prove a useful companion to you as you live your artful, art-filled, art-committed life.

Index

absorption, 33–34, 203–4
accountants, 193
acquisitions editors, 193
action plans, 176–84, 280–93
actors
    and age, 87
    blocked, 128
    creativity practice of, 306–7
    mechanics/metaphysics of career, 168–69
    professional, 161
    and talent, 13
adaptive lifestyle, 276
addictions, 327
    See also substance abuse *and specific substances*
adolescents/young adults, madness in, 60–61
affirmations, 21, 145
age, 87
agents, 172, 196–97
aggressiveness, 39, 131
agoraphobia, 55, 250
Albert, Hermann, 86
alcohol, 67, 69, 70, 139, 211, 327, 313
Alcott, Louisa May, 119
alienation, 210–11, 328–29
ambivalence, 39, 130
amnesia, 58
analytic ability, 29, 31
Andreasen, Nancy, 48
anger, 54–55, 67, 90, 313–14
anhedonia (diminished pleasure/interest in activities), 49–50, 66
Anouilh, Jean, 114, 300
antidepressants, 67, 70
Antin, Eleanor, 234
anxiety
    anxious situations, 106
    blocks due to, 139–41, 144
    exploring, 275

    managing/reducing, 69, 97, 144, 179–81, 250
    moral, 140
    overview of, 52–54
    performance, xiv, 20, 53, 135–36
    See also fears
Applebaum, Judith, 160
Archer, Jeffrey, 163
Arrau, Claudio, 87
arrogance, 37–38, 39, 131, 174, 178
art buddies, 145, 181, 198, 269–70, 276
art colonies, 243
art-committed life/identifying as an artist
    challenges of, xiii–xvii
    meaning of, xi–xii
    motives for pursuing, 4–6, 186–87
    rewards of, xvii
    See also creativity for life
art dealers, 158–59
art-filled life/living, xi
artful living, xi
The Artist and Society (Hatterer), 7, 209
"The Artist at Work" (Camus), 216
artists
    avant-garde, 103
    "difficult," 26–27
    and growth/change, 81–82
    motives of, 4–6, 186–87
    path of, 186–87
    professional, 161–62
    vs. the public, 159–60
    and talent, 13–18
artist's world, exercises, 267–76
arts medicine, 71
art therapy, 70
art vs. life, 134
ascending spiral, 84–85
Ashton-Warner, Sylvia, xix
assertiveness, 39–40, 69, 131

assistant editors, 193–94
associate publishers, 194
audience
    exercises, 267–69
    gaining, 95
    and marketplace, 158–61, 180, 181–82
Audubon, John James, 234
Audubon, Lucy, 234
Austen, Jane, 28
authoritarianism, 327
authority issues, 236, 238, 246, 250
autogenic training, 69, 179
avant-garde artists, 103
avoiding work. *See* resistance
awareness state, 327

Baber, Alice, 204
Bach, C. P. E., 75
Bach, Johann Sebastian, 86
balance, xviii, 211–13, 215
Balanchine, George, 92
Baldessari, John, 158
Baranskaya, Natalya, 30
Barron, Frank, 63
Bartók, Béla, 78
Baselitz, Georg, 5
Bashkirtseff, Marie, 207
Batman, 163
battle fatigue, 58–59
Beatles, 84, 168–69
Beecham, Sir Thomas, 75
Beethoven, Ludwig van, 39, 48, 118, 141, 210, 234
behavioral change, 144
behavioral contracts, 291–92
behavioral therapy, 70, 180
Béjart, Maurice, 33
beliefs, blocks due to, 128
Belinsky, Vissarion, 167
Bellow, Saul, 79
Benatar, Pat, 80
Benchley, Peter, 161
Bergler, Edmund, 128
Bhagavad Gita, 282
biofeedback, 69, 179
bipolar disorder, 48–49
Black Elk, 302
Blackwell, Barry, 52–53
blind spots, 103–4
blocks, 127–45, 275
    anxieties, 139–41, 144
    and criticism, 137
    and cynicism/world criticism, 132
    and depression, 141
    environmental, 136
    examining, 20
    existential, 133–34
    and fatigue, 134–35
    and fears, 128, 130
    Freud on, 131, 222
    guided writing to overcome, 141–42
    imaterial, 328
    and myths/idealizations, 138–39
    overview of, 127–28
    and paranoia/world-wariness, 132–33
    from parental voices, 130
    and pressure paralysis, 135–36, 328
    vs. resistance, 147

and self-abuse, 139
and self-censorship, 128, 131
and self-criticism, 131–32, 143
situational, 137–38
social, 136–37
sources of, 128–41
strategies for elimination, 142–45
and the workshop setting, 34
Bloom, Robert, 168
Bogosian, Eric, 164, 237
Bolet, Jorge, 8, 10
Bolinas (CA), 243
book doctors, 194
book manufacturers, 194
book packagers, 194
bookstore event coordinators, 195
bookstore managers, 195
boredom, 49–50, 178
Bortoluzzi, Paolo, 40
Bourgeois, Louise, 107
Bowers, Malcolm, 57, 61
Brahms, Johannes, 299
Braine, John, 79
Braque, Georges, 31, 52
Braudy, Susan, 37
breathing techniques, 179
Brisebois, Danielle, 240
The Brothers Karamazov (Dostoyevsky), 62
Bruhn, Erik, 91–92
Buddhism, 7, 205, 289
Burko, Diane, 8
burnout, 38, 136
bursting-balloons syndrome, 86–88
Bury, Pol, 52
business as work, 157–84
    anxiety management/reduction, 179–81
    assessment of your personality as a seller, 177–79
    and audience/marketplace, 158–61, 180, 181–82
    business action plan, 176–84
    career and compromise, 161–64
    challenges named, 175–76
    and fame, 138–39
    financial realities, 3–4
    financial-support analysis, 183–84
    mechanics/metaphysics of career, 164–69, 176
    overview of, 157–58
    product/portfolio analysis, 182
    and self-assessment, 176–77
    strategies for, 176–84
    two writers' paths, 169–75
Butler, Samuel, 299

Caen, Herb, 78–79
Cage, John, 16, 297
Callas, Maria, 17
Camus, Albert, 92, 99, 133, 216, 232
Capone, Norberto, 87
Capote, Truman, 78, 90, 170
career
    and compromise, 161–64
    inner counseling, 312–13
    second, 183–84, 330
    supporting partner's, 262
Cariou, Len, 9
carpentry analogy, 121
Carr, Emily, 4–5, 305
Carson, Rachel, 301

Holiday, Billie, 81
Holst, Gustav, 302
Holzer, Jenny, 159
Homer, Winslow, 300
honesty, 35–36, 299
hope, 322, 324
hopelessness, 49–50, 67
Hopkins, Anthony, 58
hospital clinics, 70
How to Get Happily Published (Applebaum and Evans), 160
hozh'g (beauty of life), 4
Hubbard, Elbert, 75
humanistic view, 7
Hunt, Holman, 107
Hunt, Linda, 203
Huston, Anjelica, 133
hypersomnia (excessive sleep), 49–50, 66

idealizations, 136–37, 328
identity issues, 104–10, 221, 288
id repression, 128
imagery, guided, 283–84
Images of Man (Museum of Modern Art, 1959), 165
imagination, 30–31, 117–18, 126
immersion, 10–11
imperfection, 125–26
impulse control, 96
impulse to originate, 4
income sources, 183–84
incubation/fallow periods, 114, 141
independence, 235–39, 249–51, 326
individuation/separation, 326
inferiority feelings, 239
inflation, positive/negative, 59–60
Inness, George, 76
insecurity, 87–88
insomnia, 49–50, 66
inspiration, 11, 12, 33, 328
installation artwork, 38
integrity, 119, 206
intellectual playfulness, 28–29
intelligence, 26, 28–31
intensity
    in creativity practice, 300–301
    and madness, 55–56, 58, 59, 62, 65
interest/pleasure in activities, diminished (anhedonia), 49–50, 66
interpersonal dynamics, 69
intimate relationships, 253–65
    artist/nonartist relationships, 255–59
    being in it together, 264–65
    importance of, 321, 323
    overview of, 253–55
    partners/partisans, 263–65
    permanent, monogamous, 259–60
    and romantic love, 260
    strategies for, 265
    twenty building blocks of, 259–63
introspective stance, 32–33
introverts, 203
intuition, 11, 328
Ionesco, Eugène, 62, 300
irritability, 51, 58, 67
isolation, 201–18
    and aliveness, 207
    and aloneness/alienation/estrangement, 210–11

and contact with others, 205
and contact with the work, 203–4, 211
and free play, 204
gaining solitude, 213–14
and guided writing, 213–15
integrity and existential encounters, 206
and lack of relationships/social savvy, 207
and madness, 59–60, 64–65, 210
overview of, 201–2
and parallel-life work, 215–17
personal balance, finding, 211–13, 215
prolonged, dangers of, 207–11, 214
and prolonged unreality, 209–10
as safe haven, 205–6
and spiritual journey, 205
strategic time-outs, 217–18
strategies for, 213–18
values/benefits of, 202–7
and when to leave, 214–15
and workaholism, 208–9
issues for artists, 324–35
    of circumstance, 330–31
    creative process/work, 327–28
    culture/climate, 327
    existential, 329–30
    giving art insufficient time, 334–35
    inability to act as if you matter, 332–33
    low self-confidence, 331–32
    personality/psychological, 326–27
    world, 328–29
Istomin, Eugene, 268

Jacobi, Derek, 7–8, 301
James, William, 298
Janus, Samuel, 47–48
Jarrell, Randall, 48
Joanne (painter), 332–33
job description, 192
Johnson, Samuel, 170
joins, skillful, 121–22, 126
Joseph K. (writer), 169–73, 208
joy, 94, 302–3
Joyce, James, 62
joylessness, 39
Jude the Obscure (Hardy), 99–100
juggling/managing commitments, 275

Kafka, Franz, 169–70, 232
Kalil, Michael, 52
Kaprow, Allan, 204
Karnosh, K. J., 64
Keane, Molly, 29
Kerouac, Jack, 78
King, Stephen, 172
Klee, Paul, 28, 48, 53, 65, 212–13
knowing, 7, 10–12, 19, 23
Komar, Vitaly, 53
Kosinski, Jerzy, 14–15
Kumin, Maxine, 48
Kundera, Milan, 299

Laing, R. D., 61
Lam, William, 74
L'Amour, Louis, 172
Landowska, Wanda, 302
lawyers, literary, 197
left brain, 29

About the Author

Eric Maisel, PhD, is the author of more than thirty works of fiction and nonfiction. His nonfiction titles include *Coaching the Artist Within, Fearless Creating, The Van Gogh Blues, The Creativity Book, Performance Anxiety, Ten Zen Seconds, A Writer's San Francisco,* and *A Writer's Paris.* A columnist for *Art Calendar* magazine, Maisel is a creativity coach and creativity coach trainer who presents keynote addresses and workshops nationally and internationally.

Maisel holds undergraduate degrees in philosophy and psychology, Master's degrees in counseling and creative writing, and a doctorate in counseling psychology. He is also a California-licensed marriage and family therapist. He lives with his family in San Francisco.

Visit www.ericmaisel.com to learn more about Dr. Maisel, or drop him a line at ericmaisel@hotmail.com. To learn about his innovative breathing-and-thinking techniques, visit www.tenzenseconds.com.